OUR LIVES

Publication of this book was made possible with the generous support of Kayden Research Grant Committee, University of Colorado, and The Brown Foundation, Inc., of Houston, Texas.

School for Advanced Research

Resident Scholar Series

OUR LIVES

Collaboration, Native Voice, and the Making
of the National Museum of the American Indian

Jennifer A. Shannon

SAR
PRESS

School for Advanced Research Press
Post Office Box 2188
Santa Fe, New Mexico 87504-2188
www.sarpress.org

Managing Editor: Lisa Pacheco
Editorial Assistant: Ellen Goldberg
Designer and Production Manager: Cynthia Dyer
Manuscript Editor: Merryl Sloane
Proofreader: Kate Whelan
Indexer: Margaret Moore Booker
Printer: Sheridan Books, Inc.

Library of Congress Cataloging-in-Publication Data

Shannon, Jennifer A.
  Our lives : collaboration, native voice, and the making of the National Museum of the American Indian / Jennifer A. Shannon.
       pages cm. — (Resident scholar series)
  Includes bibliographical references and index.
  ISBN 978-1-938645-27-3 (alk. paper)
  1. National Museum of the American Indian (U.S.)—History. 2. Indians of North America—Museums—Washington (D.C.)—History. I. Title.
  E76.86.W182S43 2014
  973.04'970074753—dc23
                              2013034046

MIX
Paper from
responsible sources
FSC® C014174
FSC
www.fsc.org

This book was printed on paper containing 30% PCW.

Cover illustrations: *left, Our Lives* gallery introduction detail (see plate 8), photo by Walter Larrimore, reproduced with permission of the NMAI, Smithsonian Institution; *right,* Chicago exhibit feature detail (see plate 14), photo by author, reproduced with permission of the NMAI, Smithsonian Institution.

The School for Advanced Research (SAR) promotes the furthering of scholarship on—and public understanding of—human culture, behavior, and evolution. SAR Press publishes cutting-edge scholarly and general-interest books that encourage critical thinking and present new perspectives on topics of interest to all humans. Contributions by authors reflect their own opinions and viewpoints and do not necessarily express the opinions of SAR Press.

For Ida Trilli and Mirella Shannon,
two extraordinary, inspirational women

Contents

Figures

Plates

Color plates follow page 142.

Preface

Who Killed Curatorial?

In 2004 the National Museum of the American Indian (NMAI)—the newest Smithsonian museum to be constructed on the National Mall in Washington, DC— opened to the general public. This book, in the broadest sense, is about how it became what it is today.

Although stereotyped images of Native Americans are prevalent in popular culture, Native Americans themselves are virtually absent from contemporary national media and politics in the United States. For many Native individuals, the NMAI, a prominent and permanent symbol of Native presence in America, in the shadow of the Capitol and at the center of federal power, is a triumph. At the grand opening, the museum's main message was "We are still here." This message was most directly displayed in *Our Lives: Contemporary Life and Identities*, one of the NMAI's inaugural exhibitions and the main focus of this book.

Delegations from tribes have been coming to the Capitol to address treaty rights and treaty violations for more than two hundred years, and Congress has figured prominently in tribal life through policies of termination, assimilation, and, more recently, self-determination. The identities of Native peoples in the United States have been circumscribed and litigated by the people in power since before the country was founded. The difficult history of relations not just between the government and tribes but also between Native Americans and museums has been well documented. It was thus a daunting task for the Smithsonian's NMAI, a federal and bureaucratic institution, to create positive and trusting relations with Native tribes. At a 1995 conference about museums and Native people, NMAI director Rick West promised an "authentic Native voice," which was to be produced through collaboration with Native people. The establishment of trust and of authenticity would be accomplished through a particular kind of exhibit-making practice called "community curating."

This museum, then, is the grandest experiment to date in the ethical representation of Native Americans. Along with West's refiguring of the relationship between museums and Native people, there has been a call more broadly to "decolonize the museum." Community curating and other forms of collaboration with Native people, such as welcoming and encouraging Native people to connect with museum collections, to interpret and advise on exhibits, and to work in museums, are some of the institutional responses to the movement to decolonize museums. In many ways, community curating is what decolonizing the museum means *in practice*. When NMAI staff emphasized its desire to effect a paradigm shift in museum practice, it was in line with this push for greater inclusion and wider acknowledgment of the troubled history of museum–Native American relations.

Just as Sally Price (2007) acknowledged at the start of her account of the birth of the Musée du quai Branly in Paris, there are many different people and places and times that could begin the story of the NMAI. For example, it could begin in 1897 when George Gustav Heye began his "obsessive" collecting practices with the purchase of a deerskin shirt (Force 1999:4; McMullen 2009:70); in 1916 when Heye's collection was officially transitioned into the Museum of the American Indian–Heye Foundation (Force 1999:9); in 1967 when young American Indians embarked on a fight for Native American religious freedom;[1] or in 1989 when the National Museum of the American Indian Act was signed, a result due in large part to the advocacy of Senator Daniel Inouye (Force 1999:401, 441–445). But I choose to begin my story in 1999 when the groundbreaking for the new museum was celebrated on the National Mall; when the new home for Heye's collected objects was completed in Suitland, Maryland; and when I, along with a host of other individuals, was hired to work at a new facility called the Cultural Resources Center.

Much has been written about the NMAI—by the museum itself and in newspapers, scholarly publications, and online (the companion book for the inaugural exhibitions is McMaster et al. 2004). I do not go over the same ground here but instead offer what is available uniquely through ethnographic fieldwork: the everyday practices involved in making the inaugural exhibitions, the diverse perspectives of the participants, and the ways in which those participants made sense of their own experiences. Although my account is focused on this specific museum at this particular moment in history, the issues that arose during the planning and execution of the inaugural exhibitions and after the museum opened continue to be significant to those of us who work in museums and museum anthropology, to Native communities, and to the general public. Whose voice is heard in museums? Whose expertise counts as authoritative?

Midway through my fieldwork, there was a dramatic and unexpected turn of events. The Curatorial Department, which was most closely associated with and the leading advocate of the much lauded (in contemporary museology and more specifically in the NMAI) practice of community curating, was being disbanded. It was to be eradicated from the bureaucratic structure in an upcoming major reorganization, which was referred to as a "flattening of the organization"—a concept in the business world designed to make bureaucratic practice more efficient. The curators were surprised, as was I. Later, we found out that other museums were also reorganizing and curatorial departments being dismantled.

I never would have predicted in 1999 or when I began my fieldwork in 2004 that this department would be wiped from the organizational structure of the museum by the time my fieldwork came to a close in 2006. Much as Chris Paine (2006) questioned, "Who killed the electric car?" when introducing his documentary of the same name, I invite you to consider the question "Who killed Curatorial?" At the end of Paine's film, rather than a single culprit, he presents a variety of agents and a complex web of factors that led to the disappearance of the electric car. We will find a similar web of factors as this story unfolds. Along with that question comes an equally significant one: What is the future of community curating?

Notes on Language and Names

Like any bureaucracy, the NMAI has many acronyms and shorthand terms that staff members sometimes referred to as "NMAI-speak." One NMAI curator commented, after watching an exhibit video segment in which a Pamunkey man used the term "Natives," that the man, too, had been "infected with NMAI-speak." So some of this language traveled not only within the institution but also among its partners in collaboration while making the exhibitions.

The terms "Curatorial" and "Exhibits," or other NMAI department names, refer to both agents and locations. For example, one can say, "Curatorial held a meeting yesterday" or "I went into Curatorial but couldn't find where people were meeting." Likewise, "Chicago" or "Kalinago" are terms that can refer to agents (the community as a whole or a small group of co-curators), the exhibit, or a location, depending on the context of the conversation. For example, someone might say, "Chicago wants the walls to be green," referring to the co-curators. Another might say, "*Chicago* has a nice video segment in it," referring to the exhibit.

The term "community" is widely used at the NMAI. I use "community" as an indigenous term of the people with whom I worked; I do not intend to undermine the political or legal status of tribes by using this language. "Native" is a term that is used by the NMAI precisely for its lack of specificity, no doubt a result of the institution's hemispheric scope. This term is interchangeable with "American Indian," "Native American," "Alaska Native," "Native Hawaiian," "indigenous person," "Aboriginal," "First Nations person," and so on. These more specific terms are used regionally throughout the western hemisphere.

The terms "community curator" and "co-curator" are also interchangeable. Whereas some staff told me that there was a switch from using the former to the latter term, my research suggests that this was not the case. However, this perception was important because it suggested that staff felt Native community members were less in control of the process over time (they had moved from being curators to co-curators). *Our Lives* community liaisons, or Native community members assigned to facilitate NMAI staff visits to their communities, were often lumped into the category of "co-curators" and functionally contributed to the exhibits as such.

I provide individuals' full names, tribal affiliation(s), and job titles in appendix A, and some of that information is also in the text. I follow the practice of putting tribal affiliation(s) in parentheses, for example, W. Richard West Jr. (Southern Cheyenne). Each person's job title refers to the position held at the time of the interview or event being described. Individuals' jobs have likely changed since then, and many people no longer work at the NMAI. For instance, I refer to Rick West as the director, but he has since retired from that position. In quotations from interviews or speeches, italics indicate where speakers placed emphasis as they were talking, to provide the reader with a sense of the cadence of the dialogue.

Since many of the people I discuss are well known within the museum world, I want to make a final note on the use of individuals' names. When researching a public and highly publicized institution like the NMAI, the issue of whether to use real names in a written ethnography has been resolved differently by a number of anthropologists working in similar contexts (see, for example, Born 1995:11; Gusterson 1996:xvii; Latour and Woolgar 1986:40). To credit individuals for their contributions, the names used in the book are real. Although all the participants in this research were offered anonymity, none asked for it. In the course of dozens of interviews and conversations, there were only two statements that individuals specifically requested be attributed anonymously. I occasionally have generalized statements or professional positions to protect a person's identity, however, when I felt that it was prudent. I thank all of those who contributed to this research for their time, candor, and courage. I have tried to represent their concerns, ideas, and experiences accurately, appropriately, and with sensitivity to the nature of fieldwork relations, as well as to the possible impacts on their professional development.

Ultimately, this book is a record of the sincere efforts, and conflicts and triumphs, of those who made the NMAI's inaugural exhibitions. It is a narrowly focused snapshot of a particular kind of curatorial practice during an exciting time in the history of the National Museum of the American Indian, from 1999 to 2006. It is also an account of many different kinds of people struggling to do their best under the weight of a monumental task: to represent all Native peoples of the Americas in the first institution of its kind, a national museum dedicated to the first peoples of the hemisphere.

Acknowledgments

I would first like to thank the NMAI staff and the Kalinago and Chicago community members for welcoming me so kindly into their lives and for their contributions to this research through thoughtful conversations with me over the years—especially Cynthia Chavez Lamar and Cécile Ganteaume, who encouraged me to embark on this work, and Garnette Joseph and Joe Podlasek, who encouraged me to complete it. Working at the NMAI was an amazing learning experience, and my more recent endeavors in collaborative museum practice demonstrate its impact on and continuing relevance in my life.

My deepest appreciation goes to all the people I have cited in this book for their time and consideration (see appendix A). It was a privilege to spend time with my interlocutors—often, for hours and over multiple years—and to think critically and productively with so many people invested in the mission and success of the NMAI. In addition to those mentioned above, some people I worked with deserve special mention for being so generous with their time and contributions: Ann McMullen, Bruce Bernstein, Elaine Heumann Gurian, Jim Volkert, Teresa Tate, Taryn Salinas, Arwen Nuttall, Terry Snowball, Maria McWilliams, Casey MacPherson, Fran Biehl, Prosper Paris, Sylvanie Burton, Cozier Frederick, Irvince Auguiste, Jacinta Bruney, Gerard Langlais, Eli Suzukovich, Cyndee Fox-Starr, Mavis Neconish, and Rita Hodge. Others, not cited here, nonetheless left a lasting impression and made me feel particularly welcome, including Marian Paris, Melanius Darroux, Jacqueline Corbette, and

Paulinas Frederick in Dominica; Angie Decorah, Nizhoni Hodge, Nora Lloyd, and Sharon Skolnik in Chicago; and Christine Redcloud at the NMAI.

George Horse Capture passed away in 2013; he was a mentor and supportive colleague while I worked at the NMAI and after. In the early 1990s, he traveled the country to attend regional consultations about the NMAI with Native people, and he stayed on through the opening of the museum. In an interview with me on June 16, 2004, he said of these early consultations, "We had to go to all the meetings. And it was *heaven*. To see so many Indian people, so many *shades* of Indian people, into so many things, and they're very successful. And they're outside the box, they're inside the box, they're just so many things.... I don't think I ever felt so proud."

I am also grateful to Annelise Riles, Dominic Boyer, Pamela Smart, and Hiro Miyazaki for their guidance in my research and to my Cornell University peers Eric Henry, Kim Couvson, and Elana Chipman for their comments on early chapters. Sue Rowley at the University of British Columbia shared her knowledge and provided inspiration through the example she has set in her work with various First Nations. Teaching a course with her during my postdoctoral fellowship at UBC advanced my understanding of museum anthropology and community-museum collaborations and influenced what I teach and how I practice museum anthropology at the University of Colorado. I would also like to acknowledge anthropologists A. Terry Straus and Terry Turner for their inspiration along the way.

This research was made possible with support from the Wenner-Gren Foundation, a Cornell University Sage Fellowship, and a Society for the Humanities research travel grant from Cornell University. Substantive revision was accomplished while in the company of new colleagues at the University of Colorado, Boulder, and in the wonderful intellectual environment of the School for Advanced Research in Santa Fe, New Mexico, through the support of an Ethel-Jane Westfeldt Bunting Summer Scholar Fellowship in 2011. I thank Patricia Erikson for a preliminary review of the manuscript, facilitated by SAR Press, and SAR senior scholar Linda Cordell, Indian Arts Research Center director Cynthia Chavez Lamar, SAR president James Brooks, Corinne Kratz, Ivan Karp, and others for their helpful feedback after a colloquium I presented at SAR about the manuscript. I also thank fellow summer scholar Sascha Scott for the ideas sparked by our discussions and for her detailed comments as I rewrote the conclusion. Special acknowledgment goes to Haidy Geismar for her close reading and comments.

It was a pleasure to work with Lisa Pacheco, managing editor at SAR Press, who was extremely accessible and supportive throughout. Since this was my first book project, Lisa selected an excellent copy editor for me to work with, Merryl Sloane. Merryl helped me to shape the book into its final form after I had gone through many stages of editing on my own. I have truly appreciated and benefited greatly from collaborating with these editors.

An early draft of the manuscript was circulated to key interlocutors from the three communities with which I worked, and I am grateful to those who responded with comments, which were taken into account in my revisions. Although I write about the process of collaboration, this particular account was not, however, a collaborative writing project. Therefore, any errors are my own.

I especially want to acknowledge Mirella Shannon and Mary Ann Wilhelm— thank you for being there for me, and with me, throughout this journey. Finally, I want to express my gratitude to Craig Howe for guiding me along the right path at the start—a path that eventually, surprisingly, led to this account.

one
Anticipation

THEO: And this is exciting for us!

JEN: Why is it exciting?

THEO: Because we can show the world how we live today.

TERRI: Yeah.

THEO: How much impact the world has on us today.

JEN: Has it been frustrating always having people ask you how things were before you were born?

THEO: Yeah, uh-huh.

TERRI: Yes.

...

TERRI: Some people ask us if we still live in igloos. So this is what we're doing now—it's going to tell the world that we don't live in igloos any more [*laughs*].

JEN: Well, if that's something that's really exciting for you...

THEO: It is exciting!

TERRI: It's very exciting.[1]

In September 2004, the National Museum of the American Indian (NMAI) presented its inaugural exhibitions to the public on the National Mall in Washington, DC. As NMAI founding director Richard West Jr. (Southern Cheyenne) explained at the time, the NMAI represents "the culmination of nearly 15 years of planning and collaboration with tribal communities from across the hemisphere" (Smithsonian Institution 2004). Although the museum on the mall was not completed until 2004, it had existed for years in the imaginations, documents, hopes, and dreams of countless individuals who labored to make it a reality. NMAI staff, members of Congress, Native American community members, activists, and many more had great expectations for this site. In the years leading to its grand opening, staff often talked in the future tense about the museum; they also often talked as if the structure already existed, because in many ways it did—in their minds. They all were dedicated to the promise of, and felt anticipation for, this future museum. They also labored under the heavy responsibility of preparing a museum that was to represent all Native peoples in the western hemisphere, for all time, in one place.

The Changing Presentation of the American Indian: Museums and Native Cultures, published in 2000, can be seen as both a part of and a prescription for the "paradigm shift"—a phrase that museum staff widely used by 2004 to explain the nature of their work—that Rick West and other NMAI staff hoped to implement through their museum. In the introduction to that edited volume, West (2000:7, emphasis added) places Native voice at the center of this paradigm: "From the start, our new museum has been dedicated to a fresh and, some would say, radically different approach to museum exhibitions. To put it in the most basic way, we insist that *the authentic Native voice and perspective* guide all our policies, including, of course, our exhibition philosophy." Five years later, West (2005) stated in a speech at the World Archaeological Conference in Australia that the museum is "a cultural and spiritual emblem on the National Mall in Washington, DC…[that] exemplifies decolonisation in practice" (citing C. Smith 2005). This was the new language of the paradigm shift NMAI staff had been advocating from the start.

Nowhere are collaboration, the commitment to Native voice, and the NMAI exhibition philosophy more evident than in the "community-curated" exhibits in the museum. To show what this form of collaboration entailed, this book examines both the NMAI as a whole and the making of one specific exhibition: *Our Lives: Contemporary Life and Identities (OL)*. *Our Lives* is about Native lives today, and two other galleries in the museum depict Native cosmologies (*Our Universes: Traditional Knowledge Shapes Our World* [*OU*]) and Native histories (*Our Peoples: Giving Voice to Our Histories* [*OP*]).

In June 2003, as a contract researcher for the *Our Lives* gallery and a staff field worker assigned to the Inuit community of Igloolik in Nunavut, Canada, I conducted a final exhibit script review with the Igloolik community curators. I asked the co-curators, considering that over four million people per year would read their introduction to the exhibit, what did they most want people to know about them? Their resounding response: "We don't live in igloos any more!" We all laughed because it seemed silly to have to put it in writing, but they insisted that this is what the world needed to know. They explained that it was the most common question they were asked by non-Inuit people. So the last line on the introductory panel in the Igloolik exhibit in the *Our Lives* gallery would declare precisely that.[2]

As this exchange shows, Native communities that worked on the *Our Lives* gallery hoped that they would be able to counter pervasive stereotypes in the Americas, and they were excited to be able to communicate with the public in their own words. This scene is emblematic of the subject matter of this book: it shows that the co-curators had both direction over the content of their exhibit and a particular understanding of who their audience would be; it highlights the ubiquitous practice of transforming recorded conversation into exhibit display text; it shows the desire of the co-curators to tell what their life is like *today*, in their own words; and it reflects the high level of excitement and anticipation about the NMAI that was present not just among community curators and NMAI staff but also throughout Indian country. It also shows that I was both a participant in and an observer of the curating process, and it acknowledges that my work on behalf of the museum contributed to my perspective in writing about it.

Reflection on my work with the Igloolik community in many ways motivated the questions and methodological approach of my research about community curating. My ethnographic engagement with the people with whom I did my fieldwork resembles the methods and ethical concerns espoused by the NMAI curatorial staff about community curating. This is not surprising, as this methodology and the commitment to presenting "Native voice" were responses to the critiques of representation in anthropology and in museums that I was concerned with when I entered the discipline, and the NMAI's approach was one of the reasons I applied to work there in 1999. There were many reasons I felt compelled to conduct research about the community-curating process, but mainly, like others who worked on the inaugural exhibitions, I believed that it was history in the making. The scale of the endeavor provided visibility to and increased scrutiny of the products of collaboration—but less so its process, which is why I elaborate upon that here. This book is also a direct response to the fact that the museum never asked Native community curators for feedback on the curating process or on the exhibits, nor did staff do the kind of postmortem within the museum that was conducted about the *Listening to Our Ancestors* exhibit (see epilogue).

I argue that the inaugural exhibition process—community curating—was essential to the establishment of the NMAI as a "Native place" (Blue Spruce and NMAI 2004) presenting Native voice, regardless of what kinds of curatorial methods or exhibitions have followed. Collaboration through community curating laid the foundation of the NMAI's legitimacy and its acceptance by Native people. Through foregrounding Native voice, the museum has sought to address issues of museum authority and power often central to indigenous and scholarly critiques of how indigenous people have been represented in museums and in public media, shorthanded as the "politics of representation" in anthropology. As I show, collaboration alone does not overcome the problems and politics of representation. But this particular form of collaboration was essential to building relations of trust and accountability that were foundational to creating exhibitions that Native people claimed as their own.

History and Background of the NMAI

The National Museum of the American Indian was created by the NMAI Act of 1989 (Public Law 101-185),[3] a law that is applicable to the Smithsonian Institution and includes some provisions similar to the Native American Graves Protection and Repatriation Act (NAGPRA) of 1990 (Public Law 101-601). An outcome of the decades-long movement for Native American religious freedom and social justice by Native Americans and their allies, these laws empower federally recognized US tribes to request that museums return to the tribes specific categories of items in their collections, including Native ancestors (human remains), sacred objects, and objects of cultural patrimony (Echo-Hawk 2002; Fine-Dare 2002; Mihesuah 2000; Nash and Colwell-Chanthaphonh 2010). Whereas these laws provide guidance and structure for consultations between museums and tribes regarding these particular items, the mission of the NMAI calls for consultation with tribes in all of its endeavors.

Today, the National Museum of the American Indian has three main sites: a display venue in New York City (the George Gustav Heye Center, or GGHC); a research and collection housing facility in Suitland, Maryland (the Cultural Resources Center, or CRC); and the main public exhibition space, or mall museum, on the National Mall in Washington, DC. It was estimated at the time of its opening in 2004 that the mall museum would have more than four million national and international visitors each year due to its location next to the National Air and Space Museum, which is the second most-visited museum in the world (Zafar 2012).[4]

In 1922, George Gustav Heye, known as an "obsessive" collector, opened his large private collection to the public of New York City in a space he called the Museum of the American Indian (Force 1999:3; for a critique of Force's account by a former trustee, see Carpenter 2005:167; for a more nuanced view of Heye, see McMullen 2009). In 1989, with the NMAI Act, the US Congress transformed the Museum of the American Indian into the Smithsonian's National Museum of the American Indian, and plans began for its occupation of the last spot on the National Mall.[5] In 1990, Rick West was appointed the founding director. The George Gustav Heye Center, a permanent exhibition space, opened in 1994 in the Customs House in lower Manhattan. In 1999, there was a groundbreaking ceremony in DC as construction on the National Mall got under way, and in 2001, a welcome center opened at the site. It was a small trailer with information panels containing details about the planning, design, and construction of the museum. Reflected in those information panels, as well as in various other forms of publicity, the mission statement and guiding principles of the NMAI (see appendix C) stressed the contemporary presence of Native people and their participation in every aspect of the NMAI's development and exhibition-making practices.

The NMAI is one of the most recent additions to the Smithsonian Institution, which since the bequest of James Smithson in 1829 has strived for the "increase and diffusion of knowledge." The original interpretation of this mission was to record and display for posterity dying American Indian lifeways that were going to become extinct or be completely acculturated (Fitzhugh 1997:214). To the contrary, the NMAI's guiding principles answer back in the twenty-first century, "We are here now," or as the main message of the museum in 2004 declared, "We are still here."

Among the Smithsonian museums, the NMAI is distinct in that it explicitly recognizes in its literature and staff discourse two groups to which the museum is responsible: its "constituency," or Native people, and its "audience," or non-Native visitors. This division was delineated at least as early as 1991, when it was mentioned in the master facilities plan, *The Way of the People: National Museum of the American Indian*:

> [The] NMAI has as its primary *constituency* all Native American people. However, the largest *audience* to visit NMAI facilities, especially the Mall Museum, will be non-Native. The wider public will come with a different perspective than that of Native Americans, and will have different informational expectations and needs. While programs and exhibitions will address these informational needs, they will do so with Native American voices and perspectives and in multi-sensory environments to enhance them. It is believed that all people will respond to this approach and value its *authenticity*. (Scott Brown Venturi and Associates 1991:36, emphases added)

The issue of authenticity is raised often in NMAI discourse, but anthropologists recognize authenticity to be a value judgment rather than an inherent characteristic. Therefore, it is important to ask who is using the term, what the category includes, and what is at stake. For these reasons, I do not seek to determine whether the Native voice at the NMAI is "authentic," but rather how it is produced and valued and by whom.

Critical Museology

The NMAI is in line with the approach of critical museology, which is considered to be an outgrowth of the "new museology." This approach, rooted in the social movements of the 1960s and 1970s, introduced questions of power to the analysis of museums and is derived from cultural studies, critical social theory, and anthropological theory (Kreps 2003a; Shelton 2001b:146–147; Witcomb 2003:129; see also Vergo 1989). Christina Kreps (2003a) explains, "To new museologists the 'old museology' was too concerned with museum methods and techniques, and did not pay enough attention to the purposes and interests museums serve in society. Conventional museums were seen as object-centered. The 'new museum' was to be people-centered, action-oriented, and devoted to social change and development." In short, the terms "critical museology" and "new museum theory" (Marstine 2006) point to changing forms of analysis and new expectations for museums in recent decades.

By changing the museum from a temple to a forum, critical museology advocates for the democratization of museums and greater accountability to visitors. This has been interpreted as a shift in emphasis from objects to stories (Macdonald and Silverstone 1992) and from collections to audiences. Shelton (1995:6) explains that, as a result of critical museology, "museums have the ability to empower rather than dominate, to forge dialogical rather than monological relations with their publics and to reveal and encourage the transformation of contemporary realities rather than masking them." The museum has increasingly been envisioned as an educational space and more recently as an institution for civic engagement (American Association of Museums 2002) and social change (Sandell and Nightingale 2012). Rather than a dusty place where knowledge is bestowed upon visitors and research is conducted behind closed doors, the museum is reconceived as a participatory space (Simon 2010).

In the introduction to *Reinventing the Museum* (2012:2–4), Gail Anderson provides a table that outlines the "trends in the paradigm shift" from the "traditional museum" to the "reinvented museum" advocated in new museum theory. Changes include "information provider [to] knowledge facilitator," "ethnocentric [to] multicultural," "assumed value [to] earned value," "good intentions [to] public accountability," "assumptions about audiences [to] knowledge about audiences," "individual work [to] collaboration," "one-way communication [to] two-way communication," "presenting [to] facilitating," and "protective [to] welcoming."

In the nineteenth century, the first profession established in the museum was that of the curator, who cared for and researched the collections (Kreps 2003a); typically, curators had Ph.D.s and were considered subject matter specialists. Since then, the responsibilities of curators have broadened, and collections managers, conservators, registrars, educators, and evaluators have been added as museums have become bureaucratized and as professionals have become more specialized. Museum anthropologist Michael Ames notes the changing nature of professionalism in museums as they have become more audience focused and consumer based. As the museum becomes a more public-oriented enterprise, he explains, "the work of the newer professions [those concerned with audience development and satisfaction, such as marketing, promotion, programming, and interpretation] necessarily encroaches upon traditional curatorial territories and traditions, altering the balance of power and status and upping the levels of internal tension and dispute" (Ames 1992:9). My research at the NMAI substantiates Ames's observation (see also Terrell 1991; Witcomb 2003).

As new professions—most recently, education (Roberts 1997) and visitor studies (Hooper-Greenhill 2006)—have been established in the museum, they have often justified their contributions through a critique of curators, characterizing curators as isolated in an ivory tower and unable to communicate with the public. Traditionally, curators provided the intellectual content of exhibitions; more and more, that role is being filled by educators and exhibit developers. As Macdonald and Silverstone (1990:187) explain, there has been a "displacement of attention and concern away from the curatorial achievement—the authority and coherence of the collection—to the visitor's experience—the authority and coherence of the person.... The visitor is invited to become the curator." But they and Terrell (1991) caution against the pendulum swinging too far toward the visitor.

Curators argue that they have changed with the times: "The isolated scholar and manager becomes a facilitator and collaborator who shares, rather than represents, authority" (Nicks 2003:24). Christina Kreps (2003a) writes that there is a "new reality that curators and curating can no longer be defined solely on the basis of their relation to objects. Just as the museum has become more people- and socially-oriented, so too has curating." Consequently, Kreps suggests that we view "curating as social practice" to "become more aware of how curatorial work is relative to particular cultural contexts" (ibid.).

Ironically, critical museology has been embraced by curators at the same time it has enabled the conditions in which their contributions are devalued in the museum. Museums, particularly those that house ethnographic or anthropological materials, are being democratized in two distinct ways. First, there is the wider museum trend toward inclusion of the audience in planning exhibitions and in creating more interactive experiences on the exhibit floor and through programming. Second, there is the trend toward the inclusion and participation of indigenous people when conducting research or developing an exhibition that relates to them. This latter form of inclusion is one aspect of what is referred to as "decolonizing the museum" and is considered to be part of new museum theory (Marstine 2006:5). These two different commitments to inclusion were championed by different departments at the NMAI and consequently created tensions within the museum (see chapter 3).

Decolonizing the Museum

The term "decolonization" has become quite common in museum and anthropological practice and discourse, where it points to efforts in Native communities, museums, and social sciences more broadly to acknowledge the past and to engage in ethical research, representation, and writing practices in the present.[6] Decolonizing the museum can be seen as part of a larger movement to decolonize Native communities, Native minds, and non-Native research practices (see, for example, Atalay 2006; Bowechop and Erikson 2005; Kreps 1988; Phillips 2000; C. Smith 2005; C. Smith and Jackson 2006; L. T. Smith 1999; Waziyatawin and Yellow Bird 2012; Wilson and Yellow Bird 2005).

The perspective of decolonization began in the political sphere, referring to the process by which a colony transitions to independence. But it has since taken on far greater meaning in relation to settler colonialism, internalized racism, and museums. The European museum was born from the colonization process and is an artifact of colonialism and dispossession (Simpson 1996). The United States, through settler colonialism, through force and government policy, subjected Native American communities to spiritual, cultural, and material dispossession in the nineteenth and twentieth centuries. Museums were complicit in this process; collectors and anthropologists assumed the demise of Native peoples and the loss of Native knowledges during the forced assimilation process, collecting indigenous material culture and depositing objects in museums around the world for future study. In addition, museums served ideologies of the nineteenth century that posited Native Americans to be lower in social evolution than Europeans; one result was that Native American material culture was collected and housed in the Smithsonian's National Museum of Natural History rather than in the National Museum of American History.

Government assimilation policies, scientific racism (Thomas 2000), and salvage anthropology empowered museums to collect Native ancestors and cultural artifacts,[7] some of which are considered to be breathing, living beings in need of ritual feeding or other kinds of "traditional care" (Clavir 2002; Cobb 2005; Rosoff 1998). Consequently, Native communities are spiritually, culturally, and ideologically invested in, committed to, and connected to museum collections. Collaboration with Native communities has become a key aspect of the movement to decolonize the museum; it has also been described as a commitment to "restorative justice" in light of this history (Colwell-Chanthaphonh 2007:111). Although not labeled as such at the start, the decolonizing practices the NMAI would endorse included returning ancestors' remains and sacred objects, hiring Native staff, incorporating Native voices and perspectives into exhibits, and collaborating with those whose objects are housed in the museum and whose cultural knowledge and images are placed on display.

Decolonizing the museum was at the heart of the NMAI's insistence on collaboration, which was seen as an ethical commitment to upsetting the historical power relations between tribes and museums, between those who are represented and those with the power to represent, between those who originally possessed cultural knowledge and artifacts and those who collected and stored them away from the communities in which these originated. Although this history and its injustices were legally acknowledged and addressed in the landmark legislation of the NMAI Act and NAGPRA, museum staffs and Native communities have struggled for years prior and since these acts to work productively together to restore justice (see, for example, Merrill et al. 1993).

There are many reasons that museums collaborate with originating communities, whether they are Navajos, Kalinagos, World War II veterans, people of the African diaspora, or Holocaust survivors. Collaboration can enhance participation in the museum, improve community–museum relations, help provide research resources, and ensure content accuracy. But there are other reasons as well. As a matter of politics, when working with Native peoples in particular, those interested in decolonization want to enhance the originating community's rights and public visibility. Museum professionals also want to maintain a positive public image and avoid political protests, although some of the latter have driven positive changes in museum practice over time.[8] Ethically, we want to empower Native people to have control over how they are represented to the public, redress past injustices, and include originating communities that have been represented yet often silenced in the museum. We want the museum to serve the communities whose objects they house. Finally, epistemologically, we value other ways of knowing the world around us and do not want to continue to privilege only western ways of knowing the world and western views of Native objects and Native life experiences.[9]

Historically, the non-Native public has considered museums and anthropologists as competing and, often, more-valued sources of authority or recognized expertise about Native Americans than the Native people themselves. Therefore, it was significant that the NMAI referred to community curators as "experts" on their own experience and cultures and as "co-curators" of the exhibits. By using these terms, NMAI staff clearly aimed to refigure the authority of Native peoples in museum representation and practice, a key component to decolonizing the museum. This language is at the heart of NMAI museology, which has changed over the years but has maintained the centrality of Native knowledge as authoritative and Native voice as the main vehicle for this knowledge.

Although staff did not talk about it in such terms from the beginning, because their work commenced before it was a major discourse in museum practice, Rick West's embrace of Claire Smith's (2005) description of the NMAI as a decolonizing museum certainly reflected what staff felt that they were doing and how a number of scholars have interpreted the museum. In contrast, in *Decolonizing Museums: Representing Native America in National and Tribal Museums*, Amy Lonetree offers a thoughtful and forceful critique of the NMAI. She argues that, although the museum's collaborative methodologies are laudable, collaboration alone is not decolonization. Decolonization, in her view, includes "speaking the hard truths of colonialism" and providing a space for healing (Lonetree 2012:6). She argues that the NMAI has failed to address the genocide of the Americas directly enough, and she provides a counterexample of a tribal museum that has accomplished this. It is not my purpose here to determine whether the NMAI is a decolonized museum, but rather I seek to understand the "native point of view."[10] What matters is that by 2005 the staff defined their work in such terms.

Anthropology of Museums

According to the American Alliance of Museums (formerly the American Association of Museums), as of September 2012, there were 17,774 museums in America—more than the number of Starbucks and McDonald's combined. Studies show that museums are among the most trusted sources of information in the United States, more so than books and teachers and more so than commercial, government, or private websites (American Alliance of Museums 2012; Griffins and King 2008).[11] In addition to their association with colonialism and the construction of indigenous peoples as Other, as contemporary institutions with such presence and authority in society, museums certainly merit anthropological study.

Museum anthropology is a diverse field that includes both practice-oriented and critical theoretical scholarship. The anthropology of museums uses the methods and theories of cultural anthropology to understand the role of museums in history and society, as well as the practices of culture producers within the museum. In the seminal book of this subfield, first published in 1986 and then revised under the title *Cannibal Tours and Glass Boxes: The Anthropology of Museums*, Michael Ames (1992:5) focuses on "how museums, especially those concerned with the works of humankind, cope with the two historical forces or developments of democratization and professionalization." These two forces are at the heart of the story of the NMAI: democratization in the sense of inclusion, whether of the museum's audience or its constituency, and professionalization in the sense of increasing staff specialization in a bureaucratic institution. In addition, Ames (ibid.:14) asks some key questions that are relevant to the NMAI story: "We are now entering an era [when] formerly dominated and underrepresented populations—at least those who survived—are asserting their rights to self-determination and to control of their own histories. Museums will be expected to respond creatively. Will they be able to? Will the museum professions show sufficient flexibility to enable them to respond effectively to the competing demands for popularity, integrity, responsiveness, and financial responsibility?"

Historically, the anthropology of museums mainly resembled an "anthropology of things" (Appadurai 1986), and it was more theoretical than ethnographic. For example, it focused on the context and history of collecting (O'Hanlon 1993; Shelton 2001a), the historical and changing methods of display and curatorial practice (Ames 1992; Kurin 1997; Peers and Brown 2003), and the circulation and valuation of art and museum objects (Errington 1994; Kirshenblatt-Gimblett 1998; Phillips and Steiner 1999; Price 1989). Nelson Graburn and Kathryn Mathers (2000:692) characterized the anthropology of museums as lacking a "thick" ethnographic engagement with the museum and its subjects and objects.[12] *The New History in an Old Museum: Creating the Past at Colonial Williamsburg* by Richard Handler and Eric Gable (1997), however, is one early and influential "thick" museum ethnography. In an article summing up this genre of writing, Gable (2010[2009]:[9–10]) explains that although "anthropologists of museums read, respond to, and borrow from the multidisciplinary world of cultural studies, they also tend to be more concerned with process than with representation. Like Geertz, we are fascinated with the ways that texts are produced and read by their interlocutors; like Malinowski, we want to understand this process from the native's point of view. Like Nader, we assume that when we study museums, we are 'studying up.'"[13]

The more recent work of Gwyneira Isaac on mediation and Sharon Macdonald on knowledge production provides useful interpretive frameworks for understanding the community-curating process at the NMAI. Isaac (2007) shows how a Zuni tribal museum, the A:shiwi A:wan Museum and Heritage Center, mediates between Zuni and Anglo American ideologies and approaches to knowledge. Mediation is a culturally defined practice, she explains, but in general "involves the negotiation and reconciliation of differences" and "places the museum as [an] agent" (Isaac 2007:17). The framework of mediation, then, provides an opportunity to name and analyze what these differences are. Although the NMAI certainly could be described as mediating between tribal and national interests, discourses, and expectations, in this book, I am more concerned with understanding what this process looked like in the everyday practices of individuals rather than in the museum writ large. NMAI staff did use the term "mediation" to describe their role in the community-curating process, and I use "mediation" as an analytical concept through which to view community curating a different way, to understand the role of the imagined audience in the choices made by individuals working on exhibitions (see chapter 5). Isaac's attention to different knowledge systems is akin to the approach I take in understanding the politics of expertise and how particular kinds of knowledge are valued differently.

Like Macdonald, I conducted research on an exhibition that was in the making, and we both examine the production of knowledge. Macdonald's *Behind the Scenes at the Science Museum* (2002) focuses on the unintended consequences of particular actions and decisions during the exhibit-making process. Her account of changing curatorial practices and internal departmental dynamics is helpful to compare with the story I tell here. I did not read her ethnography until well into writing my own, and I was astounded by how similar our approaches and analyses were, which became a major insight about the nature of museum institutions more generally. Reading Macdonald's work suggested to me that the museum institution as a field site moves the ethnographer to see in certain ways, bringing particular kinds of relations to the foreground. In my copy of her book, the margins are filled with "yes!"and "yep!" as I recognized the issues, tensions, and experiences common to her descriptions of the science museum and to my fieldwork at the NMAI. I would argue, however, that the introduction of community curators—outside content producers with particular subject positions with respect to the museum professionals and exhibition content—added a distinct complexity to, and increased tensions in, the exhibition-making process at the NMAI. Through describing these tensions, I, too, hope to illustrate that "an anthropological-ethnographic perspective helps to recover not just a degree of agency for museum staff but also some of their critical and informed reflexivity" (Macdonald 2002:138).

Macdonald's (2002:114) illustration of how expertise was considered an obstacle to developing museum exhibits that were more accessible to the public helped me to understand the changes at the NMAI as emblematic of the wider museum landscape. Expertise was seen by museum professionals as a "barrier" to communicating with everyday people. Macdonald (ibid.:113) situates this development within the more general trend of the declining number of jobs requiring "traditional expertise" in museums and the greater reliance on contractors. She chronicles one way that democratization and professionalization have been interpreted in museum practice, including the rise of more public-oriented professions and the decline of subject matter specialists. This trend is key to interpreting the shifting dynamics at the NMAI over time.

Ethnography of Collaboration

Whether the approach is called "critical museology" (Shelton 1995, 2001b), "analytical reflexivity" (Macdonald 2001:94), or "strong collaboration" (Matsutake Worlds Research Group 2009), this book exemplifies the theoretical position that we should collaborate and also be reflexive about the process as we do so (see Shannon n.d.).[14] There is a growing movement toward this form of knowledge production in museums and anthropology.

What makes the NMAI a fortuitous site, and indeed the inspiration for my orientation to collaboration, is that the museum's modus operandi in all its endeavors—from early consultations about the nature of the museum to architectural design features and exhibition content—has been an iterative and specifically collaborative process with Native peoples. This is an outcome of both the museum's reason for being and the shifts happening in museum practice more generally. Collaboration with Native people in anthropology and museums was not a new practice when the NMAI was being planned and implemented, but there was certainly something different about the scale, visibility, and commitment of the NMAI to this methodology and its desired outcome, the expression of Native voice.[15]

During the development of the inaugural exhibitions, collaboration was not just a buzz word among museum people and a call from Indian country; it was also the method of exhibit development, described the exhibit form, and was an ethical stance—the "right way" to make exhibits about Native peoples. A common description of this process is of someone going to a community and saying, "This is what I heard you say. Did I get that right?" The idea is not just to listen as a symbolic behavior of respect or a ritual practice, but to develop content based on accurate representations of the intent and information produced in the encounters between museum staff and Native community members.

Over the course of my fieldwork (June 2004–June 2006), I documented the production of the *Our Lives* gallery as it unfolded from an imaginary entity to its materialization in September 2004 and its subsequent reception and interpretation by its collaborators. Taking seriously NMAI references to Native American community members as co-curators of the inaugural exhibitions, I conducted my research as a multisited ethnography of "experts," both museum and cultural. For comparative purposes, my fieldwork lasted six months or more in three of the nine communities involved in the making of the *Our Lives* exhibition: the museum professionals in Washington, DC; the Kalinago community in the Carib Territory on Dominica in the Caribbean; and the American Indian community in Chicago. This book thus brings together the perspectives of people both near to and far from the center of power and cultural production.

I also attended academic and professional conferences in which museum staff presented their own interpretations and theoretical analyses of their work at the NMAI. I saw these events as moments in which NMAI staff members were both making sense of their own work to themselves and indicating how they wanted their work to be received by others in their field. Following the work of Boyer (2004) and Myers (2006), my work has illustrated that an exhibition is not just what is built on the museum floor, but also how its makers present it to others. Along with me, countless individuals were writing about the NMAI and participating in the same academic and professional arenas.[16] At academic conferences, NMAI staff presented—framed, interpreted, critiqued, and translated—their work at the museum. Just as Myers recognizes the interplay between museology and anthropology and Boyer insists that we recognize the politics of expertise, I show that anthropological methods, critiques, and theories infused NMAI curatorial practice and Native communities' expectations in their collaborations with the institution.

This account is also rooted in my experience in the NMAI's Curatorial Department from August 1999 to May 2002, first as a research assistant for the *Our Peoples* gallery and later as the lead researcher for the *Our Lives* gallery. I was also assigned as the main field worker and museum representative to the Igloolik community of Inuit in Nunavut, Canada, in 2001–2002 and continued as a consultant for the scriptwriting process and the NMAI media team's visit to that community in 2003.

A Neo-Boasian Approach

The NMAI's emphasis on collaboration manifested in the framing of Native communities as experts in their own experiences and cultures and as co-curators of the exhibits. Refiguring fieldwork as an anthropology with experts (a characterization that came *from* the field site rather than was applied *to* it), I basically went into the field asking experts on community curating and exhibition development about their collaborative process. Based on my training in anthropology, which included Vine Deloria Jr.'s *Custer Died for Your Sins* (1988[1969]),[17] as well as my experience working at the NMAI, I was not comfortable with the notion of "studying people." By focusing on knowledge production, I placed the exhibition itself as a third aspect of the fieldwork relation. The exhibition process was something that the participants in my research could look at, reflect on, and study *with* me.

In many ways, the (re)orientation to the ethnographic subject, as something the ethnographer and her interlocutors puzzle over together, resonates with the neo-Boasian approach to anthropology that Matti Bunzl (2004) proposes. Writing against the notion that anthropological knowledge must be produced through a distance between the ethnographic self and the Native Other (or a studying *of* the Other), thus reifying and sustaining a hierarchy of difference, Bunzl combines Boasian ethnography with Foucauldian genealogy. He suggests that both insiders and outsiders to a culture have a common "epistemic position" with respect to the "ethnographic subject," which he suggests is a "history of the present" (ibid.:440). This approach follows Boas in turning our attention to "the production of historical differences" and their "ethnographic reproduction"; in short, rather than simply "find" (and thus reify) cultural differences and boundaries, we should look to how they were produced, including through anthropological practice (ibid.). The neo-Boasian approach, then, makes the temporal dimension of difference, rather than the cultural dimension of difference, the focal point of analysis. In this book, it is the exhibition (that is, the history and analysis of the exhibition) that is the shared focal point of analysis.

Collaboration as Subject and Method

This shared epistemic position between the ethnographer and her interlocutors can be seen as a form of collaboration. Since the 1980s, collaboration has emerged as a solution to issues of representation in such fields as anthropology, media production, and museum studies when working with indigenous people; it has also been posited as "good practice" in business administration, state–citizen relations, and international development projects, among other endeavors. Unfortunately, "collaboration" is also an opaque, feel-good term that often passes for a description of practice when instead it can obscure the details of this particular form of knowledge production, which is tension filled, time-consuming, difficult, and rewarding.

In the museum world, collaboration is considered to be both research method and ethical practice by Native and non-Native people.[18] There are many different models for collaboration with indigenous communities; this book discusses how the process worked in just one case. Because it is seen as an ethical practice, collaboration is often assumed to be positive and productive—and consequently has been overlooked or at least underdescribed by theorists. Miriam Kahn, a curator and professor of anthropology at the University of Washington, believes that much is missing in our analysis. In her article "Not Really Pacific Voices: Politics of Representation in Collaborative Museum Exhibits," she explains that, following the critiques of representation in the 1980s,

> today, most self-respecting anthropology museums in the United States, Canada, Australia, New Zealand, and many European countries rally around the same set of principles and practices of including native advisors, advisory boards, community councils, task forces, etc.… Several accounts have appeared describing these collaborative processes and the results. With few exceptions, these reports relate mainly problem-free processes, with little or no mention of miscommunications, tensions, or factionalism, and almost no discussion of how successful these collaborations are in solving problems of representation. (Kahn 2000:58)[19]

Taking up collaboration as both subject and method opens up certain analytical opportunities and challenges. This book does not address or seek to describe or illuminate the inner workings of "cultures," in the conventional sense of the term.

Instead, I use collaboration as a lens through which to view social relations, knowledge production, and the representational strategies of culture producers—to describe and analyze the inner workings and representational consequences of this process.

Ethnography with Experts

Two methodological challenges in this multisited study were continuity and distance. In my fieldwork, I followed the *Our Lives* exhibit through time and space, mainly in three locations. This, of course, proved a challenge to the continuity of my experience and my ethnographic record keeping: as the exhibition was developed and then when it opened in September 2004, for example, events and discourse associated with *Our Lives* were occurring simultaneously in all three communities. Much of past anthropological analysis relied in general on distance, both literal and figurative, between the "modern" and the "traditional," the "anthropologist" and her "informants," "us" and "them," "here" and "there." The challenges associated with an anthropology of experts are, I believe, the latest predicaments for contemporary anthropological theory and methods (Clifford 1988; cf. Boyer 2008).

Analytical distance was also a challenge, since the participants in my research were at the same time cultural experts, anthropologists, and bureaucrats; in other words, their knowledge practices were much like mine. This particular challenge has been noted by a number of scholars doing ethnography in institutions (see, for example, Boyer 2003; Holmes 2000; Holmes and Marcus 2005; Riles 2000; Zabusky 2002) and is often shorthanded as a "lack of distance." In common conceptions of anthropological practice, the act of going somewhere unfamiliar and distant from home provides a "space" for reflection and analysis. My fieldwork provided both opportunities—anthropology at home (Chicago and DC) and anthropology abroad (Dominica).

Since this was an experimental approach for me, there were some questions that propelled my research: What might an anthropology of experts look like? Is the framework of "expertise" or even "exhibit making" appropriate to considering the processes of this kind of knowledge production? Can it adequately address such disparate locations, knowledge practices, and cultural communities in an analytically useful way? What, then, becomes the role and interpretive activity of the anthropologist in such a framework?

Although there are many ways in which the National Museum of the American Indian—its staff and its content—can be rendered through tropes like local knowledge and cosmopolitan expertise, indigenous and bureaucrat, here, I am interested in what happens when we symmetrically consider the various participants as experts, when we examine the "cultures of expertise" (Holmes and Marcus 2005).[20] Therefore, this book is a "symmetrical ethnography" (Latour 1993) of *Our Lives*, in which the subjects are both we and they and the participants in the making of the exhibit are both human and nonhuman (keeping in mind that design diagrams, content worksheets, bureaucratic forms, and computer imaging programs also impact social relations and exhibit content and design). This symmetry also means that the museum professionals, both Native and non-Native, and the Native co-curators with whom I worked are treated equally: they have all been engaged and invited to interpret the exhibition and its process and impact. Finally, it is important to recognize that I have been just as involved as the "subjects" within the frame and in the framing of the ethnography.

A number of anthropologists have discussed the challenges of doing anthropology with experts. Dominic Boyer's "The Dilemma of the Anthropology of Experts" (2004) resonates in many ways with what I found during my fieldwork: he noticed that culture was a category that experts would offer to explain particular social arrangements, already there in the "auto-analysis" (as I call it) of the interlocutors of his research. Community curators who worked with the NMAI, in this sense, are very much theorists in the ways they think, define, and speculate about their identities for the sake of exhibitions and other public presentations.

Boyer's interlocutors provided ready-made theories and analyses for his dissertation through their critical inquiries into their own social environments. Stacia Zabusky's (1995:21) interlocutors in the European Space Agency, when questioned, would theorize about "cooperation"—the focus of her research—but generally did not have such discussions during the workday. Similarly, NMAI staff and consultants were quite adept at explaining what was anthropologically interesting about the museum. In the first month of my fieldwork, a museum consultant told me that the type of tensions found at the NMAI were everywhere—they were not a product of just this particular museum, and, in that way, they were "anthropological." Some tensions were between Natives and non-Natives, and some were the historical and classic "design versus curatorial" tensions. But the consultant added, "Really, it's all about power."[21]

Like Boyer, I believe that this kind of analysis of analysis has always been present in some way in anthropological engagements with "informants," for, in translating their lived experience to outsiders, they are bound to theorize about why things are the way they are. But what is changing perhaps is that the (culture) concepts, attentions, and professional standings of expert and ethnographer are now more alike. I discussed my analysis with the people with whom I worked in all three communities, asking them about ideas I had about what was going on around us, not separating the data from the analysis or keeping my theorizing to myself. Like Zabusky's space mission members, the participants in my research were "expert theoreticians" on the concept of collaboration that I was studying. At times, I was interrogated by participants; at other times, we puzzled together about the notions of collaboration and community curating.

Circling Back

I began my fieldwork by returning to three communities where I had formerly been in a professional relationship, to live with them for an extended period of time. In explaining the term "circling back," Annelise Riles (2006a:63) recounts how she was educated in human rights law and it is in that field she formed the problems and questions that motivated her to study anthropology: "I then came to anthropology as an anthropologist comes to the field—in search of solutions to those problems." Circling back, as Riles notes, "poses certain challenges" in the relationships with one's former colleagues, who are now participants in the research, and there are certain politics of ethnography and ethnographic writing to be considered, since the participants will read and be affected by any publications (see also Brettell 1993). Thus, there is an emphasis on ethics in the way in which one interacts with, writes, and imagines the readers of the ethnography (Riles 2006a:64).

This was certainly evident when I presented a paper at the 2007 American Anthropological Association meeting in Washington, DC. Over the years, NMAI staff had been friends, colleagues, and participants in my research, but on this day, they were my audience. I began with a provocative question from Michael Ames (2000): "Are changing representations of First Peoples in Canadian museums and galleries challenging the curatorial prerogative?" I was terribly nervous as I gave a presentation that included some of the content of this book. I quoted conversations with current and former NMAI curators, some of whom were sitting in the rows of chairs facing me. My hands were shaking. At one point, I dropped the paper from which I was reading, quickly dipped down to pick it up with a nervous laugh, squared once again to the podium, and continued speaking. I gave details and analysis from an anthropological perspective and described events and practices that these anthropologists themselves had theorized, deliberated over, and put into practice. After the talk, some people said that they appreciated my presentation and that it "sounded right." But speaking for others, selecting or summarizing their conversations and perspectives and organizing their experiences according to my own perspective and purposes, continues to be an anxious exercise.

I could tell many stories based on my fieldwork, but I have chosen to maintain a narrow focus on the community-curating process. This means that my experiences of the 2005 national election in Dominica, the NMAI staff picnics and seasonal blessings, the American Indian Center's annual powwow in Chicago, and countless other events and encounters are unwritten here. But they are not unacknowledged: they have informed and guided my understanding of the relationships between community members, NMAI staff, and the subject matter of the exhibition.

My first field site was the NMAI itself in 2004, as it was preparing to open. The co-curators with whom I would later be working were flown in to participate in the Native Nations Procession and the grand opening of the museum (see chapter 7). That was a brief encounter and very museum centered, but returning to the Carib Territory and to Chicago for fieldwork was quite a different experience. Unlike working as a lead researcher for the NMAI, I had no community liaison to aid me in meeting people, no one to explain who was the right person to talk to about particular subjects, no structured agenda, and no focused group meetings with tangible goals to achieve (although I did host a co-curator meeting in each community to present what my research was about and to invite people to contribute). However, also unlike NMAI curatorial fieldwork, I had more than a week or two to spend with community members.

Comparative Methods

In each community, I confronted existing ideas of what an anthropologist does and what a volunteer can do—and, more specifically, what someone who had worked at the NMAI could do. At the NMAI field site, I was received as a former curatorial research assistant, an expert of sorts on the inaugural exhibitions, and was welcomed to assist in the plans for the opening; at one point, a new associate director questioned me at length about the history of the *Our Lives* exhibition. Among the Kalinagos, I was first greeted as an expert in computers and computer literacy training, but my administrative skills proved to be most valued by a number of different task forces. In Chicago, I was greeted as a museum specialist and assigned to keep a Native arts gallery running until a replacement could be found for the former arts director; they even surprised me with personalized business cards stamped with the American Indian Center's logo: "Jennifer Shannon, Program/Public Relations."

In each location, I engaged in the day-to-day activities of fieldwork in different ways, responding to the volunteer work I was asked to do, the different sensibilities of each community, the experiences that each community had with researchers in their midst, and the particularities of each field site, such as ease of access to community members and events or modes of transportation. For example, at the NMAI's Cultural Resources Center, recognizing that I had been an employee there and that I blended in almost too well, I sent an email to the staff about my research and carried my ethnographer's notebook much of the time—pencil in hand—to remind people that I was there as a researcher as much as a volunteer. In the other sites, I employed multiple devices suggested by Native community members to let people know that I was an anthropological researcher, including introducing myself in community newsletters and making presentations in community centers with co-curators.

My daily life in each community was quite different as well, according to the pace of life, access to transportation, nature of my volunteer work, frequency of contact with co-curators, and community gathering practices. The volunteer work I did in each community was participant observation, which provided me with ethnographic data, rewarding professional relationships, and rich learning experiences. It meant that many of the social interactions I shared with participants occurred in work environments.

Professional-to-Professional Relations

I agree with Darnell (2001:169), who states that "fieldwork may be the most theoretical of the things anthropologists do, because it forces us to reflect on the premises of our personal traditions, both culture-of-origin and professional." In addition, our approach to fieldwork, how we conceptualize and implement it, is based on particular theoretical commitments. With all of the locations (workplaces, professional conferences, Native communities, Native art and cultural centers, the museum, and the exhibition space itself) included in the "field site," research about an exhibition can provide an opportunity to reconceptualize not only what the field is, but also the nature of fieldwork relations. For example, I remember an interview with Cynthia Chavez (San Felipe Pueblo/Hopi/Tewa/Navajo), the lead curator of the *Our Lives* gallery, during which both she and I were taking notes on our conversation. (This happened often.) From my field notes:

> [Cynthia] asked me what we had talked about yesterday...so I looked back at my handwritten notes from the day before and told her. She said thanks and wrote some thoughts down. I asked if it was for the AAM [American Association of Museums conference] paper, and she said it's for herself in general and that this is really helping. She wants to make note of things so that she can start writing papers about her experiences. It's clear that talking with me is helping her process things and that she is taking notes as I am on our conversations. (July 29, 2004)

In general, NMAI staff welcomed my presence and were quite engaged in thinking with me about the museum, its exhibitions, and the process of community curating.

This mutual learning and creative thinking was one of the greatest benefits of working with people in this capacity. One of my conversations with Cynthia, focused on interdepartmental power struggles to control exhibit content and design,[22] resulted in two different publications: for me, it was "The Construction of Native Voice at the National Museum of the American Indian" (Shannon 2009), which was published in a book about Native peoples and museums and contributed to chapters 4 and 5 here; for Cynthia, it was "Collaborative Exhibit Development at the Smithsonian's National Museum of the American Indian" (Chavez Lamar 2008) in *The National Museum of the American Indian: Critical Conversations*, in which she writes about what it means to be an NMAI curator and a Native woman seeking to establish trust relationships with Native communities.

But it was not only at the NMAI, among museum experts, that I maintained this approach to ethnographic practice. Because the communities with which I worked included both a small island society and a large bustling metropolis, rural farmers and bureaucratic professionals, I was given opportunities to challenge and rethink approaches to and the classification of anthropological "subjects." I suggest an alternative metaphor for fieldwork relations: work, or professional engagement—as opposed to informant, friendship (fictional or otherwise), teacher, and so on. This is based on what I found myself saying in the course of fieldwork—"I'm going to work"—on days I would head to my volunteer positions. And I often referred to participants in my research as "the people I work with" (this phrasing has become increasingly common among cultural anthropologists more generally). Taking that language seriously, for lack of a better term, I call this approach a "professional-to-professional" relationship in ethnography.

Similar to the notion of "collegiality" in fieldwork that Rena Lederman and Annelise Riles have separately written and talked about, a professional-to-professional relationship means that there is a basic agreed-upon and stated purpose to our discussions and meetings—the exhibition—and a more structured context for our encounters. Of course, during my fieldwork, other kinds of interactions and subjects became part of our dialogue and practice, but my purpose was never to see what goes on behind closed doors at home or to create fictional friendships to access insider information.[23]

What surprised me was my overwhelming sense that people did not want me to leave. As my departure loomed closer in each place, community members often would ask, "Did you get what you need?" or "What else can we help you with?" We had forged a partnership of sorts. I do not write this to demonstrate how appreciated or "in" I was in a community—something I have heard some anthropologists and graduate students boast about. It was not my goal to be "in," if that includes being adopted into a local family, being asked to join regularly in private or religious activities, or getting a behind-the-scenes look at the underbelly of a community. And when I *was* privy to such experiences and relationships, I made it clear that, without explicit instructions and consent, the information would not be recorded or published but it did improve my understanding of the circumstances of my fieldwork.[24] Although all fieldwork encounters are inevitably imbalanced, this was my approach to creating an ethical response to these concerns and to the broader critiques of anthropological methods by indigenous people.

There were times during my fieldwork when I was placed in the position of an informant or was confronted with the stereotype of the anthropologist in a Native community, both at the museum and in other sites. In conversations, NMAI staff often asked me what I thought about the exhibitions or what other interviewees talked about. One new associate director at the NMAI extended our conversation for almost six hours, through lunch and on to dinner time, asking me questions about the history of the institution. She also requested that I let her know if, in the course of my research, I heard that her employees had issues she could address.

Despite my intentions, three instances cut to the quick, when staff members with whom I had worked in the past made a comment or explained my presence to an outsider. An NMAI associate director with a Ph.D. in anthropology said to a colleague, "I see you have your academic observer with you." My former colleague and peer responded, "Like germs under a microscope."[25] Another former colleague explained my presence to a newer hire, saying that I was studying them as if they were in a "fishbowl." We all laughed, and I took the lighthearted ribbing as an opportunity to describe my research project.[26] In another instance, a staff member commented while describing my project to another, "She has us all under a magnifying glass, and when the sun comes out, we're going to burn to a crisp."[27] Although my methods were developed to allay these anticipated fears of exposure and feelings of being studied, this type of uneasiness and the imbalance of power with respect to authorship and publication are always factors in the social relations of anthropological practice.

The Anthropologist Slot

In "Anthropology and the Savage Slot" (1991), Michel-Rolph Trouillot outlines how anthropology filled a "savage slot" in the existing tropes of western discourse and how the Other in anthropological discourse was a reproduction of this larger trend. But Native critics and scholars, talking among themselves or in books and journals—most influentially Deloria (1988[1969]) in the chapter "Anthropologists and Other Friends"[28]—created an inverse trope through their counterdiscourse: an "anthropologist slot."[29] This is a figure that, especially among tribes in the United States, the researcher often meets in the field and must come to terms with through sincerity and a commitment to reciprocity (Bodinger de Uriarte 2007:27; see also Shannon n.d.).

One evening, I interviewed a member of the Chicago urban Indian community, Eli Suzukovich (Cree/Serbian), who was about to enroll in an anthropology Ph.D. program. He noted:

> Everybody [in the Chicago community] reads Vine Deloria's *Custer Died for Your Sins*, and they stop at page 99 [the end of "Anthropologists and Other Friends"]. So they're, like [*speaks in a dopey voice*], "Oh, anthropologists are bad and blah blah blah" [*returns to normal voice*] this sort of antiquated view. So what I always liked about [elders] Angie and Susan and Josephine is that they remember Boas and they have a higher opinion of [anthropologists]. So having them kind of quell that "So what? They're anthropologists, *big deal*. Then make sure you tell the right story." So I think it changed a lot of attitudes, that Indians have always had a say in their interviews and that you can *direct*—I mean the community co-curator thing.[30] I think it was *good* in that it kind of showed people that they are empowered.[31]

He was cautioning members of his community not to automatically place museum workers from the NMAI in the anthropologist slot when they came to work with the community. Instead, he saw NMAI staff as providing an empowering rather than an extractive experience. It is important to note that his exception to the kind of anthropologist that Deloria describes is Franz Boas.[32]

Another example of how anthropology is "slotted" in a community, is a certain expectation about a white, young woman like myself in some places that reflects a tension between anthropological researcher and local community. During my first week in Dominica, I was walking along the road when a young Afro-Dominican man said, "Go home to your own country! We're not apes in a fucking zoo!"[33] Needless to say, the proliferation of tourists and investigators in the area had left some people displeased; one co-curator said that the community was tired of researchers coming and asking questions all the time. In general, Native Americans do not have a rosy view of "anthros." In Chicago, one elder, while glaring at a non-Native man who was sitting at a table after serving meals at an elders lunch, was outraged and said that she thought he was "studying" her and the other elders, because all he did was sit and watch them.[34]

These are legacies we encounter in the field. As the people with whom we work become more aware of the history of anthropology and what we do (or, more likely, what people *think* we do), we encounter this antagonism toward the anthropological expert as a category, even if we feel far from being an expert and more like a student in the situation. It is rewarding when we move past seeing each other through categories and instead create lasting working relations. Of course, we focus on the instances of critique because they are moments of anxiety in the research process and they cut to the quick in light of the professional-to-professional methodology I espouse. Therefore, this book is based on positive and productive professional relationships with NMAI staff and Native community members and also acknowledges the anxieties and concerns that inhere in anthropological work more generally.

Invisible Genealogies

What people think we do in Indian country has been greatly influenced by critiques of anthropologists such as Deloria's (see also L. T. Smith 1999); these critiques in turn have had an impact on the discipline of anthropology and on museum practice. But the critical assessment of anthropology had been going on in Native communities long before Deloria penned his witty and biting caricature of the "anthro." In fact, as Regna Darnell (2001:29, 170) mentions in her description of the Americanist tradition in anthropology, Native Americans were pivotal in shaping the nature of anthropological practice in America from Boas onward. This impact of Native Americans on the discipline of anthropology began, in part, at the Smithsonian Institution's Bureau of American Ethnology and at Columbia University, where Boas institutionalized his vision for the discipline in America.

The contemporary narrative about the development of anthropology notes two major periods of "crisis" and experimentation in anthropology over the past thirty years that have converged on the notion of collaboration as anthropological method and ethical practice. During the 1980s, epitomized by *Writing Culture* (Clifford and Marcus 1986), *Anthropology as Cultural Critique* (Marcus and Fischer 1999[1986]), and *The Predicament of Culture* (Clifford 1988), the notion of ethnography as a literary genre brought to light issues of representation and authority in ethnographic texts. It was a crisis of representation, and the collaborative strategies posited in response to these critiques included multivocal or dialogic text and co-authorship.

In the 1990s, epitomized by *Anthropological Locations* (Gupta and Ferguson 1997), *Ethnography through Thick and Thin* (Marcus 1998), and *Routes* (Clifford 1997), there was a sense that changing how one writes is not enough; the implicit assumptions of what "the field" is and how anthropologists relate to it were deeply questioned—a result of changing theoretical orientations, especially toward issues of globalization, as well as what is perceived as the changing nature and growing complexity of "the field." From this examination, multisited research methods and collaborative strategies in fieldwork relations were posited in response, illustrated by the reformulation of "informants" as "alliances" (Clifford 1997) or "counterparts" (Holmes and Marcus 2005). These developments can be characterized as a shift from locating the problem of representation and authority within the text ("writing" ethnography) to locating it in the practice of fieldwork ("doing" ethnography).

Matti Bunzl (2005:188–189) asserts that the insights of the "writing culture" group were influential but not new and, "like many paradigm-shifting contributions, that work tended to obfuscate its own historicity." Bunzl situates this work in response to the "crisis in anthropology" that occurred in the 1960s–1970s, with Dell Hymes's *Reinventing Anthropology* (1972) as emblematic of the times. In that edited volume, Hymes begins with Boas and traces his influence to Herder and German Enlightenment tradition. However, the influence of Boas is absent in later renditions of the crisis in the discipline. Regna Darnell seeks to address this absence in *Invisible Genealogies: A History of Americanist Anthropology* (2001). Her preface states that the Boasians "laid the groundwork for a number of contemporary developments," including the "reflexive moment" of "writing culture" (Darnell 2001:xviii).

Earlier, I mentioned the neo-Boasian approach, following Matti Bunzl (2004). It was through Bunzl that I began to trace my own "invisible genealogies," implicit not only in how I developed my methodological practice but also in my concerns for the perspectives of the people with whom I worked. Seeking a greater understanding about the Boasian nature of this work, I turned to Darnell. All the "signs" indicating that one is an "Americanist" rang true to me. Like J. Peter Denny (1999:365), I backed into an understanding of my own—and the NMAI's, for that matter—debts to the Americanist tradition through Darnell's work.

My concerns over how to do anthropology, and over how the NMAI went about its curatorial practices, were shaped by the same constituencies as the Americanists': Native American peoples. In Darnell's terms, Americanist anthropology is not about where you do fieldwork—although its approach was created in the context of fieldwork in the United States with American Indian tribes—but rather it denotes particular concerns and methods for practicing anthropology.[35] She also writes against the notion that Boas, his followers, or Americanists in general are "anti-theory."[36] According to Darnell (2001:12), the "Americanist tradition" has seven "distinctive features" that "form an interrelated package, [but] this is not a finite system model." Briefly, these features are as follows:

> (1) Culture is a set of symbols in people's heads, not (or at least not merely) the behavior that arises from them; (2) Language, thought, and reality are mutually entailed in ways that are accessible to investigation; (3) Texts from Native

speakers of Native languages are the appropriate database for both ethnology and linguistics; (4) There is considerable urgency to record the knowledge encoded in oral traditions as part of the permanent record of human achievement; (5) "Traditional" culture is a moving target, always changing and adapting to new circumstances; (6) Native people are subjects and collaborators, not objects for study; and, (7) Fieldwork takes a long time. (Darnell 2001:12–20)

Some basic tenets of the Boasian tradition are foundational to this Americanist approach, to the NMAI, and to my own work, and I want to highlight these before moving on.[37] First, I want to reiterate that Native Americans, their critique of and proximity to anthropologists, and their demand for accountability are part of what has shaped the nature of the Americanist tradition as a diverse but recognizable body of theory. As Darnell (2001:29) notes of the reciprocal relationship between Native peoples and anthropologists, "for a long time Native Americans have been teaching anthropologists how to behave in a civilized fashion and respond to local communities' needs and concerns" (see also Cruikshank 1992; Jones 1993:212). Second, for Boas and those who followed him, working with Native Americans entailed particular kinds of ethics and commitments, including respect for the Native point of view and the belief that the explanations by informants in their own words were crucial information. When Boas collected objects or recorded ceremonies, he felt it important to record the community member's own perspective on why they were meaningful ("Native texts"). Boas brought together psychology (what people think) and history, and the neo-Boasian approach and the NMAI community-curating process reflect this.

In this book, I document how the NMAI sought to be a "museum different" and what this meant in everyday practice and from the various perspectives of those involved. As the collaborative exhibit at the heart of this book is about Native identity, I attend to the process of creating representations of indigenous peoples and how Native communities interpret and produce notions of identity explicitly for public consumption. I also illustrate how individual identities and choices contribute to collaborative products.

Structure of the Book

Native community co-curators were tasked by the NMAI with producing the content for their exhibits in the inaugural exhibitions, since they were the "experts about what it is to be Native." Each chapter in this book considers two concepts—content development and relations with community curators—from different perspectives, and each chapter presents artifacts of the museum, but they are not (or not only) the objects in the collection. They are instead artifacts of bureaucracy, collaboration, and media production. They are the things that were created along the way to making the exhibit, what informed or organized or became the exhibit, and the varied responses to it.

This book figures the museum as both a federal bureaucracy and an institution of media and cultural production, as both a workplace and a context for collaboration among experts. Chapter 2, *"Our Lives,"* considers the exhibition as a symbolic vehicle not only for the communities represented but also for the museum professionals who worked on it. I explain what community curating is, who is involved in the process, and how the life histories of individuals and the gallery influenced the changing content of the exhibition over time. Chapter 3, "Bureaucracy," presents the institutional context of community curating. I examine how the bureaucratic nature and departmental structure of the museum impact exhibition development and relations among different cultures of expertise. Chapter 4, "Expertise," provides more focused attention to the antagonism between departments, (re)presenting the departmental dynamics of the institution through cultures of expertise and illustrating how relationships to community curators complicated the normal tensions that exist between departments in museums. Chapter 5, "Authorship," views collaboration in terms of how Native voice is produced through community curating, focusing on the collaborative authorship of exhibition concepts and text. Chapter 6, "Exhibition," is a photographic tour of the *Our Lives* exhibit. Chapter 7, "Reception," is about the performance of cultural and professional expertise, and it documents the experiences of the co-curators at the museum opening and the evaluation of the exhibition by art critics, NMAI staff, and community curators. I also include some of the impacts on the communities as a result of working on the exhibition. Chapter 8, "Reflection," in part explains how community curating—its process and product—was seen as essential to fulfilling the museum's mission and at the same time was at the center of ideological differences in the museum.

Throughout, I argue for the politics of expertise as a different way to understand the representation and reception of Native peoples and their knowledge in museums. I can say in retrospect that the museum did indeed establish itself as a Native place. Although it may not be the "museum different" that many originally imagined, it surely has become the primary institution for representing Native peoples in the Americas.

two
Our Lives

The National Museum of the American Indian shall recognize and affirm to Native communities and the non-Native public the historical and contemporary culture and cultural achievements of the Natives of the Western Hemisphere by advancing— in consultation, collaboration and cooperation with Natives—knowledge and understanding of Native cultures, including art, history and language, and by recognizing the museum's special responsibility, through innovative public programming, research and collections, to protect, support and enhance the development, maintenance and perpetuation of Native culture and community.

—*NMAI mission statement, ca. 2002*

Community Activism

The original mission statement of the National Museum of the American Indian specifically called for collaboration between the museum and Native peoples,[1] and the collaboration for the inaugural exhibitions was most visible in the form of community-curated exhibits. Viewed as an ethnographic subject, the *Our Lives* exhibition was a medium for cultural production, a history of ideas, a process that engendered a particular form of social relations, and an artifact of our identities. As Barbara Kirshenblatt-Gimblett (1998:78) has stated, "Exhibitions, whether of objects or people, are displays of the artifacts of our disciplines. They are for this reason also exhibits of those who make them, no matter what their ostensible subject."

My approach to the field site of the exhibition was to look at it from multiple perspectives, in multiple locations, with the various co-producers of the community-curated exhibits. I focus mostly on two groups of actors involved in its making—NMAI curators and Native community curators—among many in the exhibition process. This narrow focus reflects my interest in an empirical and ethnographically grounded understanding of collaboration, as well as my "situated knowledge" (Haraway 1991), which offers a view on the process from particular perspectives—mainly those of the Cultural Resources Center and of the Native communities—rather than what some might call an "objective" account from all sides.

Mine is not the first account to address the NMAI as an institution. In *Politics and the Museum of the American Indian: The Heye and the Mighty*, Roland Force explains that from 1977 to 1990 he recorded data "as a participant observer while serving as Director (and then Director and President) of the Museum of the American Indian–Heye Foundation (MAI)":

> The account chronicles the trials and tribulations of the transition of that Museum to a new status as part of the Smithsonian Institution, the National Museum of the American Indian (NMAI). I have come to consider that era, representing my "New York fieldwork," [as] comparable to research I did decades earlier in the Palau Islands of Micronesia. A time when I sat through hours of meetings with chiefs in traditional structures and additional hours with elected representatives in contemporary buildings. The leaders in both the Pacific and New York were equally skilled and all sought their own agendas. (Force 1999:xv)

Whereas Force describes his account as being about "Museums, Money, and Politics" (ibid.:xvi), mine focuses on collaboration, expertise, and knowledge production. However, we both observed "turf wars" (see chapter 3).

Rather than focus on institutional and city politics at the top, as Force did among board members and trustees, I did fieldwork with the employees of the institution and their counterparts in Native American communities (during my fieldwork, I did not have access to senior management meetings or board of trustees meetings). In this chapter, I provide some historical background and a description of the NMAI museum professionals and the Chicago and Kalinago communities with which I worked. I also describe the historical development of the *Our Lives* gallery and how community curating came to be the taken-for-granted method for creating the inaugural exhibitions.

It is clear that, in all three communities, there was a history of activism among the core participants in the *OL* gallery, of seeking political or social change in their communities, whether Native (maintaining indigenous identity) or museum (effecting a "paradigm shift"). Here, activist sentiment includes a commitment to increasing Native participation and self-representation, to communicating through Native voice, or to raising awareness about Native experiences—and those who worked on

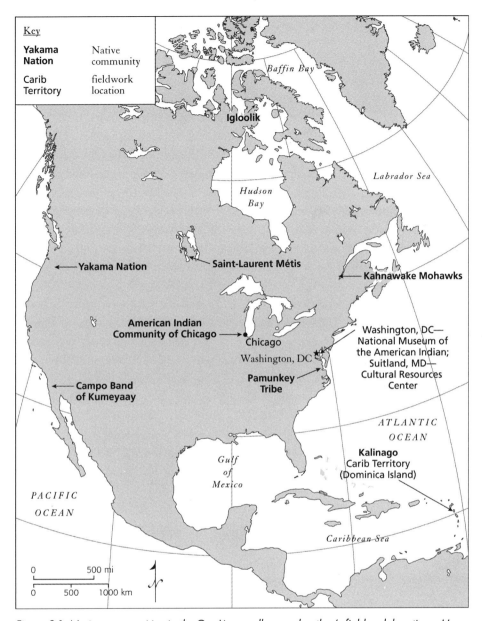

Figure 2.1. Native communities in the Our Lives *gallery and author's fieldwork locations. Map by Molly O'Halloran.*

the exhibitions at the NMAI, both in the museum and in Native communities, considered their work an extension of this sentiment and commitment.

A Multisited Approach to Museum Ethnography

I see the museum, or rather the process of exhibit development, as an ideal location for the study of collaboration—its methods, subjects, ethics, and limits—as well as for the study of cultural production, tensions between creative and bureaucratic practices, decolonizing the museum, and the coming together and negotiation of diverse knowledge practices. I followed the *Our Lives* exhibit content through the various sites of knowledge production involved in the "practical aspects of translation into design that actually make knowledge materialize" (Bouquet 2001:179). My approach, then, follows George Marcus's notion of "tracking the thing" in multisited ethnography (1998:39).[2]

I did fieldwork for six months or more in three locations. The first was the Cultural Resources Center (CRC), a research building that houses the NMAI collection in Suitland, Maryland, just outside Washington, DC. This is where the curators, collections staff, conservators, and researchers involved in exhibit development were located, along with the Community Services and Repatriation Departments. After the museum opened in DC, this central location moved to the periphery, so to speak, as the NMAI shifted its focus to the mall museum and the visiting public on the National Mall.

The other two fieldwork sites were Chicago and the Commonwealth of Dominica, two of the eight Native communities featured in the *Our Lives* exhibition (figure 2.1). The urban Indian community in Chicago is an eclectic bunch of individuals (eclectic in terms of their tribes, origins, spiritual practices, number of years of urban experience, relations to reservations, and so on) who are brought together through the institution and activities of the American Indian Center (AIC). The Carib Territory, where the Kalinago community is located, is in a remote and rural location on the tropical island of Dominica in the Caribbean. Cynthia Chavez had suggested these two Native communities for my fieldwork in part because both had requested help from the museum for projects they wanted to conduct in their own locales.

At the NMAI, I helped prepare for the opening week and provided feedback from communities about the collaborative exhibit-making process. In Chicago, I volunteered at the American Indian Center and its Trickster Gallery for Native American arts. And in the Kalinago community, I aided in the development of a history curriculum for Carib Territory schools that reflected their own experiences and history as Kalinago people, and I also served as a note taker on multiple task force committees related to tourism and development.[3]

The term "community" has multiple meanings. In "Reconceptualizing Community," Vered Amit (2002:18) seeks to "balance [the] polarizing tendencies" of scholarly discourse about communities, advocating a rapprochement of the two main theorizing trends in anthropology: imagined communities and sociologically defined ones. She stresses that communities are both social and conceptual, an "idea and/or form of sociality" (ibid.:1); "community" also denotes the interaction between the concept of community and the "actual and limited social relations and practices through which it's realized" (ibid.:18). But the Chicago and Kalinago communities could too easily be juxtaposed along this spectrum as "imagined" (Chicago) and territorially bounded (Carib Territory). Susan Lobo (2001:83) writes that urban Indian communities are "primarily abstract" and "based on a series of very dynamic relationships and shared meanings, history and symbols" rather than on residence. The Kalinagos have been described as "absorbed" into the surrounding Creole society but distinct as a community mainly because of their territorial boundary (Honychurch 1997:292). However, as Amit suggests, these communities, along with the NMAI museum professionals, are both conceptual *and* located. Chicago's Indian community is embodied in scattered sites, such as the AIC and the Ho-Chunk tribal office, and throughout the city, in which the community materializes through events and daily work; the Kalinagos are conceptualized as an indigenous community by some, but not all, residents of the territory.

Whereas Amit considers the term "community" to be an analytical one, "community" in my experience was an indigenous term—meaning that it was used in local discourse at all three field sites. Therefore, I use that term in accordance with each group's self-definition or delineation of membership, often rooted in place, common heritage, and common practices and commitments. The term "community" is specifically indigenous to the NMAI in defining units of agency, or who authors its exhibits, as in "community-curated" exhibits. Because my focus is on the *community*-curated exhibits, "community" is defined here according to the boundaries inherent in the NMAI vision of these groups. Based on NMAI staff practices and discourse, I would describe this vision as assuming a government-to-government relation with tribes (situated groups that identify themselves as communities) and the right to self-definition.

Amit (2002:1) also notes that the term "community" (like "identity" and "culture," I would add) has become analytically "sterile." I believe that this is part of what made it such a useful—and neutral—term for the museum. "Community" can be applied to many groups while masking, or not discriminating among, a host of different characteristics. For example, group inclusion (single reservation or geographically distributed, large tribe), term preference (clan, tribe, reservation), size (two hundred individuals or two thousand), and tribal status (legally recognized by a state or federal government, or neither) can all be subsumed under the same name/unit. And finally, unlike "tribe," "community" is neither political (in its legal definition with associated rights) nor specifically anthropological (or anthropologically imposed).

The Museum Professionals Community at the NMAI

In the beginning, there was the Curatorial Department. Or at least, that was how it felt to the curatorial staff when I arrived in 1999. The feeling of beginning something brand-new stemmed from the fact that most CRC staff members were new hires, many from other states, who came specifically to be a part of the NMAI institution and to contribute to its mission. However, the NMAI had been in existence since 1989, so for staff members working in New York or DC before 1999, the work likely seemed a continuation of what they had already been doing.

Curatorial staff felt that they were at the center of the museum's mission, hired to work with more than twenty-four Native communities and develop the relationships and content necessary for the inaugural exhibitions. Likely, that was how each department at the Cultural Resources Center envisioned its unique position in the monumental task of opening the latest museum on the National Mall. For example, the Collections and Registration Departments were tasked with moving and recataloging over eight hundred thousand objects from New York to the CRC in Suitland, Maryland. Each object (whether a feather warbonnet or a miniscule potsherd) was to be uniquely packaged, shipped, unpackaged, photographed, cataloged by bar code, and positioned in the allocated section of the collections space in the CRC. For Curatorial, the task was to create the most progressive, coherent, ethical, and large-scale exhibitions with and about Native Americans to date.

In 1999, the NMAI departments began imagining and preparing to create exhibitions for a building that was yet to be constructed. The departments operated largely in isolation from one another, but the staff often socialized together. Over the course of the following five years, this trend would be inverted: staff increasingly became more professionally interdependent yet socially distant from one another.

When I was there, from 1999 to 2004, the two institutional locations in Washington, DC and Suitland, MD were characterized quite distinctly by staff and referred to as "downtown" and the "CRC" respectively. Before 1999, NMAI staff and exhibitions were located at the George Gustav Heye Center in New York City, and additional staff offices in Washington, DC, were located at various buildings over the years, including the Victor Building, the Aerospace Building, and L'Enfant Plaza Hotel. One staff member who worked in Washington put it this way:

> Proximity does make a difference. And I still think that it's a huge problem for CRC to be in Maryland and for us to be here. I mean, even that fifteen-minute, twenty-minute drive—whatever it is—is still a proximity issue of *them* and *us*. Whoever, whichever site you're at...we're the them, and they're the us. There's not that water-cooler chitchat...that running into people in the break room or having somebody walk by your office and go, "Oh...I wanted to tell you, [to] talk to you about this!" It just doesn't happen.[4]

"Downtown" included most senior managers and the Exhibits, Publications, Media Services, and Human Resources Departments and then the Education, Public Programs, and Visitor Services Departments as the museum was about to open. Downtown had always been the center of power in terms of the control of finances and proximity to senior staff and the director of the museum, and it was close to a main source of funding for the museum: Congress.[5] These staff members later became known as "the fifth floor" because that was where downtown NMAI staff were relocated in the museum building on the National Mall when construction of the office space was completed in the summer of 2004.

The NMAI in general put a lot of emphasis on design and aesthetics and paid

Figure 2.2. National Museum of the American Indian mall museum. Photo by author. Reproduced with permission of the National Museum of the American Indian, Smithsonian Institution.

great attention to symbolism in both the Cultural Resources Center and the mall museum. Each design plan was developed through consultation with Native peoples and Native architects. The mall museum is now well known for its unique, curvy architecture and sandstone exterior (figure 2.2). It is located along the grassy expanse of the National Mall, next to the Capitol, and surrounded by the other Smithsonian museums. The NMAI contrasts with the other museums, which are largely rectangular and have Greek-inspired architecture. The color of the sandstone, the water features, and the wild landscaped exterior also distinguish this museum from other buildings in the area. These unique design features were considered to reflect an "Indian aesthetic" through the absence of right angles and the return of the land to its original state with the reintroduction of local indigenous plant species.

The Cultural Resources Center is within the DC metropolitan area, but it is isolated, along with the Museum of Natural History's Museum Support Center, in Suitland, Maryland, about eight miles outside the city. Both centers house Smithsonian museum collections and are located on a landscaped site enclosed by a high, imposing, black metal fence with gated entrances and security guards. Across the internal drive from the boxy, hangar-like Museum Support Center is the CRC, a salmon-colored building surrounded by trees and shrubbery, with a metal nautilus-like

Figure 2.3. Cultural Resources Center, June 15, 2006. Photo by author. Reproduced with permission of the National Museum of the American Indian, Smithsonian Institution.

structure rising above its entryway—a rare architectural beauty for the area (figure 2.3). Many staff members considered Suitland an unsafe place due to its crime rate, and, unlike the mall museum, there is no cafeteria, nor nearby cultural attractions. There are few locations to eat out in the area, the main restaurants being a Chinese buffet and a pizza joint in a small strip mall. In other words, it is both a remarkable building *and* isolated and seemingly out of context—socioeconomically and architecturally—in the area in which it sits.[6]

Designed to house the collection and to host tribal visits and research-related activities, the CRC originally included a library, archives, and the Curatorial, Conservation, Collections, Registration, Community Services, Photo Services, and Information Technology Departments. From 1999 to 2004, the entire Heye collection (except human remains [Native ancestors] that were to be repatriated) was moved from the NMAI Research Branch in the Bronx to the CRC by the "move team."[7]

The main purpose of the CRC building becomes clear when one enters the collections space. With three floors of motorized moving cabinets and shelves of various sizes, the collections space is bright and airy and has windows. It is unlike most collection spaces in museums. This is because, as any staff member would explain, the CRC is not a storage facility, but a "home" for the objects. The windows are there for the items to connect with the outside world, to "breathe." The third-floor collection space is a small loft, created for those objects that should never be walked above. These design considerations are connected to concepts of "traditional care": providing for the collection's items according to Native communities' input on how best to care for their material culture. The collections are housed according to tribal affiliation, rather than object type.

The CRC is a welcoming space where Native people come to view—and to touch and to use—their material culture. In addition, there are two ceremonial spaces: a wooded area behind the building, which can be reached by a path that ends in a circular clearing, and a small room inside the building, with floor-to-ceiling windows that face this exterior wooded area. A clothes-changing room is nearby and a fire pit in the small room, where smudging (purification through smoke) and other traditional care activities can take place.

Within the NMAI, there were common understandings of the two institutional locations (downtown and the CRC), which were represented by the Exhibits and Curatorial Departments, located in Washington and Suitland, respectively. As characterized by staff members, downtown was considered the locus of power and decision making, often referred to as the "public face" of the museum (and I heard consultants and downtown staff call it the "NMAI for the public"). In contrast, the CRC was described as the "heart" of the museum, where the mission was carried out on the ground and where tribal members came to be with the collection objects.

A Life History of the Our Lives *Gallery*

Although the *Our Lives* gallery began downtown, it was later situated in the politics and practices of the CRC as it moved conceptually from a thematic exhibit to a community-curated one, which was reflected in its name change from *Living in the Native Universe* to *Our Lives*. The gallery had many contributors over its history, and at one point, it was thought that it might not open when the rest of the museum did. Here, I focus narrowly on the different conceptual incarnations that people proposed over time, rather than on the effort to physically create the gallery (which I develop in the following chapters). Perhaps surprising to those who have visited the museum, especially in light of its methodological centrality to the NMAI's mission, the *Our Lives* gallery did not start out as a community-centered exhibition.

Long before the CRC was built and its staff hired, plans circulated as early as 1991 about the galleries' exhibition contents. A document produced from nationwide consultations with Native people, called *The Way of the People: National Museum of the American Indian*, included general prescriptions: the exhibitions should have "Indian interpreters from the tribes represented" and be "multisensory environments analogous to Native American architectures and landscapes"; "in other words, NMAI's galleries will be more like theaters, but with the audience in the middle." In addition, the document stated, "Non-Indians are novices with little knowledge and many stereotypes about Indians and they need to understand some fundamentals before they proceed to other exhibitions and performances" (Scott Brown Venturi and Associates 1991:88–89).

By 1995, a "Mall Facility Exhibition Master Plan" produced with professional consultants included a description of three "broad overarching themes" that the permanent exhibitions would address—"spirituality; lifeways; [and] history"—and emphasized the diversity among tribes and among individuals. The "Storyline and Emotional Pathway" section described the gallery as the "Museum of Native Lifeways" and explained, "Visitors will 'meet' individual native people and learn about their experiences while passing through the cycle of life, from childhood to old age." The text went on to describe the "emotion" of the exhibit: "The ideas in this section—family, tradition and generational change—are very familiar to non-Indians and should help establish their sense of comfort and connection with native peoples" (Gerard Hilferty and Associates 1995). Detailing this conception, the summary of the gallery read:

> *Living in the Native Universe*, or the Museum of Native Lifeways, will be organized into divisions representing the cycle of life: birth, childhood, adulthood, death and afterlife. Exhibits in this area will explore the notion of *process as being as important as product*. Here native people of different ages, genders, and culture groups will tell stories of their own experiences while passing through the cycle of life. These stories will recount how doing things in a native way made profound differences in these lives. Exhibits in these galleries will be about Indian ways of growing and learning; Indian ways of being in the world; passages from one stage of life to the next; relationships between generations; and the wisdom of elders. (Gerard Hilferty and Associates 1995:sec. 5.1:6, emphasis added)

Visitors would meet individuals from many tribes talking about, for example, what it was like to "grow up Zuni," and there was an emphasis on audiovisual technologies to tell these stories. The text explained that an exhibit "might use four tribal groups within the hemisphere to portray a diversity of voices with each stage of life for each culture" (Gerard Hilferty and Associates 1995:16–17). A conceptual diagram labeled "Storyline Diagram Showing Content Sequence and Visitor Flow" of the gallery included a small circle representing an introductory exhibit, leading to a kidney-bean-shaped "bubble" that says "Life Cycle." Three small circles interrupted the outline of the kidney bean: a "Resource Center satellite" station that showed computers linking to the main Resource Center and two changing or temporary exhibit areas.

In 1997, after additional consultations, a revised draft of the mall exhibition plan was circulated to staff, who referred to it as the "Duck Book" (there was a duck decoy artifact on its cover). The participants who created the content for the book were divided under the titles of core planning team (NMAI Exhibits Department and Hilferty staff), content development mentors (one for each permanent exhibition), circle of advisors (including prominent Native scholars and museum consultants), content researchers, extended review group (mainly NMAI staff, both Native and non-Native), architectural design core team, and design advisory group (Native advisors for architectural design) (Gerard Hilferty and Associates 1997:7–9). The NMAI director, Rick West, introduced the plan, writing, "Part of our task has been to synthesize a number of different realities. We have had to find a way to create an

Indian place within the context of a Smithsonian museum on the National Mall. We have had to develop approaches to bring together the Native voice with the scholar's insight, tradition with innovation, aesthetics with harsh realities" (Gerard Hilferty and Associates 1997:n.p.).

This draft included a significantly different conceptual plan for *Living in the Native Universe*. The gallery had been moved from the second to the third floor, and a "Mentor's Statement," provided by Gerald McMaster (Plains Cree/Siksika First Nation),[8] reoriented the subject matter and framing of the gallery to identity and survival:

> Indigenous people of the Americas continue to strive for a sense of identity. For us, defining who we are as individuals or people is a complex, contingent, and sensitive matter. Our identity has many aspects. Prior to the arrival of strangers, we did not think of ourselves as sharing a unified identity. Even today this idea obscures the extraordinary diversity of our culture[s] and of our individual experiences. Yet, it is our commonality that brings us together under the term "Indian." Above all, our identities persist as an important part of everyday life against the backdrop of a constantly changing world: we continue to be Indians.
>
> For many indigenous peoples today, fundamental principles and philosophies continue being guides for our survival, even for those who no longer live in their culture's homelands. These foundations stress the importance of language, family, community, ceremony, and respect for the environment. Some of our deepest connections are with the places and people we associate with "home"—where we come from; the family that nurtures us; the community that cements its relationships through tradition and ceremony; and the languages we speak. We take these principles and weave them together into a life that makes sense for us and keeps our cultures alive.
>
> As the indigenous people of the Americas, we have always expressed ourselves in distinctive ways, whether it is in art, music, dance, language, architecture, attire, literature, environment, ceremony, everyday practice, or our relationships with others. We continue balancing our enduring principles to meet the needs of living in a contemporary world. We sustain customs and traditions by adapting them to the world around us. Our cultures provide us with traditional ways that enrich our everyday lives and empower us to thrive in a continually changing world.
>
> In the words of Simon Ortiz, "We persist and insist on living, believing, hoping, loving, speaking, and writing as Indians" into the twenty-first century.
> (Gerard Hilferty and Associates 1997:55)

The vision for the gallery in 1997 continued to be focused on individual "conversations" in which visitors would "meet" Native people in thematic areas of the exhibition. But instead of the life cycle, the pathway of the exhibition now followed subthemes listed under the main title, "Heritage": language and tradition; family and community; place; names; relations with others; public and private gatherings; contemporary artistic expression; everyday practice; and fundamental principles

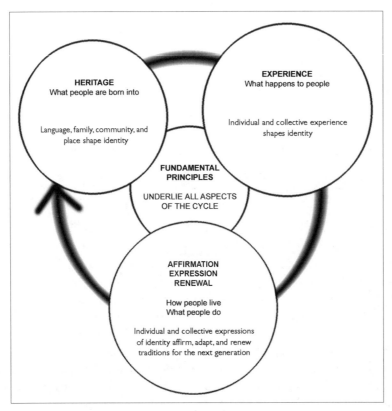

HERITAGE
What people are born into

Language, family, community, and
place shape identity

EXPERIENCE
What happens to people

Individual and collective experience
shapes identity

FUNDAMENTAL
PRINCIPLES

UNDERLIE ALL ASPECTS
OF THE CYCLE

AFFIRMATION
EXPRESSION
RENEWAL

How people live
What people do

Individual and collective expressions
of identity affirm, adapt, and renew
traditions for the next generation

Figure 2.4. Living in the Native Universe *concept diagram of the "Cycle of Identity and Continuity" (redrawn by author).*

(Gerard Hilferty and Associates 1997:56–63).[9] The *Living in the Native Universe* concept diagram now included the "Cycle of Identity and Continuity" (figure 2.4).

The Duck Book was widely trashed in vetting sessions with scholars, museum professionals, and tribal leaders.[10] Bruce Bernstein, reflecting on his time at the NMAI as assistant director for cultural resources, provides some explanation for the criticism of the plan—it was "regular, expected"—and recalls the director's consent to depart from it:

> Rick [West] provided approval to fully disregard the Duck Book and to work directly with Native communities and to have their voices on the floor of the exhibitions.... I remember reading [the plans] in Santa Fe before leaving for Washington [for his new position as head of the CRC] and being dumbfounded that they were so regular, expected, and ordinary. They thought the method of interpretation was correct, although there was not really community involvement as the museum promised. Rick asked me to do two specific tasks: to produce exhibitions that were Native voice centered, as the museum (Rick) promised, and...to get community people involved (not the Rolodex crowd).[11]

Note Bruce's use of the term "Rolodex crowd," whom he suggests the planners had relied on. This desire to work with Native community members who were not the usual representatives to museums—an indicator of what some museum professionals at the NMAI felt was and was not the "authentic Native voice"—led to the selection of community curators from the communities themselves. Some Native intellectuals would later critique the NMAI for working with amateurs, one person calling them "informants" rather than collaborators.[12]

Duane Blue Spruce (Laguna/San Juan Pueblo), an NMAI staff member and architect who worked on the mall museum, said of the Duck Book that, although the exhibit concepts were thrown out, the visitor experience information basically stayed the same and was still relevant.[13] These critical review meetings were the impetus for the community-centered approach to exhibit making that was later implemented in the three inaugural exhibitions.

Bruce Bernstein was hired by Rick West as assistant director for cultural resources, Bruce felt, in part due to his experience as curator at the Museum of New Mexico and participation in the community-curated exhibition *Here, Now, and Always: Voices of the First Peoples of the Southwest* (1997) at the Museum of Indian Arts and Culture in Santa Fe. This exhibition was an early forerunner in incorporating Native advisors in content development and presenting Native voice in exhibition displays.

Craig Howe (Oglala Lakota) was hired as deputy assistant director of cultural resources in 1999, and he oversaw the curatorial work on the inaugural exhibitions. Through "incredible sessions" with "a talented group" that included Rick Hill, Ruth Phillips, Tessie Naranjo, Ramiro Matos, and Gerald McMaster, Craig developed a "braid of feathers" concept to connect the three permanent exhibitions.[14] Craig was key to reconceptualizing how the exhibits would be tribal centered, and Bruce championed the tribal-centered and community-curating approach against much opposition at times within the institution (see chapter 4). On September 24, 1999, Bruce distributed Craig's proposed diagram of the galleries, revised narratives for *Our Universes* and *Our Peoples*, and the museum's mission statement and guiding principles to the newly hired curatorial researchers. This sketch became a well-known, often referenced image for the galleries among curatorial staff (figure 2.5). By this time, the inaugural exhibitions' names had shifted to *Our Universes*, *Our Peoples*, and *Our Lives*.[15] Although *OP* and *OU* were relatively far along in conceptual design, *OL* was the last to be developed and the last to be assigned a lead curator. Until a curator was hired in 2000, Tristine Smart, the lead researcher, was compiling research and liaising with possible contributors to the gallery.

Craig Howe left the NMAI in 2000, and Ann McMullen arrived shortly after to become the head of the Curatorial Department. Gerald McMaster was hired in August 2001 to take over the position of deputy assistant director of cultural resources. A meeting about the gallery in 2000 concluded that, with Gerald's addition to the staff and his role as the gallery's original mentor, there would likely be changes in the *Our Lives* plan.

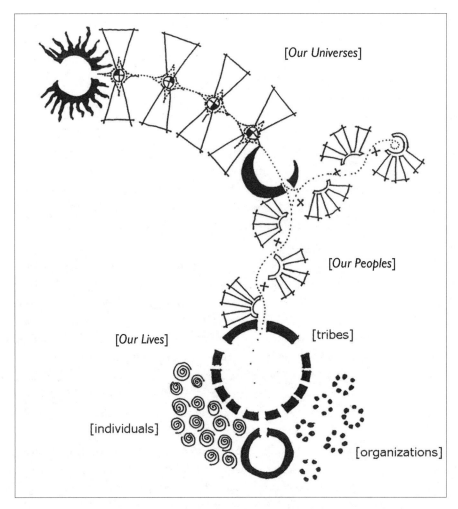

Figure 2.5. Craig Howe's conceptual drawing of OP, OU, and OL galleries (labels added).

In Craig's preliminary conceptual diagram, the *OL* gallery's focus had shifted, with thematic sections titled "Individuals," "Tribes," and "Indigenous Intertribal Organizations." By June 1999, the gallery had a walk-through narrative and was divided into four sections: "communities/tribes; intertribal organizations; individuals; and an NMAI-curated section dealing with the impact of education policy on Native individuals."[16] As Ann recalled, Craig's idea of *OL* at the time had tribal flags and resembled the halls of justice; the emphasis was on sovereignty, and the gallery had a "united indigenous nations" feel to it.[17] A list of possible tribes and intertribal organizations was prepared, but many were left out of the final exhibition plan.

In the summer of 2000, staff had completed preliminary research into possible *OL* tribes and organizations, but no formal contacts had been made. At this point, I was asked to take over the lead researcher position because Tristine was leaving the NMAI, and Cynthia was transitioning from an NMAI assistant curator position in contemporary art to the lead curator for the *OL* gallery. In January 2001, then, the gallery began anew with a full curatorial team in place: Cynthia as lead curator, me as lead researcher, and Taryn Costanzo as research assistant. Arwen Nuttall (Cherokee) would later be hired as a research assistant, and when I left in 2002, Taryn became the lead researcher. Cynthia developed a new walk-through narrative in consultation with Gerald McMaster. This marked a shift back to an emphasis on cultural identity, more closely resembling Gerald's original mentor statement, rather than political identity or sovereignty, which had been emphasized by Craig Howe during his tenure at the museum.

After several different drafts of the narrative for the gallery, the final conceptual organization consisted of "Tribes/Nations/Communities," which would be Native community curated, and a "Personal Stories" section, which would be NMAI curated (developed by NMAI curators, whether Native or non-Native).[18] The final exhibition layout for the gallery included community-curated exhibits and an NMAI-curated thematic introductory section in the central space of the gallery (see chapters 6 and 7).

As staff changed over time, so, too, did the conceptual organization of the gallery; these changes reflected staff critiques of earlier models, as well as their commitments, identities, and values. The *Our Lives* gallery moved from a classic life cycle display, to conversations with Native people, to a presentation of tribal sovereignty and life stories, to a community-focused representation of cultural identity. In addition, the notion of identity changed over time. First, it was linked to growing up and the life stages from birth to death, then it was about heritage and language and place, then it was tied to sovereignty and government policy, and then it was about cultural identity and change. In the final rendition, it was left in the hands of the community members themselves to define how they would interpret the overall identity-focused theme of the gallery, and identity became "what it's like to live today" in their communities.

Cynthia, the lead curator, wanted to leave to the communities much of the interpretation of what "contemporary Native identities" meant to them, and so she gave little guidance as to how they should approach "identity" as an exhibit theme. But she did give the co-curators three guidelines for what their exhibit should *not* be:

1. A history of the community. History will undoubtedly be part of each community's exhibition, but it should not be the focal point. History should be referenced as it relates to a contemporary event, organization, activity, etc.

2. A sanitized, tourism office version of the community.

3. Focused solely on traditional or historical practices of the community. Every community has changed over the years. This is what has contributed to their vitality and survival.

And she listed what "every community component *should* be":

1. An honest, complex representation of the community.

2. A presentation about the specific community, not the culture in general. For example, if a community is Mohawk, the focus should be on that specific Mohawk community and not Mohawk culture in general.

These instructions were intended to encourage communities to create authentic representations of their experience. They also demonstrated Cynthia's desire for a nuanced exhibition about Native identity; she was the curator, but, at the same time, she did not have control over the specific issues that would be represented in the exhibits. From these sparse guidelines, the content for the exhibits in the *Our Lives* gallery was developed through community curating.

The Process of Community Curating

Except for the opening week celebrations in 2004, all interactions between curators and co-curators described in this book are in the context of the community-curating process or community visits by NMAI staff. There were some rare instances in which co-curators visited the NMAI, such as members of the Pamunkey tribe from Virginia who lived nearby, but, due to the late start of the *Our Lives* exhibition team and because the NMAI had few contemporary collections related to the *OL* communities, most of the time and money available was spent traveling to communities rather than bringing co-curators to the museum. This meant that, for object selection, co-curators viewed binders of photographs of the collection rather than visited the objects in person (co-curators from the other two inaugural galleries visited the collection onsite). Therefore, this brief description represents the community-curating process specifically as it was practiced by the *Our Lives* team.

Cynthia took a flexible approach to community curating, providing some general guidelines and leaving it to each community to determine a proper method for co-curator selection. The co-curator committees were therefore organized in different ways and included anywhere between four and ten people.[19] The American Indian community of Chicago selected its co-curators through nomination and election at the American Indian Center; I learned later that this was a familiar process for the Chicago community. For the Kalinagos in Dominica, the chief of the Carib Territory selected the co-curator committee, making sure that there was representation of people who were male and female, lived in each hamlet, and participated in particular professions, including basket makers, canoe builders, political figures, and cultural group leaders (see chapter 4). The dynamics among the co-curators varied in each community according to gender, age, expertise, and cultural protocol. Regardless of the composition of the various co-curator groups, the committee form resulted in a unified, authoritative voice in each exhibit—and the community curators authored as a group each of the main sections of their exhibit (see chapter 5).

The process of community curating for all the inaugural exhibitions was unique in that the NMAI curators spent a significant amount of time in each community. There were regular meetings between Cynthia and the co-curator committees from 2001 to 2003. For example, in Chicago, first there was an introductory meeting to invite the Chicago American Indian community to participate in the exhibition. After the community agreed to participate, periodic meetings at the American Indian Center between NMAI staff and selected co-curators began.[20] The meetings were recorded, and the dialogue from those discussions and individual interviews with co-curators and other community members was intended to inform, or be used as, the text of the exhibit. In the first meetings, the NMAI curatorial representative listened to the co-curators as they began to formulate what it means to be a member of the American Indian community of Chicago today, including activities that bring them together, such as powwows, community gathering places like the Anawim Center and the American Indian Center, and the various ways in which individuals maintain their Native American identity in the midst of a large metropolis. The emphasis was on the Chicago community as a multitribal and widely diverse group of people. Cynthia listened and returned to the community with themes that represented the various issues discussed—and the co-curators helped to further define these themes.[21]

Then, co-curators selected objects from the NMAI, using the object binders, or booklets of photographs of the collection. For the *Our Lives* gallery, there was often no NMAI collection of contemporary items, and the museum had no collection associated with Chicago. To provide objects for display, some co-curators and community members offered material items from their own homes, and new artworks were commissioned to represent exhibit themes. The co-curators were later visited by the design team, discussed their visions for presentation, and reviewed the design team's sketches and layouts of the exhibit. An NMAI media team also went to Chicago, interviewing community members on video and recording important events during the week they were there, including a powwow and a graduation ceremony. At each stage, people working on the exhibit went to the community—to talk with co-curators and community members and get a sense of the people and the place in order to better represent them in the museum.

Overall, the community members were very involved in the development of content for the exhibit, and their recorded conversations and interviews were the source for label copy and video displays. In addition, everything in the exhibit was authored—a mandate from Rick West. For general introductory panels, the author was "Chicago co-curators." For specific quotations, the label included the person's name and tribal affiliation. Photographs of community members and their children, and objects they had made, such as beadwork, were all authored or attributed to specific individuals.

The co-curators were also responsible for determining the main message of their exhibit. The Kahnawake co-curators decided that their contemporary identity was best captured with the message "Kahnawakehro:non assert their sovereignty in all aspects of their lives." The Pamunkey co-curators chose "The Pamunkey proudly serve the Creator as stewards of the land and waters that have sustained them for thousands of years" (for a complete list of the gallery's main messages, see appendix B).

Many people wondered why certain communities were selected for the inaugural exhibitions instead of others. Even those chosen asked, "Why us?" A number of factors contributed to community selection, but NMAI curators primarily chose communities according to a particular distribution logic that was tied to the collection: each gallery was to present tribes in four "zones" of the hemisphere that proportionally matched the geographic distribution of collection objects from each region. In other words, if 75 percent of the collection is from North America, then 75 percent of the tribes in each gallery should be from that region. Because the inaugural exhibitions were all being curated at once, in many cases, particular communities within these zones were selected because NMAI staff had some form of connection to them through community members or other scholars, which helped speed up the process of locating and contacting the appropriate people with whom to create the exhibits. However, the reasons that a community may have been interesting to staff to include in a gallery about identity were often not mentioned in the exhibit content developed through the community-curating process (see chapter 5).

The Kalinago and Chicago communities were selected for inclusion in the *Our Lives* gallery for a number of reasons. Though often thought to no longer exist, the Carib, or Kalinago, people are the only Native people to have their own territory in the Caribbean. Chicago boasts the oldest multitribal Indian center in the nation. There has been an ongoing Native population in Chicago since the nineteenth century despite a lack of Indian reservations in the state of Illinois, but the urban Indian community of Chicago was also a kind of "invisible" (Beck 1998:167) community: few city residents were aware of this history or of the Native presence in Chicago more generally. Because the *OL* gallery was a year behind in development compared with the other two inaugural exhibitions, it was helpful that NMAI staff already had contacts in the Chicago community. In addition, communication with both Chicago and Kalinago was anticipated to be easier because the majority of both communities speak English. Although most Kalinagos also speak Kweyol (a local patois with French and Carib words)[22] and some Chicago community members also speak Native languages, as a result of colonization, the official language in each place, and what is learned in schools there, is English.

The Kalinago Community of the Carib Territory

The island of Dominica, where the Kalinago people live, is located halfway between Puerto Rico and the Venezuelan coast in the West Indies. Most people know the Kalinagos (as they prefer to be called), or Caribs, to be one of the first indigenous groups that Christopher Columbus encountered in the Caribbean on his second voyage in 1493. Through contact and colonization, the Kalinagos were decimated by disease, slave raiding, and genocidal warfare to the point where, today, most people think that there are no indigenous peoples left in the Caribbean. However, a small

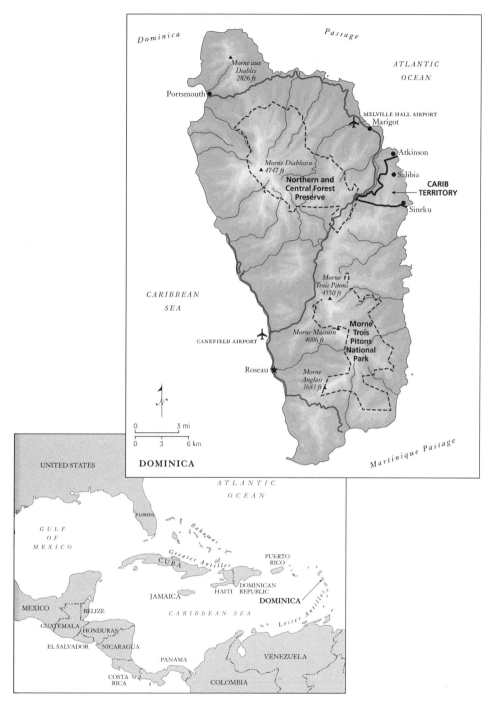

Figure 2.6. Dominica with Carib Territory. Maps by Molly O'Halloran.

population survived on the inaccessible, rugged east coast of Dominica, and a Kali-nago community remains there to this day (Baker 1994:24).

The Kalinagos are recognized for their long campaign of resistance to colonial powers (Spanish, British, and French), missionization, and enslavement between 1492 and 1700 (Beckles 1992). By the year 1700, the population may have decreased by as much as 90 percent to no more than two thousand people (ibid.:13), but their resistance affected the Caribbean economy and politics more broadly. Beginning in 1635, settlement and possession of Dominica went back and forth between the French and British, but after 1763, it was formally a British possession. In 1764, the Kalinagos had jurisdiction over 223 acres set aside by the British government on the eastern coast of the island (Gregoire and Kanem 1989). In 1903, as part of an allotment process instigated by the British colonial government, a sympathetic administrator, Hesketh Bell, enlarged this area and set aside an allotment that was labeled the Carib Reserve to be held in common by the Carib people. Today, with eight hamlets and a population of around four thousand (Special Projects Assistance Team 2000), this 3,700-acre plot of land is administered by the Carib Council and referred to as the Carib Territory (Joseph 1997:215; figure 2.6). The Carib Territory was wired for telephones in the 1960s and for electricity in the late 1980s. One main paved road, littered with potholes, runs through the territory.

The Carib people are the origin—along with the "peaceful Arawaks"—of the enduring stereotypes of Native peoples as either "noble savages" or "fierce cannibals" that were conjured by Columbus in the late fifteenth century (Thomas 2000). Even in 2005, these stereotypes were part of the popularly imagined Carib history, which Kalinagos were confronting daily in their school textbooks and national politics, and these provided the context in which the Kalinagos were attempting to take control of the process of representation or, as Terry Turner (2002:88) puts it, to "take control over the process of objectification itself." The most notable and publicly visible exercise of doing so was the Kalinago portion of the *Our Lives* exhibit.

The Kalinago co-curators were asked how they wanted to be acknowledged on the introductory panel of their NMAI exhibit. Each person offered only one position, held among many: Gerard Langlais, Karina Cultural Group manager; Jacinta Bruney, craftmaker; Prosper Paris, Karifuna Cultural Group artistic director; Chief Garnette Joseph; Sylvanie Burton, community development worker; Alexis Valmond, Carib Council member; Cozier Frederick, teacher; and Irvince Auguiste, tour operator (figure 2.7). Through formal interviews and everyday conversations, I was able to learn more about each individual than from these brief descriptions and to better understand how their roles in their community led them to be selected as co-curators.

While I was in Dominica in 2005, Kalinago community members were talking about whether to participate in the movie *Pirates of the Caribbean: Dead Man's Chest* (2006), in which they were asked to portray cannibals; how to represent themselves in the soon-to-be-opened heritage center in the Carib Territory; and what they wanted to teach their children about Kalinago culture. They invited me to participate in the task forces and community meetings about these projects, which I viewed as forms of "collective self-production" (Ginsburg 1996:2). As I listened to their concerns, the

Figure 2.7. Kalinago community curators, 2005. From left: *Garnette Joseph, Sylvanie Burton, Irvince Auguiste, Prosper Paris, Cozier Frederick, Jacinta Bruney, Gerard Langlais, and Alexis Valmond. Photo by author.*

Kalinagos contributed to my understanding of the contemporary politics of representation and indigeneity and the rise of "cultural consciousness," as the Kalinagos call it, in Native communities (Joseph and Shannon 2009).[23]

Today, the Kalinagos are listed as one of Dominica's "special features" for tourism because they are the only indigenous people to have a territory in the Caribbean. Celebrating Dominica as "the nature island," due to its "unspoiled" lush forests, mountains, geothermal attractions, and many waterfalls and rivers (figure 2.8), the island's tourism advertising also emphasizes that it is the home of a living population of "Pre-Columbian Carib Indians."[24] Packaged "Carib Tours" and "Nature Tours" offered by cruise ships are the island's main source of tourism dollars. The decline of banana production and the island's need for more tourism revenue have no doubt contributed to the increased recognition and celebration of the Carib presence in Dominica and the 2006 opening of the Kalinago Barana Autê, The Carib Cultural Village by the Sea, a heritage center thirty years in the planning. Although the Kalinagos have been historically discriminated against, they are now celebrated as a main attraction for tourists.

Not just these economic factors but also social movements contributed to a higher self-valuation by the Kalinago people, beginning in the late 1970s. Lennox Honychurch,[25] author of the definitive contemporary history of the island, *The Dominica Story* (1984:242), says of the arrival of the rights movement in Dominica, "It takes time for ideas or fashions to drift down to the Caribbean, and so the effects of

Figure 2.8. View from the Kalinago Barana Autê: Carib Village by the Sea (formerly known as the Carib Model Village), Carib Territory, November 17, 2007. Photo by author.

the protests in the US were not felt until the very end of the 1960s." But while he discusses the "Black Power boys" and the Rasta movement and how in Dominica in the 1970s there was a "wave of animosity" among Afro-Dominican urban youth (ibid.:243), neither Honychurch nor other authors who write about Dominican history or Caribs consider the late twentieth-century political formulations or community organizing created in response to the heightened race consciousness of the era from within the territory by Kalinago people.

In the 1970s, Kalinagos, including the core group of Kalinago co-curators, finally had access to secondary school education, and with this opportunity came a greater awareness that they were "not alone"—that other indigenous groups, like them, were experiencing discrimination and struggles. Co-curator Prosper Paris explained:

> To me, the whole consciousness of [the] 1970s was getting up. We had the black power, for example, in the US—it filtered through the Caribbean. So we had the Dread people getting into identifying themselves as Africans and Rasta men.... Now, we couldn't identify with *that*. We had to find *our* roots also.... There was a new image that we should rise up as Carib people. That new generation had to stand up, because everything was not lost.... People who went through education had a lot of problems, being discriminated against as being a Carib or inferior race.[26]

The same people who received a secondary education, learned about other Native communities, and experienced severe discrimination in close contact with the wider Afro-Dominican population were the first generation collectively committed to raising Carib cultural consciousness in the territory. This generation included the founders of the Karifuna Cultural Group, which was formed in 1978 to raise cultural consciousness about Carib people within and outside the territory. The Carib Liberation Movement (CLM) was created around the same time to raise political consciousness about Carib rights in Dominica (Joseph and Shannon 2009). Garnette Joseph, Irvince Auguiste, Prosper Paris, and Worrell Sanford were early key members of each of these groups, and they continue to advocate for Kalinago political and cultural consciousness today. Sylvanie Burton and Gerard Langlais were Karifuna members in its early days. Prosper, a former member of the CLM, explained, "It didn't last very long, but it did put us in a new energy by just meeting and discussing what is the next move and what is out there and how people are looking at us. It builds you into another level."[27]

Therefore, the strong cultural awareness that the Kalinago co-curators speak about today has roots in their experiences of community organizing around political and cultural consciousness. The organizers of the short-lived CLM through a concerted effort at one point took control of the Carib Council: Irvince was chief (at age twenty-one in 1980, until 1990), with Prosper and Garnette as councilors and Sylvanie as the council clerk. In addition to the Carib Council members, two served in the office of Carib chief, one later hosted a Kalinago Voices radio program, and several held leadership positions in the Karifuna Cultural Group. They all volunteered with various community organizations and development projects during my fieldwork time in Dominica, and they contributed to Carib Week cultural celebration activities as well.

After living in the Carib Territory for six months, I learned that many issues divided the Kalinago co-curators: for example, national political party affiliation, religious affiliation, being for or against Carib chief Charles Williams, what cultural group they affiliated with in the territory, and whether they had "mixed" parentage (Kalinago and Afro-Dominican). However, these divisions were not apparent to NMAI staff at meetings with the co-curators during the development of the Kalinago exhibit.

In Dominica, I intersected with many community curators on almost a daily basis, through participating in various volunteer projects or attending cultural group meetings or just walking through the territory along the main road. In contrast, I found the Chicago community to be difficult to intersect with, although not difficult to interact with, because I always felt welcomed by community members. But it was rare for our paths to cross outside of the American Indian Center or at planned community events. I did not have chance meetings with them in the city, and I was also on my own for a good portion of my volunteer work at the Trickster Gallery.

The Urban Indian Community of Chicago

I am originally from Chicago, and most of my family still lives there. One Saturday night, I was at the movies in Chicago with some family members who live in the area, and I realized that I felt out of contact with the community of the AIC, with the Indian experience in general in the city. I never felt that way at my other field sites. Was I too outside the community or too inside my own experience to be doing this ethnography? This was markedly different from how immersed I felt with the people, the media, and the concerns of the Kalinagos in Dominica. I always felt surrounded by the community there. Then I realized that perhaps this is exactly the feeling that the Chicago American Indian community members themselves face: a desire to feel surrounded by their own cultural perspectives, peoples, and values in a place where they are constantly bombarded by media, workplace encounters, and individuals who are not part of the community they have created through the American Indian Center.

Many Chicagoans are unaware that the city was a meeting ground for Native peoples long before the onset of the fur trade. The Illini and Miami, confederations of Algonquian-speaking peoples, were the first known residents in the area. Potawatomi, Ojibwe (Chippewa), and Ottawa (Odawa) tribes later pushed them out; they, too, were supplanted when, through the Treaty of Chicago (1833), they relinquished their claim to the land. Since then, no tribes have had demarcated or federally recognized homelands in the state of Illinois. Native Americans would later be viewed as curiosities in displays at the World's Columbian Exposition in Chicago in 1893. In 1923, American Indians who chose to stay in the area formed the first intertribal organization in Chicago: the Indian Council Fire.

Although World War I brought some additional Native residents to the city, it was not until after World War II that they arrived in larger numbers (Straus and Valentino 2001:87). In 1940, around 10 percent of Native Americans lived in cities; by 1980, 53 percent lived in cities; and by 2000, 64 percent were living in cities (Public Broadcasting Service 2006). The federal policy of termination was well under way when the Urban Indian Relocation Program was initiated in 1952 (see Public Broadcasting Service 2006). "Termination" was a general policy position of the US government in the mid-twentieth century in which it attempted to end the special rights and obligations that tribes were due according to treaty agreements. The relocation program after World War II was part of this effort. The assumption was that, if the US government could encourage American Indians to move to cities and away from reservations, this would hasten the breakup of the reservations and terminate the government's fiduciary and legal responsibilities to the tribes.[28]

Chicago was one of nine cities selected to host the participants in the relocation program. Promised money, counseling, and a job, many who were recruited or joined the program "found these promises were not kept.... It's estimated that as many as 750,000 Native Americans migrated to the cities between 1950 and 1980. Some came through the Relocation Program. Others came on their own" (Public

Broadcasting Service 2006). The growing concentration of Native Americans in cities is one factor that contributed to the momentum of American Indian political activism in the 1960s–1970s.

As David Beck (2002:117) notes, "more American Indians live in urban areas than anywhere else in the United States." However, one would be hard pressed to find representations of urban Indians, or urban Indian communities, in museums or the national press. In Chicago, Native Americans are "one of the least visible minority groups" (Beck 1998:167). Beck tells of a community member, a student at a suburban grade school, who in 1998 was instructed, "There are no Indians alive anymore," by her teacher (ibid.:169).

There was a particular moment when it seemed that all Native Americans looked to Chicago. The American Indian Chicago Conference took place from June 13 to June 20, 1961. The conference was an important moment in American Indian activism (often called Red Power) and community building, and its location in Chicago highlighted the active and growing Native community there. Ninety tribes were represented by more than 450 delegates from all over the western hemisphere. The meeting was hosted and paid for by the University of Chicago, its professors and students, and granting foundations. Sol Tax, Nancy Lurie, and Robert Reitz coordinated the project. Mayor Richard Daley declared June 13–20 American Indian Week.

The Declaration of Indian Purpose was a policy statement created by participants and demanded, among other things, a reversal of the federal government's termination process, increased Indian educational opportunities, more economic development programs, better health care, the abolition of ten Bureau of Indian Affairs area offices, and the protection of Native water rights. This document is credited with promoting development and a greater awareness of American Indian concerns nationwide, as well as sparking the creation of the National Indian Youth Council.[29] The Chicago community would become known for its organizations, and its members for being consummate organizers, as seen in the Chicago American Indian Community Organizations Conference in 1981.

Anthropologist Terry Straus and AIC member Debra Valentino (Oneida/Menominee), who was the AIC board president in 2009, explain that "in the early twentieth century, Chicago had an Indian population (188 were counted in the 1910 census), but no Indian *community*" (Straus and Valentino 2003:523). They locate the beginning of this community, marked by "purposeful gatherings," in the 1920s (ibid.:524). What began as social organizations eventually turned to social services as more Natives were pushed (through federal relocation programs) or pulled (with the hope of jobs) to the city.[30] Today, some nations have established tribal offices in Chicago that, along with other Native organizations in the city, help enroll individuals in their tribes and serve both enrolled and non-enrolled Native individuals. The city has become a place to maintain, reconnect, or connect for the first time with one's tribal identity and community; the American Indian Center is often the first step

Figure 2.9. American Indian Center of Chicago, 2005. Photo by author.

in this process (Straus and Valentino 2001:89–92). Straus and Valentino (2001:92) call this "retribalization:" contrary to common conceptions of city life, an individual moves from a pan-Indian to a tribally specific Indian identity. In times past, American Indians concentrated in Chicago's Uptown neighborhood, but today they live throughout the city and suburbs, reflected in the two locations the American Indian Center now manages: the center itself on Wilson Avenue in the city (figure 2.9) and the Trickster Gallery in Schaumburg, Illinois. Community members live in both neighborhoods.

The American Indian Center of Chicago, first called the All Tribes Indian Center, was established in 1953, shortly after the relocation program began. In 1954, the AIC hosted its first powwow; by 1957, the AIC had broken away from BIA support; and by the 1970s, the relocation era was over (Arndt 1998; Beck 1998). Beck explains that "people created new 'families' in their organizational affiliations" (1998:174), and during my time at the AIC, members did refer to it as a family. The different organizations in the city provide an important "web of support" for community members, who continue to suffer from economic and social hardship at disproportional rates compared with the surrounding population (ibid.:175).

The Chicago co-curators are committed to the urban Indian population as a community that maintains itself through its own tribal practices and acts of participation and volunteerism, often addressing the hardships fellow community members face. As with the Kalinagos, the Chicago co-curators defined their own tribal affiliations

Figure 2.10. Chicago community curators, 2003. Front row, from left: *Cyndee Fox-Starr, Mavis Neconish, Patricia Xerikos;* middle row: *Rita Hodge, Cynthia Soto;* back row: *David Spencer, Susan Power, Ansel Deon, Joe Podlasek.* Reproduced with permission of the National Museum of the American Indian, Smithsonian Institution. Photo by Roger Whiteside.

and roles for the purposes of the exhibit: Cyndee Fox-Starr (Omaha/Odawa), American Indian Health Service of Chicago; Mavis Neconish (Menominee/Potawatomi), collection management assistant, Field Museum; Patricia Xerikos (Anishnaabe/ Colombian), American Indian Center advisory board; Rita Hodge (Diné), Native American Support Program, University of Illinois at Chicago; Cynthia Soto (Sicangu Lakota/Puerto Rican), Citywide American Indian Education Council; David Spencer (Chata/Diné), AIC fundraising developer; Susan Power (Dakota/Yanktonai), founding member of AIC, historian, and elder; Ansel Deon (Sioux/Navajo), AIC cultural coordinator; Joe Podlasek (Ojibwe/Polish), AIC executive director; and Jayne Wapahnok Blacker (Menominee/Potawatomi), student, University of Illinois at Chicago (figure 2.10). These co-curators represent many of the tribes of this urban community and the diverse experiences of Natives in the city—some came before relocation, others with their families, who arrived due to this legislation or on their own as job seekers; some were born in the city, others arrived with their parents; some were "Indian center babies" and became members of the AIC community as young children or teens, others connected more deeply to their Native heritage later in life. There was a concerted effort among the co-curators to include the generational perspectives of the community, from elders to middle-aged adults to youth.

When I first arrived in Chicago in the spring of 2005, the community had just celebrated the opening of the Trickster Gallery in Schaumburg. Dedicated to displaying contemporary Native American arts, the gallery was a source of excitement for most but also consternation for a few, who felt that its suburban site would divert time, money, and staff from the main, more service-oriented AIC location in the city. The AIC staff were debating what kind of displays the gallery would present and whether it should resemble, in their terms, an "art gallery" or a "museum." The other major focus of community meetings, excitement, and debate was the AIC powwow: how to run it, how to advertise it, and to what extent AIC staff should formally be involved in its operation. This powwow is a major annual event every November that draws Native Americans from many different tribes and from all over North America to the University of Illinois arena to dance competitively, to visit the various craft booths, and to reunite with old friends or make new ones.

The Kalinago and Chicago communities were partially forged, or reconstituted, through the work of activism and increased cultural awareness and pride linked to the Red Power movement in the United States. Grant Arndt (1998:126–127) explains the irony of one unintended consequence of the US assimilationist policy embodied in the relocation program: rather than "dismantle" the reservations, it created a "new form of community through which American Indians could take a unified stand on behalf of both their reservation homelands and their lives in urban America." With the American Indian Center as their "platform," in the words of an AIC director cited in a newspaper article in 1957, "it is a sad mistake to say Indians are a voiceless people": "We have a voice and we are voicing a unified stand" (ibid.:126).

The Core of the Community-Curating Process

It is important to understand not only the communities but also the individuals who were immersed in them, and who represented them, during the curatorial process. There was a "core team" for *OL*, and I noticed that co-curators in Chicago and the Carib Territory also called three individuals from each committee the "core" members contributing to exhibit development. The Kalinago and Chicago co-curators said that one of the greatest challenges was to get all the co-curators to come to the meetings; those who showed up most consistently, met on their own, and worked most with the documents and scripts provided by the NMAI were considered the core. I did career and life histories with most of the co-curators in each community but provide brief introductions below of only the core members. Not only did these individuals have more intimate knowledge of the various aspects of producing the exhibition, but they also were among those who visited the NMAI for the grand opening and therefore contributed more feedback on the process (see chapters 5 and 7). I do not intend to diminish the significant contributions of the other community co-curators in any way, but in this particular account, I focus on only six of them.

All the NMAI core team members for the *OL* gallery were relatively young women, and, for many, it was their first time working on such a large project; for some, including me, it was the first time working in a museum. Cynthia Chavez, Taryn Salinas (née Costanzo), and I were core members from the Curatorial Department; we were later joined by Arwen Nuttall. Anthropologist Ann McMullen, though not listed as a core *Our Lives* team member in the documents, was the head of the Curatorial Department and was assigned as the field worker for the *OL* Pamunkey exhibit due to her expertise with New England tribes (see, for instance, McMullen 1996). Cynthia's immaculate office with bookshelves lined with uniform rows of binders was in stark contrast to Ann's cluttered and overburdened shelves and desktop, filled with books and stacks of papers and hints of color from sticky notes everywhere. Ann had jokes and comics about cats pinned up across the window to her office and mechanical punching dolls among other knickknacks on her shelves. Ann was always working in her office long before staff came in each day and after most of them left, due to the numerous projects she contributed to, as well as a love for the work itself. Cynthia, too, was deeply committed to the work she was responsible for, so for a large part of the time during exhibit development, she was out of the office, visiting *OL* communities.

The Kalinago core members were Garnette Joseph, Sylvanie Burton, and Prosper Paris. They had all been members at one point of the Karifuna Cultural Group; Prosper was still in charge of it. Garnette was the Carib chief from 1999 to 2004; he was reelected in 2009. I found during my extended stay in the Carib Territory that Garnette was well respected for his intelligence and commitment to the community, Sylvanie was a development worker referred to as a "daughter of the soil" by Dominican government officials, and Prosper was called a "cultural icon" by everyone. These three individuals were involved in almost every kind of community project that was under way. Sylvanie was well known for her successful grant writing, and Prosper for his vast knowledge about Kalinago culture and history. Both Garnette and Sylvanie had graduate degrees from an indigenous theater program in Canada; Garnette also had training in business administration, and Sylvanie had done a course in England about rural poverty alleviation. Prosper was a self-taught cultural scholar. At one point in our discussions, I asked him a question I had used with NMAI curators: what is your favorite book? His answer was Dee Brown's *Bury My Heart at Wounded Knee* (1971), which he read in the late 1980s. Prosper explained that it was first introduced by Garnette and then circulated among a close circle of Kalinagos. People in this circle included co-curators Irvince, Prosper, Garnette, and Sylvanie, all of whom shared a lasting commitment to raising cultural consciousness in the Carib Territory.

The Chicago core members were Rita Hodge, Joe Podlasek, and Cyndee Fox-Starr. These individuals, like the Kalinago co-curators, were dedicated to volunteerism and involved in many community projects, most often associated with or hosted by the American Indian Center. Rita's daughter Nizhoni worked at the AIC, Joe was its director, and Cyndee ran the elders program there. Rita worked for the University of Illinois's Native American Support Program and had a keen interest in helping Native students excel in the university and cope with life in the city. Joe had worked with computers and had been a technical engineer at the Chicago Histori-cal Society before joining the AIC; he was a fierce negotiator and an able networker, constantly on the lookout for ways to bring in revenue, to maintain staff salaries, and to improve programs for the community at large. Cyndee had a heart of gold and an infectious laugh, and she cared for both elders and youth in the community. Rita and Cyndee participated in the Enter the Circle program, teaching kids how to sew dance clothes and introducing them to powwows.

All of these individuals' histories and experiences shaped the content and expres-sion of identity in the *Our Lives* exhibition. As Cynthia and the co-curators acknowl-edged, had different people been selected to be on the co-curator committee or had the exhibit been created at a different point in time, *Our Lives* no doubt would have come out differently.

Conclusion

By framing the exhibition as a field site, I was able to document not only the interac-tions among NMAI curators and community curators in this process but also the unique personal histories of the individuals who contributed to the whole. During the development of the *Our Lives* gallery, as each new person joined the project, his or her personal history and perspective on how to represent Native identity shaped and changed the structure and content of the exhibition. Ironically, although the exhibits are about, for example, the Kalinagos or the American Indians of Chicago, the Native co-curators' everyday lives and identities were far less defined by the museum than were the lives and identities of those who worked at the NMAI. All the co-curators had other jobs and projects they were working on, besides providing for their families. This was not their life's work, even though, according to Kalinago co-curator Sylvanie, it made their life seem more meaningful for having participated in it.

During my fieldwork, I came to realize that people at the NMAI really wanted to talk about the museum and curatorial processes. It was as if they needed someone outside the office to talk to in order to sort out their thoughts, to explain what could have been. Staff often welcomed the unusual opportunity to reflect on their work or engage with the bigger questions of its meaning. Two staff members called it "thera-peutic," another "cathartic." Making the exhibitions consumed almost every day of their lives for four years or more and will continue to be a part of who they are and how they define themselves. It *was* their life's work; their career paths were affected by the results on display; and their reputations as museum professionals were influ-enced by the judgment of their colleagues and the media. Working at the NMAI also, clearly, influenced the trajectory of my own life and career.

In the Native communities, however, co-curators experienced only a few brief, intense visits by NMAI staff over the course of three years. This experiential dif-ference in exhibition making became clear exactly one month into my fieldwork in

Dominica, when I wrote in my notebook, "All of a sudden, asking people about the museum seems ridiculous. It's such a small part of their lives. There's so much else going on." The Kalinago co-curators frankly told me they were skeptical all along that anything would come of their work, until the media crew showed up in 2002. The co-curators were happy about the result of their efforts, but it was clear they did not have their professional identities and personal lives tied up in the exhibit.

The communities were hopeful that by sharing their lives in the exhibition, they would become more visible, since the museum would be visited by millions of people each year. Although both the Kalinago and Chicago communities had hosted significant historical events in the history of the hemisphere that had wide-ranging consequences for Native people—the first encounter with Europeans in the fifteenth century and the 1961 American Indian Chicago Conference—they remained largely invisible in contemporary literature, popular imagination, and public and political spheres nationally and internationally.

Both Native communities also shared a kind of common past: they had reunited after devastating campaigns against their existence and lifeways by foreign governments. For the Kalinagos, it was the Spanish who committed genocide to the point that most people, including many scholars, believe there are no longer indigenous people in the Caribbean. In Chicago, Native individuals and families came from many places and for many reasons—some escaping the impoverished conditions on the reservations due to the removal of Native peoples from their homelands, some due to a relocation program that was part of the termination policies of the US government, and some, more recently, seeking new opportunities. In both the Carib Territory and Chicago, these communities were revived *as* communities (Arndt 1998; Joseph 1997), with recognizable indigenous identities, though they remained marginalized by the dominant societies surrounding them, as well as by the wider family of indigenous peoples.

Whereas the activism of these Native individuals ensured the continuity of their communities, the activism of the NMAI Curatorial staff and managers did not have the same effect. Curators continue to make significant contributions at the NMAI, but after the museum opened, the Curatorial Department was dissolved.

three
Bureaucracy

Because we're doing something for the first time and we know, no matter what you do, whether it's creating purchase orders, feeding paper all day, or doing what you've done—talking to communities and moving objects—it's like you've touched generations. And you've truly made an impact, whether you meet those people or not, whether they say it to you or not. You can always say, "You know what? I changed, and I've impacted people."

—Tanya Thrasher, downtown staff member, 2004

There was a point three or four years ago where all of us in Curatorial had a mental picture of what we were creating, and it was an elephant.... Now, throughout this process, we have three legs of an elephant. It's got, like, a jackass's head. It's got somebody else's tail on it. Because that's basically what we've done. Each one of the exhibits is a Frankenstein monster in its own way.

—Ann McMullen, CRC staff member, 2004

First Encounter: A Return

Within minutes of my arrival at the Cultural Resources Center in Suitland, Maryland, to start my fieldwork in June 2004, I was greeted by a former curatorial colleague, who asked, "Wanna go outside?" We sat on a bench in the shade while he filled me in on what life was like there now. To our left, I saw the water feature running along the length of the entry stairs to the building; I remembered how, in times past, staff had conducted boat races in this small running stream, each department creating miniature boats out of materials at hand and cheering them on. My impression of the CRC from when I worked there several years earlier was that it was a bustling and energetic site of activity, but my colleague's characterization of the NMAI as just a "shell" indicated that great changes had occurred in the intervening years.[1] He was not alone, as a number of staff members would later say that the CRC felt like a "ghost town."

The image of a ghost town reflected a loss of personnel (mainly researchers and people who worked on the move team, transferring objects from New York to Suitland), as well as a change in morale. In 2002, there were around 145 people working in the CRC building; by 2006, there were fewer than 75.[2] In 2004, many CRC staff members had left or were facing the end of their term and knew that they would not be renewed, whereas the mall museum in DC was ramping up, hiring cultural interpreters and visitor services and public programs employees.[3]

This shift in focus and activity from the CRC to the mall museum was underway at the same time that installation—the actual building of the exhibits and placement of objects in cases—was about to begin at the *Our Lives* gallery. By the time I left the museum in December 2004, the curators and research assistants had experienced a swing from the exhilaration of seeing the exhibits materialize and the excitement of the museum's opening week to the tedium of printing, indexing, and boxing up documents to be placed in the archives in the basement of the CRC. Before being let go, they were organizing years of accumulated research documents they had produced. A number of offices in which people had worked were now occupied instead by storage boxes filled with papers and files (figure 3.1). By the time I returned in 2006 to conclude my fieldwork, even more of the individuals I had previously interviewed were no longer working at the NMAI.

In 1999, however, the CRC was a forward-looking, lively place. It was populated by a mainly young, idealistic crowd of Native and non-Native individuals, utterly excited at the opportunity to work at the museum—whether for contact with the objects or for the opportunity to support and empower Native peoples and Native voices in a museum context. So imagine a group of people working long hours on a monumental task, each department with its own contribution—designing and building a new museum, moving an entire collection of more than eight hundred thousand objects from New York to Maryland, creating the inaugural exhibitions in collaboration with more than twenty-four tribes. The staff knew that far more work was to be done than their numbers could handle, but everyone felt, as many described in similar words during my fieldwork, that "the struggle was worth it." A number of us would often scarf down our food to play hacky sack outside in the allotted thirty-minute lunch period, and after work on Fridays, we would play volleyball next door on the National Museum of Natural History's Museum Support Center lawn before heading to our respective homes or perhaps to someone's place to

Figure 3.1. Office in the Curatorial Department at the CRC, November 24, 2004. Photo by author. Reproduced with permission of the National Museum of the American Indian, Smithsonian Institution.

play cards. We were a small, hardworking, and very social group of people, and for the first couple of years, we had the energy and dedication of a start-up company.[4]

By 2004, one staff member was sad to see the "loss of naiveté" in everyone.[5] I also noticed that CRC lunchtimes were longer, people rarely spent time outside of work together in groups, no one played sports together any more, and most employees wanted to get away from the office and were reluctant to work overtime. In one staff member's terms, it had become "just a job," rather than what had, to many, felt like a vocation. Some individuals felt that senior managers were trying to "get rid" of all the early curatorial staff members, many of whom were bound to be disappointed at the final results of the exhibitions. They explained that, from this point of view, the CRC needed to hire new people without the experience of that "honeymoon period," who could be more practical and continue the work of the museum.[6]

In many ways, this story could be told as a shift from what felt like a start-up company—a mission-oriented, experimental, and tight-knit group of enthusiasts transplanted from other places to the CRC—to a large and increasingly impersonal bureaucracy that rationalized and made more "efficient" the practice of community curating and exhibition development with more oversight by other departments. By 2006, the new associate director, Tim Johnson (Mohawk), was emphasizing his goal of making the museum more "businesslike," the Curatorial Department was disbanded, and many of the CRC desks were empty. How did this come about? And what contributed to these changes?

To address these questions, I attempt to "look past objects"[7] in the museum, which are often the center of analysis. In this chapter, I emphasize the museum as a bureaucracy, as an institution that is a gathering place of diverse knowledge practices (Bouquet 2001:195), and as a "place of work" (Friedman 2001:265).[8] I am also concerned with bureaucracy as both hierarchy and form filing, structure and practice. This "cultural bureaucracy" (Born 1995) is illustrated below through its artifacts—documents.[9]

The NMAI contained at once routinized forms and creative practices, structured rules and flexible interpretations, in its attempt to fulfill its commitment to collaborate with Native communities. What comes to light through these documents is neither readily apparent in the exhibitions nor easily observable in interactions among museum staff. The documents record a changing relationship, increasingly structured by bureaucratic procedures, between Native communities and the museum. They provide insight into the various forms of social and ethical relations that the museum engendered with its Native partners—collaborative and contractual, interpersonal and institutional.

The NMAI as a Creative Bureaucracy

When the Museum of the American Indian became the National Museum of the American Indian, it was incorporated into the Smithsonian Institution, an agency of the federal government that is in part funded by allocations from Congress. Like other bureaucratic government organizations, the NMAI has fixed salary ranges ("GS levels"), purchase orders, a vendor system, and extensive regulatory oversight. But the NMAI is a different kind of bureaucracy, a "creative bureaucracy," in which there are tensions between the artistic and the bureaucratic knowledge practices of the museum as it engages in content development, scriptwriting, design, and exhibit planning. The term "creative bureaucracy" also refers to the ways in which the NMAI has dealt with the intersection between bureaucratic and Native sensibilities, the ways in which it has responded to the needs and ethics of Native peoples by creatively navigating the Smithsonian's rules and regulations in its quest for best practices in the museum.

Few studies highlight the bureaucratic dimension of museum practice, and the literature on the anthropology of institutions rarely addresses museums.[10] However, two notable exceptions are relevant here. First, in *Behind the Scenes at the Science Museum*, Sharon Macdonald (2002:248) illustrates the trend toward audience-centered museology, a shift in the focus from objects to visitors. She also documents an increasing reliance on non-experts in the museum's professional practice of exhibit making. While she does not address bureaucracy as directly as I do here, Macdonald certainly captures some of its everyday, lived experience at the Science Museum in London, including discussions of "territory" or "professional territorialism" (66), "constraints of time and money" (131), enthusiastic beginnings and "feeling flat" in the end (93), work paced to deadlines (193), and the recognition that "constant restructuring has become a feature of public organizations" (249). Macdonald suggests that the struggles between departments, the "factional warfare," is "magic" and an engine of creativity to drive new ideas (260). At the NMAI, however, the interdepartmental tensions appeared to be more of a hindrance than an engine of creativity.

The other study that addresses bureaucracy is Georgina Born's *Rationalizing Culture* (1995). She writes about the Institut de Recherche et Coordination Acoustique/Musique (IRCAM), which is a state-subsidized institution in Paris that promotes and develops avant-garde music through collaboration between computer technicians and musicians. She discusses the "collaborative ideal" and tensions between artistic and bureaucratic practices. In her description of the changes in IRCAM over time, which echoes some NMAI staff concerns, Born (1995:314) explains, "there was a change of atmosphere in the institute, and especially its research culture, toward what is seen as a 'dark age' or spoken of simply in terms of profound closure," in which cross-project collaboration efforts decreased and "projects became discrete affairs with little mutual dialogue. Researchers and composers just got on with the job.... Informants mourned the passing of the earlier spirit of IRCAM...which vanished as IRCAM's young adulthood turned into the settled and 'stabilized' maturity of the present." IRCAM became a "hierarchical, increasingly efficient bureaucratic institution" (ibid.).

The Science Museum of London, IRCAM, and the NMAI are cultural institutions that are state subsidized.[11] The similarities between the NMAI and the institutions that Macdonald and Born describe suggest that they are of similar bureaucratic type, including their classification as cultural institutions, the tensions between experts within the institution, and the coming together of technical and artistic expertise and practices in everyday work. There is also a similar desire by those of us who study these organizations to elucidate the collaborative relationships, bureaucratic pressures, and notions of crisis in the institution.

Smithsonian Institution Models of Hierarchy and Decision Making

In 2006, to better understand how the NMAI fit into the wider Smithsonian bureaucracy and family of museums, I sat down with sociologist Andrew Pekarik, who worked at the Smithsonian's Office of Policy and Analysis. His job was to conduct exhibition evaluations and to interview visitors at all the Smithsonian museums. He provided a comparison of the NMAI with the other Smithsonian museums, explaining that there are "distinctive methods" for exhibit making at each one, ranging on a continuum from a single curator in charge to a project team approach. For example, at the Freer and Sackler Galleries, the curator "calls all the shots," except for the title of the exhibition and public relations issues. The curator is the decision maker, and there is a designer-curator relation that is a "struggle of near equals." The curator is also in charge at the National Museum of American History, but the team he or she oversees includes an education person—"as the visitor voice," Andrew added—and an official project manager, who runs the meetings (and "spares" the curator from doing budgets, among other tasks). He emphasized, "Every person in the team has veto power." If the team cannot come to consensus on something, the disagreement is settled by the assistant director who does not have specialized knowledge on the issue. The assistant director usually "sides" with the person whose professional expertise is more relevant to the discrepancy—designer or curator. Because the team does not want the decision to be made by the relatively uninformed assistant director, they usually work until the "curator comes around" and there is a "compromise."[12]

But the NMAI, the sociologist explained, is a "new situation." The NMAI staff were reworking the exhibit-making model at the same time they were constructing the exhibits. The idea was that the "world of Native communities meets professionalized world of exhibit development and makes original, effective exhibits.... But neither the exhibit development nor the community people had a sense of the visitor dimension." There was "no prior testing," "no diversity in presentation." He critiqued the NMAI for using the "standard message model," in which the exhibit is a medium of communication that delivers the messages and the visitor is a "passive recipient." Only some visitors receive messages Andrew added—and no more than 50 percent of visitors at the Smithsonian Institution museums "get" the "main message." He asked, are the rest "just losers," then? In his view, the NMAI follows the "message model" as opposed to the "service model" (the model he supports). The latter focuses on "what people need" or how an exhibit can benefit them, and staff try to use resources to find the "middle ground" between "delivering and benefiting." For Andrew, the "service model" referred to serving the public or, even more specifically, a majority of Euro American visitors.[13] The NMAI Curatorial Department might have also considered its work to be in line with the service model, but with respect to serving Native communities.

The NMAI style of exhibit development resulted in "a lot of conflict," Andrew continued, and the curator's power significantly changed over time. In the past, curators were "like the god calling all the shots," and there was much conflict between them and designers. "I knew the designer was way more right," he added, and there was "no way to resolve it like at [the National Museum of] American History," with its long list of rules learned through prior failures. When the National Museum of American History team is at an impasse, it goes "upstairs." Its "rules" also prompt the team to ask whether the impasse is related more to the "expertise of the designer or curator": "content versus placement." What the NMAI lacked, he felt, was the "motivation" to build "consensus."[14]

The NMAI, in the "absence of rules," ended up being about how "two characters can or can't get along," Andrew concluded. Exhibit making became "interpersonal politics." Then, since the program manager controls the budget and schedule, in the end, the process gets taken over by "deadlines." And this is how decisions are made. At one point, he commented, "It's obvious, I'm *pro-visitor*." I responded in my field notes: "I wonder to myself—what is the opposite of pro-visitor? Anti-visitor? Pro-curator? Pro–Native communities?"[15] This turn toward the visitor, and the shift away from curatorial authority, is in part what museum consultants referred to when they recommended that the NMAI "culture must shift" (Gurian and Gorbey 2003a). An ethnographic approach to the museum shows that the conflict clearly went beyond two personalities, although the organizational structure contributed to staff's making sense of their experience in this way.

The view from the Office of Policy and Analysis was, basically, that NMAI staff were inexperienced and that there needed to be more emphasis on visitor needs and formal procedures. But since the museum has a separate constituency from its visitors, this created a problem as to which group to prioritize: the constituency (tribes) or the audience (visitors), a classification that has always been present in NMAI rhetoric and affects how staff interpret what a "paradigm shift" might mean (see chapter 4). The "standard message model" Andrew mentioned is severely critiqued as outdated in museum studies literature, which champions more participatory models and visitor-centric approaches (see, for example, Anderson 2012; Simon 2010). The NMAI, then, was seen as both in line with current trends in museum anthropology, with its extensive collaboration with Native communities, *and* behind the times, according to museum studies, due to its standard message model.

A View of Bureaucracy from the Center

At the Native American Art Studies Association conference in Salem, Massachusetts, in November 2003, I met Ruth Phillips, a widely respected curator who has long worked with Native peoples on collaborative exhibits and with exhibition teams within her own institution, the Canadian Museum of Civilization.[16] We had both elected to go on a preconference tour of the Pequot Museum in Connecticut, and she asked about my research at the NMAI. I was currently experiencing the installation process in the *Our Lives* gallery, and I mentioned something that had surprised me— the amount of waiting these professionals did.

I described how at times there were three contracted mount makers, three people from the Collections Department, two conservators, a curator, a curatorial research assistant, one person from registration, and a program manager gathered in the unfinished gallery (plate 2). The three contracted mount makers worked nonstop placing objects in cases, when the fabrication process (the construction of the walls and cases in the gallery) was not delaying this. Meanwhile, all the other individuals, much of the time, would be standing there watching them. The pressure! Their poise! Each staff member had a specific job to do: cleaning the glass case cover, rolling objects on a cart in and out of a storage room, scanning barcodes, suggesting slight changes to object placement, making object mount notes, dusting the case. But between performances of their delimited tasks, many of them stood around talking, or they would sit somewhere out of the way and read a book or do some work. Most of the time, however, was spent waiting to do a task that would take only minutes to perform. But they had to be present. Phillips explained that this was not an uncommon scene in a large museum; this apparently inefficient process was a result of the increasing professionalization of museum departments, which happens most in large museums like the NMAI and the Canadian Museum of Civilization.

Many specialized departments participate in the process of making an exhibition and installing it. Each department relies on its own technical language, documentation practices, and forms of organizing and transmitting information to contribute its part of the exhibit-making process. They are unique cultures of expertise, but they are also cooperating, participating in a choreographed performance of various knowledge practices and products that must come together in the end to create the exhibition. However, I noticed that, whereas there was constant talk of "collaboration" with Native communities, the interaction among professionals within the museum was almost never referred to as such and instead was called "teamwork." On paper, each gallery (*OP*, *OU*, and *OL*) group was referred to as a "team."[17] And, when face to face, members did appear to work toward common goals. But, in private conversations and even in formal interviews, the sports metaphor was replaced by battle metaphors, which permeated people's speech about their experiences working on the exhibitions. One staff member explained, "The more a museum is bureaucratized, the more a department has to protect its turf and [staff have] to be asserting themselves, and the more they have to be shaping the exhibition." When I asked why they have to "protect their turf" so diligently, the response was quick: "Because…they're inconsequential if they don't."[18]

The *Our Lives* core and extended team members were located in two different sites, downtown and the CRC (see chapter 2). A year after the Curatorial Department began working on the final instantiation of the *Our Lives* gallery, the whole *OL* team convened for the first time, in February 2002. In a document titled "*Our Lives* Core Team Meeting Summary" (figure 3.2), the project manager, Jennifer Miller, listed each person's "roles and responsibilities" (I have added where each person's office was located).[19] Note that the responsibilities to visitors are listed with downtown staff, and communities are mentioned only in the responsibilities of CRC staff. In addition, the curator is described as the mediator between the exhibition team and the communities. These distinctions are more directly highlighted in chapter 4.

When I talked to people in Dominica about the community projects or committees they worked on, bureaucracy in its familiar forms—delays, government inefficiency, incompetence, red tape, and "experts" who know nothing about the local situation and thus make poor decisions—came to the fore, particularly with respect to the Carib Model Village, which also was a government-sponsored cultural site. I

Carolyn Rapkievian, Educator & Public Programs Liaison [*downtown*]
- Primary task is educator assigned to Our Lives. This role helps to articulate messages to visitors, with emphasis on multiple communication methods to reach all visitors.
- As Public programs liaison, assists the team in connecting to other areas, for example Resource center, Film and Video. This role gets more emphasis later in the project.
- Public programs plans to contract with people to develop the programs for the Mall, this is a point for connecting the communities and the NMAI.

Susan Secakuku, Community Services liaison [*CRC*]
- Primary task is to work with selected communities, keeping track of initiatives that emerge from the work.
- Creates/facilitates long-term relationships with communities.
- Connects the communities with other NMAI programs – for example radio programs, training, film and video – acting as catalyst.

Cynthia Chavez, Curator [*CRC*]
- Establishes and maintains relationships with communities, working with them to develop content for the exhibition. Holds 2-3 co-curation sessions with each group.
- Role is as facilitator/collaborator in the back and forth process of developing the exhibition content.
- Mediator between internal NMAI groups (like the core team) and the communities.
- Interested in ways to give back to the communities, for example the workshop under development with the Chicago community.
- Actively creating a curatorial/community services model for future work.

Evi Oehler, Design Liaison [*Downtown*; by 2004 no longer with NMAI]
- Serves as the connection between the core team and the design and construction group for the Mall building.
- Helps contracted exhibit designers to understand the building, keeping channels open between D+C and the general contractor.
- Represents the project with other SI groups, OFEO in particular, to coordinate code compliance, etc.
- Works one-on-one with D+C to represent exhibit ideas in a buildable way.
- Brings experience of other projects to help avoid pitfalls.

Mark Hirsch, Script Editor [*Downtown*]
- Develops scripts, taking the information provided and organizing it, making voices understandable to visitors.
- Works with curatorial to understand how information connects, and how best to transfer information.
- Working with Ann McM and Karen F to develop script process, which includes editing phases, etc.

Kathy Suter, Media Coordinator [*Downtown*]
- Sees three phases to media work: communication phase – how NMAI-curated and community work is developing, what are the messages. This informs initial ideas for media. Media is defined broadly: audio/visual; combos of objects/sound/light; web casts, etc. Next is production phase – taking the standard media process and customizing it to our needs and specific situations. Final is post-production phase, including editing, etc.
- Coordinates and oversees Mall media productions, acting as executive producer.
- Has developed media production guidelines to help define process.

Jennifer Miller, Exhibit Project Manager [*Downtown*]
- Primary responsibility is the effective coordination and management of the exhibition development and production.
- Coordinates internal museum functions between offices for the exhibition.
- Resolves conflicts in schedule, budget, and tasks within project team.
- Handles requests from NMAI offices and SI divisions for specific information, images, reports on the exhibition.

Figure 3.2. Excerpt from "Our Lives *Core Team Meeting Summary" document, February 2002.*

encountered committees and task forces, *Robert's Rules of Order*, and NGO workers in both Chicago and Dominica. Between the Bureau of Indian Affairs, local tribal governments, community development organizations, and cultural institutions in these communities, people in Indian country are certainly familiar with bureaucracies.

At the NMAI, however, every time I asked people about it, the issue of bureaucracy seemed to recede into discussions of "personalities" and "turf." There were "tugs-of-war" between departments, which were called "territorial" while protecting their "turfs," and exhibit features represented "battles" won and lost. To one downtown person, "research was a weapon" used by the Curatorial Department before the opening of the museum.[20] A project manager characterized the conflict between the heads of Curatorial and Exhibits as the "contested territory of cult leaders."[21] Countless staff members, when questioned about the bureaucratic nature of the museum, replied something like "Bureaucracy is not the problem—it's more the turf business."[22] It seemed that the "turf wars" Roland Force (1999:357–367) wrote about—regarding where the Museum of the American Indian would move in 1987 (including Ross Perot's bid for it to go to Texas)—had become internalized in the Smithsonian's "Indian museum." "Personalities"—the word provided as an explanation for the state of affairs between departments—were found both downtown and at the CRC, the term most often referencing the individuals in charge of the Exhibits and Curatorial Departments.

Only one staff member, who had been at the NMAI for more than twenty years, discussed how bureaucracy was a social form that inhibited the curatorial process. Cécile Ganteaume was a curator at both the Museum of the American Indian and the George Gustav Heye Foundation. She continued on when the museum transitioned to the Smithsonian as the NMAI, and she worked extensively on the community-curated portions of the *Our Peoples* exhibition. Cécile explained the difference between a small private institution and a large federal institution as a matter of scale, responsibility, and increasing specialization. Her story provides a long-term view of changes in museum practice more generally and at the NMAI specifically.

At the Heye Foundation, which was a very small institution with few staff members, Cécile did whatever work was needed, including registration, photography, writing grants, and fundraising—"You just do a bit of everything." She started working in Latin American archaeology, switched to the Exhibits Department, then moved to North American ethnology, and later worked in the Curatorial Department. At the NMAI, on the other hand, she said, because of "the bureaucracy," "you really do work in one department, and departments are territorial. And that's the major difference...you very much get pigeonholed": "So, for example, at the Heye Foundation, I had a lot of hands-on work with the collections. But here, we have a Collections Management Department, so I don't have much hands-on work with the collections. At the Heye Foundation, I worked a lot with visiting researchers. That was a curatorial responsibility. Here, that's not a curatorial responsibility. It's a collections responsibility." She also noted that what bureaucracy introduces to the exhibit-making process is "rank," which means that "there's nothing you can do" if a senior manager makes a particular decision. "In a private institution, the curator is in control of the exhibit, and here, that is not the case. There are senior managers above the curator who are shaping exhibits and making decisions."[23]

The project managers at the NMAI began to take on a greater role as exhibition development progressed, particularly as the shift from research to production began. One downtown staff member characterized the project managers as the "watchdogs" for fabrication, installation, graphic design, and media coordinating—the "nuts and bolts of the space." She added that Jennifer Miller, the project manager for *Our Lives*, had the long-term view "all through the ranks." And the project manager, script-writer, and upper management were all in a "tug-of-war with Curatorial."[24] Elaine Heumann Gurian, a consultant to the museum who, with Ken Gorbey, advised on the post-opening organizational restructuring, said that Curatorial was a "cabal" that needed to be "broken up,"[25] and Jim Volkert commented that the problem in the institution was the "silo mentality" of the departments.[26]

A number of staff members pointed to the hierarchical organization of the museum as a source of continuing problems in exhibit making. A senior manager could radically alter the course of an exhibition by deciding who would stay or go on a project, for example. One CRC staff member explained that, in meetings, a person's position in the hierarchy would determine whether people thought his or her idea was a good one, adding, "Just because someone is high up in this institution doesn't mean their ideas are better than anyone else's.... There was a tremendous amount of frustration, on almost every level, spurred by these differences of opinion, this sort of *hierarchical crap*."[27] Staff members felt that their job assignments, the aesthetic quality of their work, and their ideas were subject to the judgment and individual tastes of senior staff members.

There was a kind of hierarchy among departments as well, a "class structure," as one staff member described it. She said that Collections Department staff felt that they were in "the lowest position in the museum." The Curatorial and Conservation Departments were afforded a higher "level of respect" than other departments, despite the fact that, for example, several people on the "move team" had master's degrees and had "worked in museums for ten, fifteen years."[28]

In addition, a kind of time hierarchy was put in place by downtown staff and museum consultants. Tanya Thrasher (Cherokee Nation of Oklahoma), a member of the Mall Transition Team, explained how "Day 1" and "Day 2" terminology from the Museum of New Zealand: Te Papa Tongarewa was basically "dropped into NMAI culture"[29] by Elaine Gurian and Jim Volkert. "Day 1" indicated projects that would be complete by the opening day of the museum. "Day 2" indicated projects that would be completed later. There was a time when *Our Lives* was "threatened" to be Day 2 because the development of the NMAI-curated introductory section was behind schedule.

Although hierarchies were experienced in several ways, clear leadership was perceived as lacking in regard to a singular guiding vision for the exhibitions. Ann McMullen explained, "There is no single vision of what [is] supposed to happen. There's no single vision of the mission of the institution, there's no single vision of what Native voice might be, there's no single vision or belief in what that dotted line or iron curtain is between community curation and NMAI design. It's always this negotiated thing" (see chapter 4). The lack of coordination among departments would sometimes lead to dissatisfying results because no one person was in charge of the vision for any given gallery (curators traditionally had this role), although many *thought* that they were in charge: "So it ends up being like this big conglomerated mess of no single vision.... It's certainly not that of the community curators, it's not that of the NMAI curatorial staff, it's not that of the designers, because they feel that their work is being compromised—everybody feels it's a compromise. And it's not usually a happy compromise, either, because there's so much at stake with people trying to get their way."[30] This was a problem of, as Cécile Ganteaume similarly identified it, "exhibit by committee." "It's all watered down by so many compromises," Cécile lamented.[31] And whereas the committee structure apparently was a positive experience for the curators when working with Native communities (see chapter 5), it was not a positive experience for curators when working within the museum.

The term "compromise" was uttered in frustration by both downtown and CRC staff—from media team members to project managers, curators to conservators—along with the issues of "time and money." Compromise necessitated dealing with other departments' requirements or changes to an exhibit, and it indicated a certain relinquishing of control in the face of the deadlines and budget restrictions that often forced decisions for staff members. Liz Brown, the *OL* conservator, explained the importance of a compromise between "design concept and object safety."[32] Cynthia Chavez, the lead curator for *OL*, said that it was the word everyone was using, and she was clearly frustrated with it. In a meeting with Media Department staff, both Cynthia and I were disappointed that interviews with Igloolik community members on video would be dubbed rather than subtitled. It was a "compromise," the media producer said.[33]

Another curator and some research assistants developed a strategy to deal with the changes other departments would inevitably want to make to the content Curatorial had developed. They decided to include extra text in their exhibit label drafts when working with other departments, so that they could negotiate out what was not important (the extraneous information), allowing them to appear to be compromising while keeping material they felt was essential to the exhibit. The curator who reported this seemed to be intimating that other departments wanted to make changes simply for the sake of placing their mark on the exhibit; it was not so much about making the final content better, but rather changing its original form to mark their intervention or participation.

Artifacts of Bureaucracy

Because the NMAI is a federally funded, bureaucratic institution, working there involved the completion and circulation of standardized vendor forms, time sheets, budget proposals, and project reports. Because it is a creative bureaucracy, the museum's departments also produced an abundance of documents that were expressive, artistic, and uniquely crafted and intended to reach a greater audience, including exhibition catalogs, design documents, and the exhibitions themselves. But there were also quintessential artifacts of bureaucracy—standardized forms for bureaucratic routines—that, through creative execution at this museum, pointed to a unique confluence of cultural and bureaucratic practices. For example, Terry Snow-ball (Ho-Chunk/Prairie Band Potawatomi) in the Repatriation Department had to complete a vendor form, a standard Smithsonian Institution document, for Maliseet people who were coming to give a seasonal blessing, so that they would be "in the system" for travel reimbursements and honorariums.[34]

I had the experience of being told to fill out a standard "burn permit" in 2006 for another blessing ceremony, to be conducted in the *Our Lives* gallery. I emailed NMAI staff members about co-curator Joe Podlasek's request to visit the Chicago exhibit to give a blessing for the drum encased in glass at the center of the display. He wanted to place some tobacco for the drum and to burn sage. The tobacco would be placed outside the case, he said, and it would be all right for it to be swept away later, as he understood the requirements of the gallery.[35] The *OL* exhibit manager, Jennifer Tozer, emailed the building operations staff to ask whether it would be possible to comply with Joe's request and, if so, who must be alerted to turn off the fire detectors during the visit. She told me that I would need to file a burn permit and have a fire extinguisher on standby; there was an extinguisher in the Potomac "green room" specifically for this purpose, she noted. The security manager emailed to let me know that if the extinguisher were discharged, another report would have to be generated. I was notified that I would be the "burn supervisor," with the responsibility of accessing the fire extinguisher and filling out the paperwork. Following the recommendations of other staff, I filled in the burn permit form and listed Joe as the "equipment officer."

Another creative bureaucratic move occurred when, as Bruce Bernstein recounted in 2007 at his American Anthropological Association presentation in Washington, DC, the *Our Universes* team bought a bull. This purchase provided the means to appease an angry deity that had brought heavy rains and forsaken a community curator's village for sharing too much religious information during the exhibit-making process without following proper protocol. Ann McMullen would later write of this experience:

> We had to fulfill our debt to [the deity Nakawe] through the sacrifice of a bull so she would stop punishing Huichol lands and people with destructive storms.... I will not go into the difficulties we faced to satisfy this requirement except to say that a bull, when delivered two years late, has to be truly fabulous.... And if the bull represented a traditional payment for hearing the flood narratives, why were the curators not told this during their initial work? The explanation lies in recognizing that museums' entrée into traditional systems of knowledge and value may present unprecedented problems and sometimes require innovative community resolutions. (McMullen 2008:59)

The NMAI paid for the bull through a "professional services contract" with the anthropologist who was working with the Huichols on behalf of the museum. As part of his trip to take photographs for their exhibit, he was tasked with "facilitating all aspects of NMAI staff's work in Bancos de Calitique and its environs," and money was allocated in the contract for "the cost of reimbursable permissions and fees paid to Huichol community leaders to secure requisite permissions," which, according to a staff member at the CRC, "certainly applied" to the bull.[36] In these cases, NMAI staff were able to navigate the institutional forms and regulations of the wider Smithsonian bureaucracy with their own categorizations of cultural specialists and cultural practices, which were then interpreted through the bureaucratic forms of a vendor in the system, a burn permit, and a professional services contract.[37]

Another quintessential bureaucratic document—the organizational chart—is also among the museum's artifacts. What is notable, however, is the relative absence of these charts for several years; I managed to find one from 2002, but staff complained of not knowing the organization of the museum, or who was in charge of what. By 2006, organizational charts abounded: eleven on the internal staff website detailed the long-awaited reorganization I had been hearing about since 2005. Each time I spoke with staff members—especially those at the CRC and, even more, in the Curatorial Department—they worried about an upcoming "restructuring" or "reorganization." They were told that it was going to happen, but not how it would happen, nor what it meant for their jobs, so there was high anxiety over job insecurity (see also Gurian and Gorbey 2003a, 2003b). One staff member described reorganization as "a response to how people worked or didn't work together."[38]

Similarly, there was a shift to using contracts to define the relationships with communities, exemplified by the different model of community curating employed to develop *Listening to Our Ancestors: The Art of Native Life along the North Pacific Coast* (2006), which was the second exhibition featured in the NMAI changing gallery. *Listening to Our Ancestors* was developed in fits and starts for about five years, including while the inaugural exhibitions were being developed. In 2005, it was "restarted" when a new project manager was hired. Unlike the inaugural exhibitions, which relied on personal relationships between curators and communities to establish trust, for *Listening to Our Ancestors*, the collaborators signed contracts to establish their rights and responsibilities. These were formal agreements, and the museum endeavored, where possible, to work with institutions rather than groups of individuals. The exhibit's community curators—specifically *not* referred to as "co-curators"—were usually professionals in a museum or cultural field. Although curatorial staff used the term "fieldwork" to describe visiting with communities during the development of the inaugural exhibitions, I was told by a member of the *Listening to Our Ancestors* team that they wrote a document about their 2003 visit with communities in which they called it "the camping trip."

In 2006, I spoke at length with a management support assistant for a newly organized department of the museum, Museum Assets and Operations. He had worked on the *Listening to Our Ancestors* exhibition (called, among staff, NPC, for "North Pacific Coast," an earlier title) and had in-depth knowledge of the contracting process. My assumption at first was that these documents were like the memorandums of understanding used at the Museum of New Zealand: Te Papa Tongarewa between the museum and the Maori. To the contrary, he corrected me, these agreements and documents were more like contracts.[39]

In late 2003, the first "collaborative agreement" was created. In the legalese of the document, the contractual partners are described as the "sole source." Accordingly, a justification was required within the contract for why it was not offered to multiple groups, like a request for proposals, before choosing a final source for the partnership, which is standard federal bureaucratic procedure. The management support assistant explained that the "sole source" aspect in the contract explains why the museum is not asking Kwakwaka'waka people from communities besides Alert Bay to participate. Nobody is questioning the selection of that one community, he added, "it's just part of the contracting process." It is what happens when you "mesh community curating with [a] contract process." In one instance, there was no cultural institution with which to forge a contractual relationship, so the contract was written between the NMAI and a hereditary chief of the Heiltsuk tribe "as if he was an organization."[40]

The major change between the inaugural exhibitions and *Listening to Our Ancestors* was that, in the later exhibition, the status of the Native communities changed from "invitational travelers" to representatives of contracted cultural institutions providing "deliverables." Because the exhibition premier was altered from New York to Washington, DC, the contract was modified a number of times. Each time, the contract had to be passed around to eleven participating communities and signed by all parties involved.

The "rights in agreement" clause was something the Makah (Neah Bay) community curators objected to, the management support assistant explained. A Makah community member said that it sounded like "The white man has Indian pictures and can do whatever he wants with them."[41] The community did not want its materials used outside the exhibition—not in books or brochures or even noncommercially—without getting renewed permission through the Makah Cultural and Research Center, the cultural institution with which the contract was made. Working with the center was slowgoing, and the letter its representatives wrote regarding their concerns was "about trusting one another." Because these contracts were between the NMAI *as an institution* and other institutions, the Smithsonian Office of Contracting (OCon) oversaw the process, rather than it being an internal NMAI matter. However, the management support assistant felt that the attorney at OCon exhibited a "good deal of flexibility, which is what [was] needed."[42]

I asked how people in the communities responded to receiving these formal contracts. The management support assistant said that the contract was "not objected to." The communities "understood." But since the contract required that the museum fulfill an obligation to send particular materials from the displays to the communities after the exhibition was over, "there was an extra bureaucratic step involved." Any changes in the exhibit travel plan, for example, meant that OCon would again have to review the contract, which meant that it had to go out to the communities again, be signed, and then be returned again. The Native cultural center was named as the "contractor," and it did the "fee payouts" to the people who worked on the exhibition.[43] When I asked what this contract was modeled on, since it was not the memorandums of understanding widely praised at Te Papa, I was told that it was based on a standard form of contract used for an "organization with a service" to be provided to the Smithsonian Institution. The *OL, OP,* and *OU* exhibitions, he continued, "dealt with people" and did not entail the same "beginning and end relationship." In other words, the contract stipulated a precise date when the formal relationship would end, whereas the inaugural exhibitions had no such written agreement. The inaugural exhibitions were framed as working primarily with people, not institutions, as with *Listening to Our Ancestors.*

It seems that, in this instance, it was the contract that was in negotiation over the years and constituted the "back and forth" between the museum and the communities. Unlike the inaugural exhibitions' community-curating process, in which the people—curators and co-curators—traveled back and forth, with *Listening to Our Ancestors,* it was the contract that traveled. The knowledge producers were largely professional culture producers, who were responsible for the selection of objects (at the start of the exhibit-making process, unlike *Our Lives;* see chapter 5) and the writing of the scripts. There was more interaction among different cultures of expertise in the making of *Listening to Our Ancestors,* which embraced the project team approach, but less collaborative knowledge production than in the inaugural exhibitions. And it was a short-term, contract-based model, rather than a long-term, personal-relationship-based model for exhibit making.

I conclude this section with a brief note about an artifact of bureaucracy that was left unfinished, a dead end, traceable only in the email archives of individuals and no longer part of institutional memory beyond a few of its contributors. Suzan Shown Harjo (Cheyenne/Hodulgee Muscogee), an artist, a writer, president of the Morning Star Institute, and an early NMAI board member, told me that when she moved from being on the board of trustees of the Museum of the American Indian to the NMAI, the board members had to craft policies—a quintessential artifact of bureaucracy—"for everything" because there was no staff at the time. She mentioned "the repatriation policy, [the] identity policy, the collections policy, [and]...the exhibits policy."[44] I hunted for the elusive "identity policy," but no one seemed to know what I was talking about, although I found traces in talk of a "research policy" that first appeared in meeting minutes from November 26, 2001 (according to internal files). One contributor said that the document began a "turf war," invoking the language and anxieties I mention above.

The curatorial staff's draft of this policy was critiqued as "too dense" and not reflecting the view of personnel in the Public Programs Department. A later document that included "overall Curatorial comments" gathered in a department-wide meeting spoke of the "need to include community feedback on processes, outside evaluations, etc.," and the "need [for a] definition of Native voice" (a definition that was not produced until 2005, when it was included in the labels for the *Listening to*

Our Ancestors exhibit; see epilogue). After several more iterations, a draft was sent out in December 2001 for additional comments, and by February 2002, a senior manager, an educator, and senior curatorial staff were working on the document. But it was never finished or submitted to the board. Ann McMullen, who originally pointed me in the direction of this policy, referred to it as a "nitty-gritty cultural resources document." It is virtually unknown by other museum staff.

A Museum in Transition

These examples of artifacts show an institution bureaucratic, creative, and in transition. But what was driving this transition, and where was it leading? There were multiple attempts to short-circuit the bureaucratic conduits of decision making in the museum, including informal groupings like the "coffee group" and the "gang of five" and more formal, institutionalized bodies like the Mall Transition Team and the Mall Action Committee.[45] These were all small groups of powerful decision makers; the actors were nearly identical. They were mainly created to bypass the large and lethargic senior management group at the NMAI. But although the participants viewed these groups as "subverting the bureaucracy" and collaborating across departments, others saw them as gatherings of elitist "powermongers" secretively doing "the smoke-filled-room thing"—especially the informal groups.

The coffee group, for example, was intended to bridge Exhibits and Curatorial, with members from both. Recognizing the schisms between the departments, it was an effort to create "water-cooler chat" at the highest level and across the separate institutional locations. The Mall Transition Team (MTT), on the other hand, included no one from Curatorial or the CRC except Fran Biehl, a member of the Collections Department who was seen as a liaison to the CRC. A member of the MTT commented, "It really *was* Exhibits versus Curatorial.... There was definitely a 'them' mentality, the 'them' being Curatorial."[46] The MTT was specifically developed to make faster decisions than the bureaucracy of the NMAI would permit as the museum neared and pushed through the grand opening.

In 2003, consultants Elaine Heumann Gurian and Ken Gorbey had been hired by the NMAI to help manage the transition to a fully operational museum and to ensure that the museum would open on time. They assessed its status and made a series of recommendations for the opening to move forward. The main theme that runs through their reports is the lack of decisive and quick decision making in the museum and the lack of adherence to decisions once they were made. The Mall Transition Team was created at the urging of these consultants, and the results of the team's streamlined decision-making process were published regularly on the museum's internal website. It was deemed such an effective body by senior management that it was later institutionalized for the long term as the Mall Action Committee (MAC).[47] The MAC, one curator noted, "got a budget" and it was powerful because "the power is where the money is."[48] Jim Volkert was put in charge of the MAC; one member suggested that his leading the committee meant that decisions would stick.

It is worth noting that Gurian and Gorbey's (2003a) report was filled, again, with battle language: "Pull the trigger" (2003a:1) (begin making decisions and stop second-guessing them), "retrenching exercise" (3) (elimination of all unnecessary work), and "This is not a review committee but rather a SWAT team" (3) (in reference to the new MTT). In "Summary Action Steps," they stated that the Mall Transition Team should "build an enforcer system that signals a final decision" and that this team should "use guerilla type action while being kind and inclusive" (Gurian and Gorbey 2003b:1). Ultimately, they asserted, the "culture must shift" (Gurian and Gorbey 2003a). They painted a picture of slow decision making and inertia in response to decisions at the museum. This and the reorganization they also contributed to were presented as methods to get around the cumbersome, bureaucratic pace of work at the NMAI, particularly as the opening loomed.

As mentioned above, the museum transition felt like a small start-up company of enthusiasts growing into a large bureaucracy of workers. By 2006, there had been an overall increase in staff at the mall museum, and its structural reorganization was complete. The same forces that were driving this transition (consultants, senior managers) were also notably trying to make the bureaucracy more efficient (MTT, reorganization). The restructuring of the departments was driven in part by the desire to shift where decision-making power resides in the museum and in part by the changing funding realities as the institution transitioned to a fully operational museum. The funding change happened almost immediately. The day before the museum opened, NMAI staff received an email saying that the government would not be so lenient about money any more: it would be transitioning to the "use-it-or-lose-it" standard fiscal policy of congressional allocations and could no longer carry over funds from year to year.[49]

During the museum's reorganization, only two departments were changed radically: administration was "decentralized" and the Curatorial Department was "broken up." Administrative staff moved to different locations in the museum according to their departmental assignments, and the curatorial staff continued to occupy the same offices but reported to different people and had different job titles. It did not go unnoticed, often with raised eyebrows, that all of the non-Native curators were now situated under collections research and the Native curators were placed mainly in public programs—non-Natives were behind the scenes, and Natives were out in public, people noted.[50]

Though many individuals remained in the same offices, the names of the departments and NMAI divisions changed, and the person they reported to changed. Tim Johnson described this transition as moving to more "corporate" and "businesslike" operations at the NMAI for greater "efficiency."[51] The CRC staff often joked about the idea that this was somehow a "flattening" of the organization, as Rick West had called it; one comment was delivered with perfect comedic timing: "Yeah, flat like a pancake—on its edge!" Although "flattening" is intended to refer to the project team approach, which brings people from different departments together, the organizational chart looked very "vertical" to staff, and even Johnson acknowledged that the museum was more hierarchical after this reorganization. The museum would be reorganized at least two more times by 2010.[52]

When I asked people what the goals for reorganizing were, one CRC staff member's comment summed up the staff's perspective well, so I quote this person at length:

> I have Rick's reasons stamped in my mind. It's to flatten out the hierarchical flow chart and encourage cross-communication, working with more flow between the departments. But then there's the gossipy side of it all that you hear, you know, to "get rid" of [the] Curatorial Department. It was this person versus that person for all these years, and then someone finds out that this person is consulting from a contract—you know, Jim [Volkert]—and then one day I find out that he's a paid consultant on this, and everyone feels enlightened when they find that out.
>
> Because the position that Bruce [Bernstein] and Jim were in all those years— it really *was* Exhibits versus Curatorial.... But do I agree with that? I hope that Rick West is above that.... There are a couple things that I've observed about the reorganization, that I've found really puzzling.... Why do the other three major departments [besides Curatorial] still have assistant directors, but Museum Assets and Operations does not? Why is there still that middle area for other departments?[53]

The institution essentially shifted from power located with the curators to power located with the project managers, and, with the opening of the mall museum, the center of activity reoriented from the CRC to downtown. In the course of this transition from imagined possibility to materialized reality, one CRC staff member felt that a "switch to practicality" was needed in the Curatorial Department but some staff could not make that transition. She said, "We had to surrender our values or dreams" along the way to make it happen. Project managers were in charge of the "drive to open" the museum, which she called a "steamroller you can't stop." She said that curatorial staff were perceived to be "obstructionist." And, as more than one person told me, if you are called "obstructionist" at the museum, you get "removed from the project." By 2004, in response to job insecurity and internal museum politics, a number of low-level curatorial staff were "depressed" and seeing an ombudsman, a counselor, or both. By 2006, the attitude in the CRC overall had changed from frustration to resignation. One person told me, with sadness, "It's just a job.... I just need to get my work done.... It didn't used to be like that."[54]

A View of Bureaucracy from the Periphery

So far, I have described the bureaucracy from the center, but the NMAI was also visible from a distance and communities on the periphery had their own experiences of bureaucratic practices. To the Kalinago co-curators, for example, the NMAI bureaucracy looked like a one dollar check.

One afternoon in April 2005, I sat with Gerard Langlais on the performance stage that was also the front porch of his family's house in the Carib Territory. I asked Gerard whether he had had any contact with the museum since he had come back from the opening. He said no, except for a check that said, "Pay to Gerard Langlais, one dollar." We both laughed as he retrieved the official-looking check from his house to show it to me. Gerard said that he had wondered, "What is that?... Is it one dollar or one hundred dollars? One dollar!" and he began laughing again.[55] I said that I would email Ann McMullen at the museum to ask about it. Neither he nor I knew what it was for.

Later in the month, I went to Jacinta Bruney's home to share a meal and work, with her guidance, on weaving a *larouma* (reed) basket for my mother. She told me about her experiences being an extra in the movie *Pirates of the Caribbean: Dead Man's Chest*, which was then being filmed on the island. When I mentioned Gerard's one dollar check, she went in the house and came back with her own one dollar check from the Smithsonian; other Kalinago co-curators had received them as well. She also showed me tax forms mailed from the Smithsonian Institution for income earned in the United States. We both cracked up after she said, in a deadpan and conspiratorial manner, that she was not planning on filing.

As promised, I emailed Ann McMullen: "None of us have a clue as to what [the one dollar check is] about. Some think perhaps the decimal was put in the wrong place. Others call it a 'souvenir' sent from the [Smithsonian]! Any ideas?... If you can forward the following information to the correct person, I think folks here would like to find out the end of the story.... Clearly, the cost to send the envelope was more than the sum on the check!"[56] Ann responded that the checks were related to the changing exchange rate between from the time they received their reimbursements at a bank in the United States and the time their reimbursements were processed at the Smithsonian, which, "in its own special way," sent out one dollar checks; she suggested that the co-curators could indeed consider them to be souvenirs of the opening.[57] As both Chicago and Kalinago co-curators attested later (see chapter 7), there was no follow-up in their communities by the NMAI; the one dollar checks were the final formal communication between the museum and the Kalinagos after the grand opening.

The NMAI was not the only bureaucracy the Kalinagos were dealing with. A number of the co-curators also were participating in the Carib Model Village task force, dedicated to planning and opening a cultural heritage center in the Carib Territory. A Canadian consultant who was hired to put together a marketing and business plan for the Carib Model Village began one of the task force meetings by passing out a list of reports that had been made over the previous twenty-five years; he said that there had been enough reports and what they needed was *action*. Describing himself as a "results-oriented" person and lamenting the "painfully slow" process of "getting things done" in Dominica, the consultant was in the Carib Territory for a year to get the long-awaited model village up and running in collaboration with Willa Cyrille, the Kalinago woman who was the manager of the site. The model village finally opened in 2006 with a new name in the Kalinago language, Kalinago Barana Autê (Carib Cultural Village by the Sea).

The project was hampered by fluctuating funds, problematic contractor relationships, and a lack of consultation with the local community that resulted in a poor selection of building materials. One of the criticisms was that no Kalinago people were employed in the (re)construction efforts of the model village, although there were competent and available Kalinagos in this field. The permanent secretary of tourism and Willa Cyrille explained that a "tendering" process was required by the Caribbean Development Bank, which was funding the project with loans. In order to put in a bid, you had to be a company or an organization—and the Kalinagos had no such organized body to do so. This was certainly not a creative bureaucracy in the sense of being flexible about the circumstances of Native peoples; the bank could have, for example, construed Kalinago individuals as organizations, as the NMAI did.

Prosper Paris did manage to be contracted to supervise the traditional thatching of the roofs of the structures in the Carib Model Village. But, over a period of three months, he and his Kalinago four-man crew finished only two buildings; there was not enough grass, and it was the wrong time in the growing season to harvest it. The Canadian consultant wondered why the grass-growing season was not taken into account and the thatching started earlier in the year. Willa explained that when Prosper put in the bid a year and a half earlier, the grass was plentiful and there was time to finish. But he was not approved by the government bureaucracy until February.

Whereas the Kalinagos had a problem of too much documentation and not enough action, the Chicago community was experiencing quite the opposite. For them, paper did not symbolize inaction, but rather a form of anonymous agency. At the American Indian Center on November 8, 2005, shortly before the annual powwow, a board meeting was brought to order under the guidelines of Robert's Rules. The meeting began with concern about how the powwow finances were being handled; there was an emphasis on making "policies"—putting rules in writing—so that the AIC would be "protected." Using documents was a way to mitigate "personal issues."

Having policies in writing was intended to address security for both the physical place and the reputation of the American Indian Center, as well as the "point system" at the annual powwow. Participants in the meeting expressed concerns over how points were assessed for competition dancers and over the tribal affiliations of the head judges; people thought it inappropriate for all the judges at an intertribal powwow to be from the same tribe. One person commented that if judges do not show up, they should be replaced, as drum groups are. Another person said, "[We] need to set policies for this—if x, then y." He wondered aloud, Who was going to be responsible for telling the judges the rules? The chairman replied, "What is a piece of paper going to do?" The response: "It sets the rules." The chairman then stated,

"If we *had* a policy, they can't just say we made the rules up just now." The director agreed that the rules would be from the board of directors, implying that these are not from the individual enforcing them. In this case, policies, as rules written on paper, provided a way to empower individuals to enforce a certain order without having to be personally accountable to a fellow community member.[58]

Conclusion

My fieldwork and interviewing turned out to be a kind of salvage ethnography of the NMAI in transition, documenting the changes that occurred as it became a fully functioning Smithsonian Institution museum. Bruce Bernstein told me, when I first approached the NMAI to do this research, that he thought it was a good idea because no one had been keeping records of the development of the museum or its inaugural exhibitions. Although there was a lack of documentation of the organization and chains of command in the museum initially, by the time I finished my fieldwork, many documents were on file, including timelines, organizational charts, lists of deadlines, and transcriptions of exhibit-related interviews (the process of community curating, by the nature of its practice, was well documented by the Curatorial Department).

A similar recuperation of process is found in Edward Linenthal's *Preserving Memory: The Struggle to Create America's Holocaust Museum*. Linenthal (2001:118–119) writes about Holocaust survivor and author Elie Wiesel's "ambivalence about the project" due to the mundane, bureaucratic nature of the institution charged with such a heavy moral responsibility. Wiesel likened the Holocaust Museum to "the invisible temple of a Talmudic story." "'I'm always afraid,' he said, that 'because of bureaucracy, because of the nature of things, because of the fact that we deal with prosaic matters, meetings, budgets, human relations, positions, honors, telephones… somehow this vision of the temple…occupying a space that is between one world and another…will disappear.'" Staff at the NMAI had the same fears, despite some innovative adaptations to bureaucratic routines.

As the institution matured, and with the guidance of prominent museum consultants, the NMAI went from (to characterize it roughly) curatorial power, to minimal curatorial power, to no Curatorial Department. Community curating moved from having personal relations at the intersection between the museum and Native communities to having contractual relations between institutions. There was also a movement from a lack of documentation of the organization to an abundance of organizational charts and contracts.

Highlighting the museum as a bureaucracy also foregrounds the different social relations that are engendered through its work with Native people. A person offering a blessing can be a "vendor" or an "operator of equipment"; a hereditary chief can be a "service organization." Exhibitions have largely been developed either through personal relationships, as in *Our Lives*, or through contracts, as in *Listening to Our*

Ancestors. I do not mean to imply that no meaningful relationships were cultivated through the latter exhibition, but I do want to emphasize its fundamentally different framing of museum-community partnerships.

Interpersonal and contractual relations can too easily be rendered simply as positive and social or as negative and bureaucratic. Each form of social relation embodies a different kind of ethics—what I have referred to elsewhere as collaborative versus contractual ethics (Shannon 2007b)—and each entails particular commitments. For example, although the trust relations developed through the community-curating process for *Our Lives* were essential for creating its exhibitions about Native identity, each community's request—to visit the museum at the opening or to have parts of its exhibit loaned or displayed in the community after objects were removed from the gallery—was consistently met by *OL* curatorial staff with something along the lines of "We'll ask, but we can't promise anything." Curators did press for these requests within the institution, but they did not have the authority to fulfill them. Co-curators were keenly aware of this dynamic—and the history of broken promises to Native peoples—when negotiating with federal institutions.[59]

The NMAI curators clearly saw themselves in a different relation to communities—more personal, long-term, and ethical—than the contractual, legally binding, and finite relations that defined *Listening to Our Ancestors'* museum–community relationship. Curators considered themselves flexible and responsive to each community as opposed to rigidly adhering to bureaucratic procedure; this included the CRC staff's representational experimentalism and openness to Native communities.

The NMAI curators were the mediators between the bureaucracy and the communities, but they had little power to make the institution accountable to the community members with whom they worked. For example, although the original plan was to have "modular" exhibits that could travel to communities, budget and time constraints eventually dictated otherwise. And although the Curatorial Department labored to have the represented communities invited to the opening, in the end, this was achieved only on a shoestring budget at the last minute (see chapter 7). For *Listening to Our Ancestors*, on the other hand, the museum was contractually obligated to send the exhibits to the communities and to provide money for community curators to attend the opening. The contract thus provided guarantees that independent actors in the museum often could not. However, it seems that the museum relied too heavily on the contract to maintain relations with communities, especially when there was a great turnover of staff and no consistent mediator, no curator, between the communities and the museum bureaucracy to advocate within the institution and ensure that Native voices were, according to community curators, faithfully maintained throughout the exhibit-making process.

This did create some problems. At the Native American Art Studies conference held during the last week of October 2005 in Scottsdale, Arizona, Lindsey Martin (Tsimshian, program director, Museum of Northern British Columbia) and

Rachel Griffin (NMAI) discussed their experiences working on *Listening to Our Ancestors*, which had not yet opened. Martin was tasked with developing the text for her community's portion of the exhibit and was candid in describing her concerns about representing her community in the museum, as well as how museum staff represented her voice in the text of the exhibit:

> We were told to write what we wanted to write to tell our story. In an ideal world we could use as many words as we want, or share the story the way we want to. Realistically though, you have museum staff telling you that this term should be changed, or this paragraph should be shortened. In some instances, it comes down to having to change your content. *What happens to Native voice then?* We were trying to share the complexity of our history, the sophistication of our people, but were told that some of the concepts would not be understood by the average visitor. I think when starting out, it is important for museums to establish not only deadlines for things such as exhibit text but also *explain who the audience is*. (Griffin and Martin 2005)

Martin went on to convey that there were times when she felt frustrated, when she asked herself, "Why continue when you [feel] your voice [is] being censored?" She would tell herself that "the aim of the project was to develop these relationships between museums and Native communities" and then acknowledge, "The staff at NMAI are not uncompromising.... They have tried to accommodate us in every way." In her ultimate assessment, the rewards outweighed the challenges: "This is establishing a new type of relationship between museums and our Native communities, opening our eyes to what museums can be in terms of bringing Native voice and Native perspective to objects in the collection at NMAI." "Overall," Martin said, "it is bringing two cultures together—First Nations culture and museum culture.... Sometimes it is like we are speaking two different languages, when in fact we are all speaking English" (Griffin and Martin 2005).

Many people are inclined to see power claims, like contracts, as negative—as about egos and hierarchical maneuvering. Access to information and the shaping of the exhibit process can too easily be considered by those involved as wielding power for power's sake. Often, decision making is indeed about politics, both professional and personal, but not always; sometimes it is about competing visions for proper and ethical action. At the NMAI, there were times when power was seized not to gain control but rather to practice quality control. People cared greatly about their work—for reasons of professional integrity or community obligations or personal commitments, or all of the above. When a commitment to doing things "properly" was interpreted differently by different actors, dedication to the integrity of the project often set individuals or groups at odds.

The museum's senior managers and consultants sought to move its bureaucratic structure from opaque to "transparent," to shift from "leisurely" decision making (according to the consultants' review) to a sleek, "flattened," and "efficient" practice. Lower-level staff, on the other hand, felt that personalities, not the bureaucracy, were "the problem." "Personalities" in this instance seems to combine the notion of "that hierarchical crap" (rank as a measure of one's intellectual contribution or as the ability to reject without explanation the intellectual contributions of those of lower status) and "aesthetics" (glossed as subjective judgment, personal taste, or the unexplained reason something gets changed). But the specific personalities, the people to whom staff mainly referred, were not just a combination of bureaucratic power and idiosyncratic creative judgment; they also represented dueling departmental ideologies and perspectives on community curating. The next chapter shows how the staff in these departments held opposing interpretations of what the "paradigm shift" might mean—some advocating that the museum be more audience focused, according to best practice in museum studies, others advocating a more Native community focus, according to best practice in contemporary museum anthropology.

The museum may not always or only use contracts in the future, and whatever form community curating takes at the NMAI, it will not be the same process as for the inaugural exhibitions—at least in detail, if not in spirit. It is clear, in talking with staff and senior managers, that the original process was not viable once the museum was in operation; it took too long, was too expensive, and relied on a particular kind of freedom from regulatory and fiscal oversight by the Smithsonian that is no longer present.

The apparent dichotomy between a focus on the audience and a focus on the constituency is also one of product versus process, and it concerns the various ways that people separate content development (associated with the Curatorial Department) from design and presentation (associated with the contracted design firms and the Exhibits Department). Not surprisingly, this is a false dichotomy.[60] Every translation from two dimensions to three—from design documents to spatial installation, from worksheet to text panel, from the juxtaposition of objects to the adding of audiovisual media—influences content, as chapter 5 illustrates. But it is important to note that this notion of division between content and design, the textual and the visual, process and product, was conceptually significant to individuals in the institutional locations and specialized departments of the NMAI.

There is another broad stroke I would like to add here. The exhibits staff, as later consultants or as project managers, were involved in "reducing" bureaucracy within the museum, and curators were involved in "mediating" bureaucracy to Native communities. At the NMAI, those who participated in the curatorial and design aspects of exhibit making often felt that overt time pressures limited their ability to do their best work. However, another view relates to the temporal quality of the NMAI as a "bureaucratic machine." Terry Turner (2001:58) cautions against proprietary research with indigenous peoples, and he describes the situation of having a "massive research apparatus waiting" for the "data" to come in. This was part of the pressure on the curators, since their collection of "data" as they did fieldwork with the communities determined the rate of progress in other departments, particularly as the new museum struggled to stay on course for its grand opening. The curatorial research staff were constantly aware of and sensitive to the need to mediate between the bureaucratic demands of this large institution and the sensibilities of the communities with which they worked.

four
Expertise

Rick Hill, who was here as assistant director of Public Programs…said, "Doug, the one thing you need to remember is that Native people are the experts about what it is to be Native people."

—Doug Evelyn, NMAI deputy director, 2004

From the standpoint of museum professionals, it is one thing to call on one's "native informant" and quite another to work with a co-curator.

—James Clifford, Routes

We're not curators. We're facilitators in your exhibitions.

—Gerald McMaster, NMAI deputy assistant director, 2004

We *do* translate from the communities to the exhibit. *Not* a bad thing—that's our job.

—Notes from an Exhibits meeting, 2004

[We were able] to work with communities in this way because…people in Cultural Resources believed in this process that had been instituted. And other people, who weren't a part of Cultural Resources, maybe they didn't all believe—some of them surely did—but even if they didn't believe in it, they still knew it was an instituted methodology that we were going to adhere to.… It became somewhat of a law around here.

—Cynthia Chavez, OL lead curator, 2004

Interpreting "the Law"

The paradigm shift that NMAI staff advocated was, at its heart, a reorientation toward Native peoples—and their knowledges—in museums. The community-curating process was the method by which the museum sought to do so in its early years. This commitment to working with communities was, as Cynthia commented, "somewhat of a law" at the museum, and essential to this process was the figuring of Native individuals in the exhibit-making process as co-curators with valuable and particular kinds of expertise. This approach is in contrast to the historical role Native Americans had in museums, as "objects of knowledge rather than the producers of knowledge" (Errington 1998:24).

The anthropology of experts usually focuses on elites in institutions of power; here, I expand this by including the Native community curators themselves as experts. This goes beyond posing the usual dichotomy of expert versus local knowledge. My approach is to look at the category of "expert" as it was constructed and contested both within and across various groups in the museum and in Native communities; to examine how working on the project of *Our Lives* mobilized certain kinds of expertise within these communities; and in turn to see what happened in the "contact zones" in which these cultures of expertise interacted (Clifford 1997).

Previous chapters discuss the Exhibits and Curatorial Departments as components of a bureaucratic structure. In this chapter, they are (re)presented as cultures of expertise in a wider context of knowledge making; they are also juxtaposed to similar processes within Native communities as those communities selected their own specialists as co-curators. The "community wishes" about exhibit content, which were generated in the process of community curating, at times were considered by NMAI staff to be expert contributions while at other times they were configured as specifically non-expert and thus not seen as credible sources for making the exhibits. Curators sometimes were seen as experts and then at other times as not enacting enough museological expertise in the course of community curating. What was at stake was whether Native knowledge should be interpreted as expert knowledge and what role this knowledge should have in collaborative exhibit making.

An Anthropology of Experts

Two main bodies of anthropological literature discuss an anthropology of experts. One employs the ethnography of elites—financial traders, scientists, political leaders—to understand the contemporary condition, addressing such concepts as globalization, multiculturalism, or postmodernism. The second body of work is a subset of the first, also studying elites but with a tighter focus on the cultural producers involved specifically in mass media production. While not usually categorized as such, an often overlooked area of research about experts is the anthropology of museums, which is also about the interaction of elite culture producers in public institutions of authority.[1]

The anthropology of experts is one way of "studying up" (Nader 1974[1969]), of understanding the everyday lives of the powerful instead of the oppressed, who were historically the focus of anthropological study. Here, my ethnographic approach to *Our Lives* provides an opportunity to both study up and study down. Community curators, as indigenous people, are most often recognized as oppressed, as non-elites. They are also very much theorists in the ways they think, define, and talk about their identities for the sake of exhibitions and other public presentations. No doubt, due to the millions of people coming to the NMAI each year, both curatorial staff and community curators contributed significantly to public discourse, but not through political or economic positions of power—rather, through the power of representation, or the "ability to produce (and control) meaning and disseminate it" (Kurin 1997:285). This, of course, is a cogent source of power, but many actors in addition to the curators and co-curators influenced the meanings of the exhibitions they were producing.

In general, the scholarly analysis of museums has put forth that they are elite institutions asserting their power and privilege (Smart 2011:12). Rarely does the research focus on how museum staff make sense of their work. I do not deny that culture producers in the NMAI are elites, nor that the power to represent is a significant one, but this is not my frame of analysis here. Although the NMAI and even more so the Smithsonian are influential and powerful institutions, my story is about the staff members working with oppressed or underrepresented peoples. I was in the unusual situation of "studying up" with culture producers who represented and empowered marginalized peoples but who felt themselves to be relatively disempowered within the museum. The NMAI curators did not feel that they had much control in the end, regardless of the view from outside or their access to and communication with the broader public.

If we take the term "expert" to mean having highly specialized knowledge through training, then in anthropology with Native Americans more generally and in my fieldwork, experts abound: religious experts, tribal historians, material culture specialists, and more. From this perspective, the anthropology of experts has been going on for a long time, even if anthropologists' interlocutors were not named as such (cf. Radin 1927:xii, 5).[2] "Expert" is a somewhat political term, a differentially valued category. Labeling Native community members as cultural experts, as NMAI staff did, is an ethical stance, a self-consciously subversive classification of sorts, a balancing of academic and oral traditional modes of knowing and knowledge training, and a form of activism in which staff were seeking to change museological language and practice in light of the historical relations between museums and Native Americans.

It is not unprecedented to consider the experts making an exhibition to include indigenous people, as well as museum staff, nor is the experience of negotiating the various interests of the parties involved unique to the NMAI, as Anita Herle illustrates in "Torres Strait Islanders: Stories from an Exhibition" (2000; see also Ames 1999; Kahn 2000). Herle explains that collaborative exhibitions with Native people include "cross-cultural collaborative work, reflecting the changing roles of museums as sites for contact and research combining curatorial expertise and indigenous knowledge" (2000:253). She continues:

> The contextualization of the collections in the centenary exhibition necessarily involved both Islander and curatorial knowledge and expertise.... There are few ethnographies of the making of an exhibition and insider evaluations usually take the form of relatively standardized visitor surveys designed with an eye towards marketing. Those actively involved in producing exhibitions are well aware of the negotiations between the different interests of specialist museum staff (curators, designers, conservators, educators) and outside experts (academic specialists, indigenous representatives, community and special interest groups), as well as the practical limitations imposed by time, space and resources. (Herle 2000:253)

This chapter is one answer to her call for a more in-depth study of the dynamics of the collaborative process.

Expertise in the Contact Zone

In *Routes: Travel and Translation in the Late Twentieth Century*, James Clifford (1997: 188–219) renders museums as "contact zones." This complex concept refers to the meeting of indigenous peoples and museums in ongoing intercultural and contentious relations connected to a colonial past, entailing uneven reciprocity and political negotiation, as well as alliances and advocacy. This analysis represents a shared acknowledgment of the inequalities inherent in the museum space and in the collaborative process.[3] Whereas Clifford considers how collections and objects traverse these contact zones, I borrow the concept and its vivid imagery to examine the contact between different forms of expertise during the making of the *Our Lives* exhibit.

Clifford (1997:208) explains that "neither community 'experience' nor curatorial 'authority' has an automatic right to the contextualization of collections or to the narration of contact histories." This is precisely where the *OL* "battle" was waged: the contextualization of the exhibit content. The constant "personalities" and "turf" issues between departments were in part a battle over jurisdiction, over boundaries of professional expertise. Expertise was contested, enacted, and located differently by various departments. The notion of Native community members as experts was very differently viewed by Exhibits and by Curatorial. Individuals both inside and outside the museum assured me that the tension between these two departments was classic and occurs in all museums. However, at the NMAI, there was a new element: the community curator.

As mentioned in the previous chapter, there is a set of dichotomies in museum structure and practice: process versus product, content versus design, and textual versus visual. The Exhibits Department was responsible for the oversight of the final product and the design and visual properties of the exhibition, and the Curatorial Department was responsible for the process, textual output, and content. Whether it is about being a visual thinker, being able to anticipate the audience, or knowing the "right" way to work with Native communities, each NMAI department had its own modus operandi.

The category of expert, and the decision about what kind of expert was necessary to the particular tasks of exhibit making, can be analyzed in a number of different ways—through the contestation of professional responsibility within the museum, through the selection of particular individuals for co-curator committees, and even through the categories of expertise that the museum used to define its consultants in its development phases. For example, documents from the 1997 meetings about the recently created exhibition master plan, much like earlier consultations about the planning of the museum itself, reveal that NMAI staff categorized guests and meetings according to specific groups of experts, such as academics, Native scholars, and museum professionals. Much like what I have termed the "representational calculus" conducted by the Kalinagos for their co-curator committee, Rick West stated in a memorandum to NMAI staff about an upcoming meeting, "I believe we have come up with lists of people for both sessions that have rough geographic balance and variety, gender balance, diverse subject expertise, and hemispheric representation," referring to both the "scholars and academics" list and the "Indian museum community" list.[4] In the 2000 "vetting session" for the *OL* gallery, which was a meeting with "Native scholars," the museum sought certain groups of specialists, as it defined them, to accomplish its goals of consultation and legitimization.

Each culture of expertise has its own ethos, material practices, technical languages, and power structures. From collections management, to curatorial, to design, there are many expert communities of practice within the museum bureaucracy. Add to these the community curators and the museum becomes a large field of collaborating experts and knowledges, a complex contact zone within which the exhibition is produced. Doug Evelyn provided a picture of this contact zone as "being a collaborative one within the museum, requiring different sets of expertise and disciplines to pull off":

> And we were anxious that there was an interplay between the design and the production side of the house and the curatorial. And there's always tension in that process. There's got to be at some point a baton pass, where the curatorial people kind of wrap up the script. Now, in this case, who were the curators? The curators were…NMAI people, who facilitated a much larger set of interactions with tribal curators. That was all very complex.[5]

The "baton pass" was at the heart of the conflict between Exhibits and Curatorial, along with the complex interactions with and on behalf of the community curators. This language suggests a relay race, a model in which content is passed from department to department (often, curatorial to design to education). More recent trends in museum studies, however, advocate instead a team approach in which all professionals work at the same time on exhibit development, from start to finish.

Each side of the institutional divide—between Curatorial and Exhibits—had its own ideas about the community-curating process and different criteria for evaluating the success of exhibits. The NMAI literature has repeated, from its earliest planning documents to today, that it has both a constituency and an audience, the former being "Native communities" and the latter being the "non-Native public." (Although the visiting public to some extent includes Native communities, it is generally envisioned as an uninformed, non-Native public.) People working at the NMAI readily acknowledged that the struggle between Exhibits and Curatorial had been going on for many years, as it often does in other museums, but they felt that in this particular case, the cause seemed to be that the departments looked to different constituencies.[6] Staff viewed Exhibits as prioritizing the non-Native public and Curatorial as prioritizing Native communities, most notably in the form of co-curators. The Curatorial Department worried about doing things the "right" way and squarely faced and served Native peoples in its philosophy and practice to accomplish this. The Exhibits and Education Departments were more consistently mindful of and directed toward doing appropriate "translation" for the non-Native museum-going public.

I am in no way suggesting that public-oriented staff did not also have a strong desire to do what is right in regard to Native communities, but this divide in language, interpretation, perception, and practice about the NMAI's mission and commitment to Native voice was a key part of the museum's internal dynamics. The two approaches were opposed and situated the locus of expertise and professional responsibilities differently. They also represented different theoretical commitments, one associated with contemporary museum studies (a greater focus on audience and participation) and the other with museum anthropology (sharing authority with the people being represented). In an interview, Rick West explained that curators were "told early on in the process to let it flow, not to filter Native voice." He said, "They've been very disciplined in that."[7] Apparently to their detriment, according to evaluations by exhibits staff.

Curatorial Experts and Advocates

As I explained earlier, the Curatorial Department at the NMAI shared authority with Native co-curators during the making of the community-curated portions of the inaugural exhibitions, considering them to be the experts of their own (cultural) experience and producers of the exhibition content.[8] There was an "intellectual openness that recognize[d] the place and the authority of indigenous peoples in their own interpretation and representation" (West 2004). This collaborative approach fundamentally changed the role of the curators and the relationship they had to the subjects and the content of the exhibits. Michael Ames explains:

> The customary method of exhibition development could be summarized by

saying it is governed by the "curatorial prerogative." By that I mean: (a) the final decision, authority, or prerogative for the exhibition usually lies with the curatorial team, subject to the approval of senior museum administration and budgetary constraints; and (b) the team is led or authorized by a content specialist or knowledge expert, designated as the curator or guest curator, rather than by a conservator, designer, educator, administrator, or specialist consultant.

The process thus is hierarchical in structure: from the governing bodies of a museum, who set its mandate, to the director and/or senior management, to the curator, to the exhibition team composed of museological specialists. The assumption underlying the key role given to the curator is that specialized research knowledge is a primary consideration, subject to the exhibition and financial policies of the museum as monitored by the director or senior administrative official. Research or "knowledge" is considered a primary good, therefore the person specializing in its production expects, and usually is accorded, privileged status in the decision-making process and in any public benefits. (Ames 1999:42)

In contrast, NMAI curators described themselves as facilitators—which is not unusual in collaborative exhibit development with originating communities, or "source communities" (see Ames 1992; Phillips 2003)—and also as "advocates" for Native communities within the museum. They saw the Native community members as content specialists and squarely placed the "prerogative" with them; NMAI staff placed themselves as intermediaries, representatives, and sometimes even protectors of the community prerogative in interdepartmental meetings.

A vetting session in 2000, at which people brainstormed the framework and content of the *Our Lives* gallery, included a small group of respected Native scholars and NMAI staff members.[9] Bruce Bernstein began the meeting by explaining:

All three [inaugural] exhibits are community curated, at least 70 percent. What we mean by that is the museum curators, the museum staff, whether Native or non-Native, serve as facilitators or advocates, that the *experts reside in the communities*. So not only should we go to the communities to get their voices. Many exhibits over the last 20 or 30 years have sought Native people to be voices. Then, however, they put them in front of the exhibit to comment on the exhibit but haven't really allowed them into the exhibit....

As we are going into the design phases for these two exhibitions, [we are seeing] the difficulty of non-Native people to hear a lot of what these experts have told us. Yesterday we were in the design session for [*Our*] *Universes*, and there is a tendency for the people who are working with these individuals to reassemble everything.

So it is our responsibility not so much to correct them—that it's not red but it's blue—but rather to get them to have a comfort that Native people know what they are speaking about. If you really think about the problem exhibitions, it's still the general public or the museum-going public's *discomfort with expertise*. Academically, as well, you can understand that museums, like academic institutions, are based upon writing, based upon publication. If you have the scholars, like myself, who write and publish, then you add Native people's narrative, *which is more legitimate*.... The power of narrative [in our society] is overwhelming. Certainly that is a lesson that comes out of Native cultures everywhere in the hemisphere. So we're trying to resituate the exhibition so that people hear narratives as important as [any other] view....

[NMAI staff are] trying to work with [Native peoples] in partnership *advocating their point of view*. It is taxing on people, to say the least. You can imagine how it is when you've worked with one community and going back and forth. Things sometimes change in communities. The governors change, and there are all those family differences. The museum has to remain as much a neutral body as we can possibly be. Therefore, the museum on the Mall becomes a venue for Native people to tell their story *without the filter, without the interpretation of NMAI*.[10]

Here, we see a reversal of the conventional notions of expertise. What is oral is more "legitimate" than what is published, and the Native community member is more legitimate than the accredited anthropologist, who represents an institution that is not to interrupt the Native story with its own "interpretation."

As Bruce's introduction to the session shows, NMAI curatorial staff viewed the co-curators as experts and had used such language to describe them since at least 1999.[11] This meant that the exhibit content and themes were to come from Native community members. As Cynthia Chavez explained, her job was to listen carefully, to group together co-curators' ideas into coherent themes, and to organize them in a way that could be visually presented in the form of an exhibit. She also commented, "Well, looking at myself as a curator within the context of the NMAI and then this particular exhibit, I see myself more as a facilitator—of information—and also someone who is a liaison. And I think that that's what I've been best at doing.... We either have to *not* call me a curator, or we have to redefine what a curator is. Because I certainly don't see myself as that in the traditional sense of that word or that definition."[12]

Having heard various staff members construe the community-curating process quite differently, I asked a number of people what being a curator *at the NMAI* meant. Did curators have any kind of role in exhibit development beyond just listening to what community members said (a characterization made by many fifth-floor staff)? One curator responded, "Curators *did* have to translate knowledge—it's a question of whether you think they have a certain expertise or they just facilitated."[13] Bruce Bernstein explained, "Although you can't be an expert in eight different cultures, you can be an expert in talking to people about their cultures.... It means we have an expert in working with Plains people. But it doesn't mean that we're *the* experts on Plains people."[14]

Speaking of how other staff members perceived the Curatorial Department, one curator commented, "I think there's sort of a feeling that there is not expertise in this department.… That pretty much anyone can curate an exhibit and that we don't have anybody around here in this department who has such a specialized body of knowledge that we need them, that they're necessary."[15] This perception was corroborated by the head of the Exhibits Department in interviews over the years (see below). Ann McMullen, on the other hand, insisted that curators did have special skills, although she confirmed that this was challenged by other departments.

On a number of occasions, Ann and I talked about the role of curators in the museum. In November 2004, shortly after the museum opened to the public, we had a long conversation in the rotunda area of the CRC while, outside the large panoramic windows, the day faded and turned to night. Ann directly addressed what she saw to be the expertise of NMAI curators and how they were indeed viewed as having little or no relevant expertise by other departments in the museum. She pointed out that curators provide what is not written down, which is essential to "get it right," and she said that there was a commitment based on intimacy—knowing the backstory, so to speak—between the NMAI curators and Native community members. What is important is "the curator's ability and the curator's *tact* and the exercise of negotiation within the communities, to be that mediator between museum forces": "There are people within NMAI—even people who *ought* to know better—who feel that *anyone* can be a curator."[16]

Ann went on to explain that the curator's knowledge was key to determining what was significant in the "raw transcripts," which "included a lot of sensitive information and a lot of irrelevant information and some relevant." Her main concern was that this information "would be given into the hands of someone who had no idea of what those relevancies were—who had no idea how the text and the things that were in the transcripts actually related to the *rest* of the exhibition as it had been developed so far." To Ann, a demand by the program manager to turn over raw transcripts, rather than have curators write exhibition scripts based on them, "was the place where curatorial authority was really at stake." "Because we ran the risk of sort of just opening up the transcripts," she explained, a situation in which community requests or even tacit understandings (for example, that particular conversations co-curators had with NMAI staff not be displayed in public) could have gone unheeded.

The fear in the Curatorial Department was that the content of the exhibits would tend to reflect what "piqued the interest of the scriptwriter," possibly presenting something "horribly overemphasized in the exhibit that resulted" or presenting something that the community did not agree with. Ann continued:

> So it was like…*the big fight*. And the *whole* thing hinges on—for me—authority. And how authority is constituted within NMAI.… In the same way that I described everybody having a piece of the exhibit and having no single picture.… Because there's *no recognition that Curatorial stands in a unique, face-to-face position with the community*, and being in the *best* position to actually, in some cases, *interpret* the feeling of the community when there's no possibility of going back and asking every single question.… *Somebody's* got to take *responsibility* for that. And it seemed at that point that…members of Curatorial, specifically the

lead curators, were the only ones who recognized that it was a *responsibility*. And it was what we *owed* communities.

[Our position was] that you couldn't understand communities and what they wanted for their exhibits solely by what was recorded on paper, what was in the transcripts, or anything else like that. Part of it had to do with the development of personal relationships and *feelings* of community, of having *heard* them, of having heard their often emotional reactions to what they're talking about. Having heard their own ideas about what the exhibit might be and try[ing] to tailor them to what might actually be possible within a physical exhibit space....

So there are all these people sticking their fingers in this pie, and if curators sit between those things, they're the only ones who can actually say, "I don't think the community's going to like that—that isn't...what they said. It's not what they stressed, when we talked to them.".....

Part of the [problem with] some of the design teams—and not all of them, but some of them—would be, they'd always be introducing their own research. They'd be going on the web, and they'd be going to the library and they'd be checking books out.... We were, like, "No! That's not what [the co-curators] said—this is supposed to be *what these community people said*. And if you want to *back* it up with something, we still have to *check* with them about whether it's okay to do that."

Ann stressed that the curators' face-to-face relationships with communities in part compel them to be advocates within the museum, where the exhibition content gets manipulated into a three-dimensional exhibit—where the content is affected by multiple experts transforming it through script editing, the juxtaposition of images and objects, and the use of colors and textual strategies of emphasis and de-emphasis. This responsibility to advocate is in part based on a particular kind of intimacy—or shared knowledge—that NMAI curators have with community curators and on their desire to participate in the exhibit-making process beyond merely collecting raw data:

And part of our understanding in Curatorial of Native voice was...the content of the exhibits went as far as the communities *wanted* it to.... Because part of the curator's relationship to the community members is also one of *intimacy*. For instance, I can remember...doing interviews with people where the person that you're speaking with automatically assumes that you *know* something, or that you *don't* know something. And if they feel that you have a shared background, they *don't* talk about the ABC's of the situation.[17]

Ann further explained that this familiarity between the NMAI curator and the Native co-curators allowed for a higher level of detail in conversations, but, as a result, sometimes the curator may "become somewhat blind to the fact that *more* introductory information is actually necessary."

Ann also described what she saw as the role of the curator in community curating: "*the mediator* between the *source*—the communities themselves—and what we've presented in the exhibits." She contrasted this with her view that exhibit developers, tasked with taking "raw content and transform[ing] it into what exhibits look like," consider the curators as simply collectors of information rather than mediators. According to exhibit developers, she explained, curators are "simply these sort of people with dust pans kind of scraping up things and collecting stories and everything and bringing [them] back and handing them over in that raw fashion to somebody else." She saw this as undermining the Curatorial Department and, consequently, community curators' authority in the process: "Because…*all* of it has to do with who's got authority over what…. Native voice was supposed to be the *representation* the communities had, physically, within the exhibit design. And it was supposed to be also some kind of empowerment of what they *said* about what [should be] in there." She talked about the "push-pull thing" within the NMAI and wondered why, "if Native voice was truly more than words and the communities were supposed to have solid input into their designs," it was decided that the designers would be the final authority on what the exhibits would look like. She explained, "[In effect,] community curators are not in a position to approve or disapprove the design…. Essentially, it sort of simultaneously *dis*empowered the community curators, and it disempowered Curatorial as a unit itself":

> If Curatorial is put in a position of representing the interests of disempowered people, how empowered can Curatorial itself be?… If no one's listening to Curatorial, then community curators themselves are effectively silenced…. And that's a question about community curation, which is, How do you actually get to that point of intimacy where you can actually guess what somebody's going to say, where you can actually judge what's going to matter and what's not going to matter? And that's the point that NMAI is at now, because there are people downtown who think that anybody can be a curator—that you can send *anybody* out there to a community and come back with what members of Curatorial have.

Ann's comments are very much representative of the Curatorial ethos in general: a desire to advocate for "community wishes" against other interests and actors within the bureaucracy and a desire to remain connected to and shepherd the exhibit content, which was developed in what was conceptualized as an intimate partnership with Native community members. Curatorial staff members felt that, since the co-curators could not always be present in departmental meetings or at important decision-making moments, they were charged with the responsibility to represent co-curators' interests throughout the exhibit's development. They were the closest staff members—socially and spatially, through repeat visits—to the communities.

Exhibits Experts and Translators

Like many Exhibits Department staff members, Mark Hirsch, the scriptwriter/editor,[18] saw his job as bringing "clarity," making it easier for visitors to understand the exhibits. He and I talked about how sometimes the co-curators would choose not to provide content for exhibits that the museum staff were interested in. He said, "I felt we often acted as supplicants at times when we should have provided direction [to communities about curating]. And I don't think that was helpful. Again, a very subjective feeling. I mean, I think that's probably heresy in Curatorial." He discussed "paying the price" for just doing what the community wants and added that it is the exhibition team that staff members should have allegiance to, not their departments.[19]

What is ironic about some of the common conceptions from outside the Curatorial Department—that there was a "cabal," as one museum consultant put it when she was explaining why Curatorial needed to be "broken up,"[20] or that curatorial staff had an allegiance to one another rather than to the wider exhibition team—is that Curatorial did not have a single meeting as a department during the entire course of my fieldwork at the NMAI and some staff members did not even speak to one another in the months before the museum opening. A number of staff complained about the lack of meetings and the lack of discussions of any kind among curators, and one Curatorial member even suggested that *I* arrange a meeting for the department. Here, I think, fifth-floor people like Mark got it wrong: there was not an allegiance among Curatorial staff to their department or to one another, but rather—and fiercely—their allegiance was to the Native communities with which they worked.

Mark also emphasized the difference between fieldwork and museum labels, stating that only politicians talk in sound bites, not Native community members. So their comments needed to be rewritten to suit the audience, for better understanding. He construed his own lack of knowledge about Native Americans as helpful in an editorial capacity ("Ignorance is bliss," he joked) because he could come at the material from the visitor's perspective. Mark is one person, among others on the fifth floor or downtown, about whom other staff members said, "They don't know Indians 101." Mark presented it as an advantage; he saw himself as representative of the museum's audience, imagined by him as an ignorant public. He also thought that what was seen as advocacy in Curatorial, was viewed in other departments as a kind of paternalism:[21]

> This is kind of hard to explain, actually. I'm not sure I'm going to do this justice. This is one of those points where I think *maybe* this is the moment where we should shut the tape recorder off. *But!* Let's not. Let's see how far we go. I felt like the opposition between Curatorial—or the tension between Curatorial and Exhibitions—here was perhaps more pronounced than I think it is naturally in other places. And I got the sense that Curatorial's main constituency was the Native communities, and they really at some level, *apparently*—I'm not saying this as *fact*—it *seemed* to me that sometimes that was the only constituency that they were particularly interested in, that the museum content that they were acquiring was important content, and that they had to defend the interests of Native people. In some ways, I tended to look at some people in Curatorial like the Indian agents.... There seemed to me to be a kind of paternalism—you know, "Indian people can't take care of themselves, so we have to take care of

them." I think the tension on the other side was that we're here to create exhibits and tell people about Native people, and the constituency for Exhibits was the public.[22] And I think that dichotomy was very pronounced.... Again, this is very subjective. You need to talk to other people about this.

In many ways, Mark bridged the two departments, working on materials provided by Curatorial while situated on the fifth floor near the senior managers and the head of the Exhibits Department. I did talk to others about this perspective, and in general, Mark's language reflected the fifth-floor speech network, which used similar phrases about, and critiques of, the curators and community curating. In a series of interviews, Jim Volkert told me that he felt the curators had not "stepped up to the table" with museological expertise, that they simply would go "to a community and say, 'Tell us your story.'" Jim believed that this approach had injured the final exhibits. The notion that curators did "whatever the communities told them to" was repeated often in criticisms of the Curatorial Department by downtown staff.

Jim contended that the problem was with using experts to talk to the museum public, regardless of what kind of experts they are:

> We simply replaced the experts with Native people *we call* experts. You know, just a different group of experts, that's all. So, if we were a museum on trains, we would have train experts. But we're about Indians, so we have Indian experts. Well, that's not enough. You know, that's not the answer. And I am in no way saying that the authority of the museum doesn't go back to the community. I'm not saying that at all. What I'm saying is, when we isolate them as experts in a nonconversational way, we've done the same thing that museums have done for a hundred years.[23]

Jim saw the role—the particular expertise—of the Exhibits Department (and, some would say, the exhibit developer) as bringing those experts into conversation in an effective way with visitors.

Jim explained in 2004 that the sharing of authority in exhibitions may have been new ten years ago, when the museum was in the planning stages, but it was not new any more. He located the authority in Native communities, but he emphasized the expertise of the Exhibits Department to bridge the conversation between the Native "cultural expert" and the non-Native museum visitor:

> You know, we're not in the forefront of that [notion of sharing authority in exhibitions] as much as we might think we are...because that's just replacing one expert with another, replacing an anthropologist, you know, with an Indian.[24] But I think what's *more* important is that we found ways to bridge that conversation, from expert to visitor, in ways that are more conversational.... I think that's what's important about the way this museum operates...on the authority transfer from the museum to Native people. Here, it's more about the communication quality of the voice, so the issue that this museum needs to focus on is taking on its own responsibility when that communication doesn't work. In other words, just because a Native person *says* it doesn't mean a non-Native person *gets* it.

Jim suggests here that, whereas Curatorial empowers communities by resting content authority in them, Exhibits improves the quality and accessibility of Native voice for museum visitors.

Much as Ann intimated, Jim did not see working with communities as a particular skill of curators, citing an earlier exhibition, *Woven by the Grandmothers: Nineteenth-Century Navajo Textiles from the National Museum of the American Indian*, which was featured at the George Gustav Heye Center in 1996. On the contrary, he saw curatorial staff as "sequestering" communities from the rest of the museum during the making of the inaugural exhibitions: "The community conversations, to some extent, took on a kind of exclusive quality...only certain people could talk with the communities. And that's what I mean by sequestered. And the show process suffered because of that—the exhibition process. Because while the conversations might have been lovely, they weren't going towards making exhibitions very well." And, in what seems a blatant disregard for what the Curatorial Department saw as its purpose and as the specific role of the communities (exhibit content), Jim stated:

> I think museums, *us* in particular, worry too much about content. You know, that some of that's the *reason* that everybody's coming to the museum. And in fact we've had *endless* discussions over the years about that. And I think we've made *far* too much of that conversation. I mean, you know...we're talking, what, three hundred square feet for the tribal areas, and we have endless days of conversation about them. When taken in the totality of the building, it's a tiny piece of it. I'm not trying to minimize the work at all, but you know, we think that it's the single piece that will have the most impact on the visitors, and in fact it's not....
>
> And I understand all about the process that we've done here, and so forth and so forth, but at the same time, I think that we've tied ourselves up a bit without fully understanding what we were trying to do. The outcome of this was *not* to have good conversations with communities, although we did. The outcome was to make a physical representation of [those conversations] that other people would walk into.... But I think what we have to be careful of is that we, the museum, bring all of our skills to bear, because otherwise it could seem like some of the communities are just...not very interesting, not very thoughtful, not very engaged.[25]

Jim in a later interview concluded that "filtering" or "translating," in common museum terms, is necessary. In many ways, this is what he saw the role of the Exhibits Department to be: to translate in a way that elevates the product of the collaboration and also makes the communities look good. Otherwise, not using that expertise is "unfair":

> I think one of the mistakes we've made—I think we've adjusted since then—but early in the process, there was this fear of the museum somehow filtering Native voice. And it came to be a kind of pejorative statement, you know, that it has to be sort of pure, unaltered, unfiltered. And I think that was a mistake.

I don't think there is such a thing, actually. Nor do I think [it] is that desirable. I think that the museum's responsibility is to synthesize and evaluate and converse about and make apparent, and those kinds of things. Not to say, whatever you, Native person, have to say is what we're going to do. Because that's—well, I talked about that before—I think it's unfair. So part of it is being better at having conversations. We're just not very good at it yet.[26]

Note that Jim is working with two concepts of "conversation": the one that worked well (interpersonal) and the one that did not (museological).

In a similar vein, a program manager in the Exhibits Department said that community curating is "not like a real job; it's a process definition" allowing people "traditionally not in the inner sanctum of the museum to enter the fold," "not as spectators, but as participants." Community curating "has value," he said, "but we went way too far in one direction…[and] abdicated our responsibilities" to visitors, including the information they wanted and the intellectual framing of the exhibits.[27]

Kerry Boyd, the head of Exhibits after Jim left to lead the Mall Action Committee, echoed the sentiment that not enough guidance was offered to the participating Native communities:

So it is challenging here…. And there were so many conflicting viewpoints. And the overriding thing is that Native voice has to be heard without, in theory, without filters. So how do we best do that?… I think part of the problem is that we let a lot of communities come in unfiltered. And not only did we not filter them, we didn't really guide them. And I think some guidance might have assisted us—the presentations in the galleries—[to] be more cohesive. Some communities—Seminole, Cherokee, Santa Clara—I mean, those communities have thriving cultural centers and museums, and they kind of know— and they've been subjects of exhibits before—and they kind of know exhibitory [standards]. Ka'apor, Tapirapé, I mean, the communities are not experienced…. I think, personally, some more guidance in assisting them…might have been better for our visitors to understand their stories.[28]

Kerry's comments show that there was a common language and conceptualization of the process among fifth-floor staff ("without filters") that was not common among the curatorial staff. It is clear that between these two cultures of expertise—Curatorial and Exhibits—not only their technical languages and tools vary, but also their common conceptions and language about the exhibition process and community curating. The view was quite different from each vantage point.

What can be gleaned from these commentaries, which are representative of the two departments, is that there was by curatorial staff a deference to communities for exhibit content and cultural expertise and they felt that their roles as mediators and advocates working with Native communities required specific skills. The exhibits staff, on the other hand, viewed the curators as not providing enough expertise, or museological guidance, to the communities to develop the best exhibition possible. This is also related to their characterization of the Curatorial Department as being too protective of communities and not letting other staff have "access" to them. In what was no doubt a reference to Curatorial, Jim Volkert expressed a sentiment I had heard from other staff members outside the Curatorial Department: "Nobody *owns* the community. Nobody *owns* the people, you know, or owns *access* to them, for that matter."[29]

One person I interviewed in 2006 specifically asked that the following be included in this book but wanted the statement to remain anonymous: "There was very much at the front end [of making the exhibitions] a total disbelief and distrust that Indian people could interpret themselves, from the Exhibits Department at this museum. And that hindered the work from the onset. And that's what the arguments between [department heads] were about, quite frankly…that Indian people could speak for themselves but needed a developer, or an Exhibits person—a pertinent person of great expertise—to interpret [them]." What many of my interlocutors, including this one, said was at stake was power, power conceived of here as the power to represent.

The politics of representation, then, was highlighted in two of its many aspects: as (re)presentating (or translating) and as acting on behalf of (or advocating). Exhibits wanted the power to represent Native life in a way that would be accessible to the audience (and, in so doing, benefit the reputation of Native communities). Curatorial wanted the power to create a faithful representation of the communities according to how they wanted to represent themselves (and, in so doing, maintain ethical and positive relationships with Native communities). While the museum as a whole recognized that Native communities are experts of their own experience, staff contested the extent that expertise should define the exhibit itself. Each department interpreted the role of expert in different ways.

Two curators revealed separately, but in similar terms, that in the museum bureaucracy, the Native communities often became "pawns" in interoffice power struggles.[30] At times, to get people in other departments to do something a specific way, a curator would say, "The community wants it that way." One curator explicitly did not like doing this, but it became a strategy. This sentence became a trump card in many ways, due to the institution's mission, and it was mobilized in response to the dwindling power of the curators in decision making and their concern that earlier decisions made by community curators regarding exhibit content would be ignored in later stages of the exhibit-making process. Even if a curator felt that the community might be willing to compromise on an issue of design, for example, the curator spoke on their behalf to maintain the plan as they had approved it, insisting that this was the way the community wanted it to be. In essence, museological expertise could be trumped by community expertise, often glossed as community wishes. Seen this way, controlling access to the community or access to legitimating knowledge could indeed be considered a form of power.

This friction between departments was also alluded to as a conflict between department heads and a clash between two "cults of personality." Other staff members suggested that the main issue was control over the exhibitions and whether it rested in the museum or outside it, in the communities. What we see here is a competition between cultures of expertise, staking out their professional territory and advancing their own interpretations of what is best practice in exhibit making and in representing Native Americans in the museum.

Cultural Experts and Community Curators

In addition to the "battle" raging inside the museum about the expertise and responsibilities of curators and co-curators, there was the evaluation and selection of experts within the Native communities.[31] During my fieldwork in both Chicago and Dominica, I learned that those who had been selected for the co-curator committees were people who often volunteered for or were recruited into various community projects or by outside organizations as representatives. Well before the NMAI came to town, these individuals were already recognized as having specialized skills or knowledge and often were asked to represent their communities to outsiders.

At the NMAI, each gallery required certain kinds of experts: for *Our Peoples*, they were elders or tribal historians who knew the stories of selected events in their tribe's history; for *Our Universes*, they were spiritual practitioners or religious leaders who had knowledge of a particular ceremony at a particular time of year; and *Our Lives* required expertise in "Native identities," as per the exhibition's theme. An expert on identity, in many ways, can be any individual in a community—anyone can be an expert on his or her own identity and life experience. But *Our Lives* was about community identity, so specific people were mobilized as having the appropriate expertise to represent each community in this way. The formation of the co-curator committees tells us about community members' expectations of the work they would be asked to do; indeed, it required a preconceived notion of what constitutes community identity, regardless of how the concept eventually was interpreted in community curator meetings. In selecting the community curator group, there was an assumption about what kinds of specialized knowledge were necessary to make an appropriate representation of a community's identity.

Each community in the *Our Lives* exhibition was charged with providing a group of community curators with whom the NMAI could work. The selection of committees in Native communities both enacted a collaboration between experts and reflected established modes of bureaucratic practice in these groups. Community curators were selected by the chief in the Carib Territory, and in Chicago, they were elected through a nomination and voting process. In each instance, the co-curator committees were developed through familiar processes of determining representatives for projects both internal and external to their communities.

One way to think about the *OL* co-curator process is that it was adapted to what were already existing practices in the communities: something foreign was made to fit into and was understood through existing local logics and practices (see Sahlins

1985). In contrast, the term "expert"—a common category among museum staff that was used to describe community curators—was not used often in the communities, and when it was, it was sometimes used disparagingly.[32] But this does not mean that there were no recognized specialists in these groups. In the Carib Territory, the term "resource person" had a meaning similar to, but not quite the same as, what "expert" meant to museum staff. The important thing to Kalinago community members was that the skills of the person be utilized in service to the community; this added component gives "resource person" a somewhat different connotation than "expert." According to Prosper Paris, a resource person is "somebody you can rely on...if the person can type, if the person does certain skills."

> If you're talking about herbal medicine and history and planning and all this... they say, "Come to Prosper." If you're talking about project writing...you go to Sylvanie [Burton]. If you want to talk about motivation of community development, you go to James Frederick. If you're talking about tourism...you go to Irvince Auguiste. So different people with different skills, we have them there— a resource person—not only that they have a *skill*, but [they are] somebody we *know* that *will* contribute. Because somebody may have the skill, they have the resource, they can do certain things...but when you put them [in the situation,] they don't do [the] work.[33]

For the Kalinago co-curator committee, Chief Garnette Joseph selected a group of resource persons who would adequately represent the territory in the making of the exhibition. He deliberately chose a mix of representatives according to their skills, residency, and gender: "The makeup of the committee co-curators was based on people's skills and different interests, and we felt that the selection was well done and covered the areas—education, tourism, craft, [and] community development."[34] Members of the committee represented a number of hamlets and included craft makers, political figures, and cultural group leaders.

While I was in the Carib Territory, I noticed that a small group of people was repeatedly tapped for cultural and community projects, not only because they had a history of working on such projects but also because they were organized, reliable, and committed to getting things done. These were the people who were selected to be on the co-curator committee. When asked, all committee members could state precisely why they had been chosen. Similar to Prosper, Garnette said, "We looked at people's involvement in different areas. Like, in craft—Jacinta," for "culture—Cozier and Prosper," "Irvince because of his involvement in tourism and culture, and Alexis Valmond because he was the councilor responsible for culture. Basically, this is how people got on board the co-curators committee." I asked whether being on a committee was a familiar way for people to work together. He replied, "Well, yes...we have a history of working together, because we are one people anyway." Garnette chose Prosper as the "coordinator," or liaison, because of his work as a tour guide. Prosper had experience "coordinating the movement of people in tours.... So it's nothing unusual [for Prosper]." Garnette continued, "I felt that the people who were selected had different roles to play. They were best chosen because they are involved in that."[35]

During my fieldwork after the NMAI opened, I learned that the process the co-curators used in working on the exhibit was the same process used for many projects undertaken in the territory, including the Carib Model Village task force and a Kalinago curriculum project, in which I was asked to participate. First, there is an initiative to accomplish something, so they form a small committee; then, they send out written letters of invitation and gather together a group of resource persons for a "community meeting" to get their ideas and give the project some legitimacy and support; and then, the committee formulates ideas and, in some cases, implements them. (This last part was often, frustratingly, not accomplished; many people said that there is plenty of talk and not much action.) But the key is to have the right people involved so that they are aware that something is going on and feel that they have some input into the process.

The resource persons, although not referred to as experts, are what I would describe as the usual suspects when rounding up knowledgeable people in the community. For instance, Sylvie Warrington was at the community meeting for the NMAI (see chapter 5), was invited to the Kalinago curriculum task force meetings, and was often called upon as a representative of women's and health issues. Irvince Auguiste was a past chief and considered one of the most knowledgeable people in the community about tourism. Sylvanie Burton was considered exceptionally successful in community development projects. Prosper Paris and Gerard Langlais, a self-described medicine man in training, are Kalinago cultural go-to men. A certain kind of expertise was recognized, then, and they were seen as competent representatives of a particular subset of the population.

The Chicago community also had a co-curator selection process and practices that reflected their usual way of doing projects. In Chicago, the co-curators were nominated and then selected by a secret ballot process. They chose a group of ten, including the liaison with alternates, and their committee structure resembled NGO practices with which their community was familiar. The co-curators were not selected based on specific specialties, however; in this multitribal community, people were loath to step forward and claim representative authority over the rest of the group.

When I was preparing this chapter, I spoke to Eli Suzukovich, a Chicago co-curator who later enrolled in an anthropology graduate program and was replaced by an alternate. I commented that, beyond Dave Spencer and Mavis Neconish, who were suggested as co-curators based on their museum experience, people seemed to be selected according to their level of community participation rather than their specialized knowledge. Eli explained that Chicago is a "polyethnic community" and no one wants to "step on" other people's expertise or be responsible for representing other people's tribes. He said that the co-curator committee was composed of people who worked for various community organizations that serve Chicago Indians, had

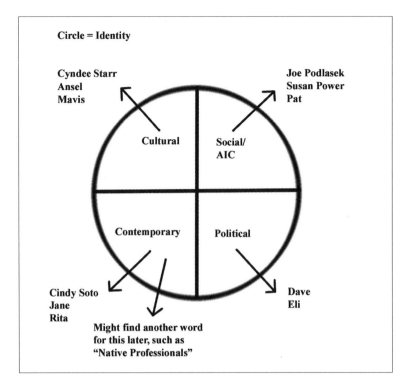

Circle = Identity

Cyndee Starr
Ansel
Mavis

Joe Podlasek
Susan Power
Pat

Cultural

Social/
AIC

Contemporary

Political

Cindy Soto
Jane
Rita

Dave
Eli

**Might find another word
for this later, such as
"Native Professionals"**

*Figure 4.1. Reproduction of the Chicago co-curator chart of subcommittees,
October 29, 2001.*

good contacts within the community, and had access to people and information that others may not have. He called this a "coalition method," similar to other types of organizational planning that are typical in the community.[36]

The Chicago urban Indian community was often described as a place where anyone could come into the community and be welcomed—it is a community based on voluntary participation. So, too, was the process for selecting co-curators. The nomination and election process was similar to how they organized the annual AIC powwow committee each year, which also was a multitribal event, attracting Natives and non-Natives from all over the United States. Furthermore, the co-curator committee was divided into subcommittees addressing particular themes: "cultural," "political," "social," and "contemporary." This was also much like how the powwow committee worked: people volunteered for specific subcommittee tasks like fundraising, vendors, and publicity, according to their interests and skills. The subcommittees were listed under the title "Circle = Identity" in notes from a Chicago co-curator meeting at the American Indian Center on October 29, 2001 (figure 4.1),[37] and each group was expected to meet on its own to work on its aspect of the exhibit. In later meetings, Rita Hodge, the NMAI liaison, would ask for updates from each subcommittee.

Conclusion

The different NMAI perspectives on expertise were evident at the 2005 American Association of Museums conference in Indianapolis. The museum sponsored several sessions, including one by Carolyn Rapkievian from the Education Department and one by Cynthia Chavez from the Curatorial Department, and had a large number of staff in attendance. The approaches that Carolyn and Cynthia took in organizing and presenting information about the NMAI showed their own conceptions of expertise, which reflected the views from downtown and the CRC, as well as what they felt they had to offer to their respective professional fields.

Titled "Are All Roads Good? Opening the National Museum of the American Indian—Lessons Learned," Carolyn's session focused on, as she wrote in her proposal,[38] "what the lessons learned at the NMAI mean for the future of museums." This session included introductions by Rick West and Jim Volkert, and then twelve NMAI staff members split into table discussions that were labeled so that attendees could gravitate to the "expert" of their choice—to learn about marketing, media production, business administration, getting projects to completion, teacher training, and so on. Jim led a discussion on "implementing change and nurturing diverse thinking throughout an organization," Carolyn addressed "evaluation at soft openings—refining operations before the grand opening," Kathy Suter talked about "making media in Native voice," and Karen Fort conducted a roundtable for "opening five major exhibitions—simultaneously." All of these individuals were from downtown.

Cynthia's session was titled "Community Curatorship: The National Museum of the American Indian and Native Peoples Working Collaboratively." Cynthia invited Native co-curators to give constructive criticism about the exhibit-making process. In her proposal, Cynthia had written, "Native representatives from communities in *Our Lives* will critique their involvement as community curators."[39] A handout promised that attendees would "learn how inclusive curatorial methods and processes can enhance the representation of Native peoples and their communities in exhibitions and understand the limitations of inclusive methods in collaborative exhibitions." Cynthia asked leading questions that the co-curators had seen beforehand. The panel included Arlen Washines (Yakama, Yakama Nation wildlife manager), Jacinte Lambert (Saint-Laurent Métis, community organizer), and David Spencer (Chata/Diné, arts director of the American Indian Center of Chicago).

At one point, Cynthia recalled that, when she first met Arlen Washines, he had said that he wanted the exhibit to be "more than beautiful objects in cases." She then asked him to comment. Arlen said that his goal was to make the exhibit something he wanted his children to see and learn from, adding that it was also to educate the people of the world. He had traveled all over the world, from Europe to Japan, and he saw that people had a fascination with Native Americans. But all they knew were beads and feathers and what he called "the Hollywood effect"—chanting and dancing around bonfires. They often asked him, "Do you still live in tepees?" He continued, "I wanted to share with those people of the world who we are…and to share we still hold onto those traditions regardless of what western civilization has done to our people."

Dave Spencer, who credited Cynthia appreciatively with encouraging him to pursue a master's degree at the Art Institute of Chicago, talked about how such educational institutions teach French theory, critique, and the perspective of large, mainstream institutions. But that is not useful to someone like him, who works in a small community gallery. What was useful from his educational experience was thinking about "the objectification of culture." He critiqued Chicago institutions like the Field Museum for involving local Indians only in the final stages of exhibition making. For example, the much lauded *Hero, Hawk and Open Hand* exhibition was five years in the making, but the museum contacted the Chicago Indian community only three weeks before the opening, when some community members were invited to sit at a table at a press luncheon. "They wanted our endorsement," Dave explained. There was a debate within the Chicago Indian community about whether to participate, but Dave "refused." In contrast, he said, when the NMAI asked the Chicago community to make an exhibit, it was "really a historical moment."

Along similar lines, in a presentation at the Native American Art Studies Association meetings in 2005, Bruce Bernstein insisted, "The most important product of our exhibitions and programs are the relationships and reciprocity that are created." He added, "The *dissolving of curatorial privilege* as a scholarship of exclusion is one of the guiding principles of an increasing number of museum-collection-based and academic projects throughout the Native art world.… NMAI's mission is to define Indian people on their own terms. Following this basic methodological premise, we can begin to conceptualize the research and scholarship agenda for the museum. *It is about the production and development of a methodology for the production and use of knowledge*" (emphases added).

One usually normalized dichotomy was particularly eschewed in the museum: expert versus local knowledge. This was at the heart of the NMAI curatorial ideology, which considered community curators to be cultural experts. In the collaborative, ethical, and community-centered paradigm, curators and the nature of their expertise are changing. They are no longer necessarily area or subject matter specialists. The main curator I worked with said that she did not feel she was a curator, but a facilitator; another curator described her role as being a mediator. The head of Exhibits, almost two years after the museum opened, also had a different idea about the curator's role. He said that "it doesn't matter the subject of the exhibition" for solid research to be done. The idea that you "must use a curator with subject expertise before" you decide whether an exhibit is a good idea is not right. What you need is a "nimble, global curator" who can work on developing good exhibits, as opposed to a curator who knows a specific subject or community: "You can always find that." But not all researchers, he added, have that "nimble global" quality.[40] Clearly, both cultures of expertise agreed that the role of curators was shifting, but they did not envision similar futures or potentials for curators.[41]

Members of each of the departments shared candid reflections and critical thinking about their experiences making the inaugural exhibitions. It is clear that the Exhibits and Curatorial Departments disagreed on the role and contribution of co-curators, which seemed to relate to how they viewed their own roles in the exhibit-making process. The exhibits staff claimed "specialized knowledge" for translating the final product to the visitor, and the curatorial staff emphasized its ethics in the process of collaborating with Native communities in the "right" way. Pamela Smart's study of the John and Dominique de Menil Collection in Houston, Texas, provides a useful comparison with the NMAI, specifically regarding what she calls the "practice of exquisite care" that was referred to among museum staff as "the Menil Way" (Smart 2007, 2010; see also Smart 2011). She describes the intentions of the Menils for the use of the objects, as well as their personal history in amassing the collection. However, her story is not just another account of collecting. She also provides insight into the daily practices and experiences of the staff, including personnel training, which is crafted according to the mission of the museum.

The Menil Collection, composed of religious objects, aims to "recuperate spirituality" in modern times—to reunite the sacred and the modern—by giving visitors an "aesthetic experience." One point Smart (2007:8) makes is that, unlike Pierre Bourdieu's unconscious, normative habitus, the routine everyday practices of the staff were "self-conscious practices of cultivation." The museum emphasized "a *training* of ethical sensibilities so as to foster the possibility of a new social and moral order" (ibid.). "The Menil Way," she explains, was not "codified" or a "mandated policy," but an often referenced "set of practices that were essentially ethical in character," which she was able to deduce through the work of ethnography. This is similar to what the NMAI Curatorial Department referred to as the "right" way to work with Native peoples. Smart clarifies that the "Menil Way" is not a set of techniques to secure particular outcomes, but instead a set of "ethical injunctions."

Like the Menil Collection, the NMAI was mission driven to provide "exquisite care" for its collection and toward its originating communities. And in some quarters of the museum, there was indeed an unwritten code for doing things the "right" way.[42] I am not suggesting that Curatorial was the only department that had an ethically informed practice in the museum, but it was the one to stress that its practices constituted a "way." A commitment to Native voices and Native peoples as authorities was recognized throughout the museum, but it was interpreted and guided professional practices differently among the various departments.

Cynthia's description of a tacit "law" is an indicator of this "way." One CRC staff member said that Native voice was "in the CRC's DNA." A curator, emphasizing the opposing ideologies of the CRC and downtown, said, "Project management doesn't teach doing things in the right way.... It teaches creating flow charts and moving your project along the flow chart and getting things done as expediently as possible."[43] In other words, the "economy of care," to borrow Smart's phrase, that was self-consciously cultivated by curatorial managers, embraced as law, and defended by curatorial staff was not an institution-wide way of managing relations with Native peoples and the collection.

Collaboration was both a method and an outcome of this imperative, and one characteristic of collaborative knowledge production is that its product is emergent and often not predictable. Like Boasians who believe that Native texts are valuable and interesting in and of themselves, the Curatorial Department believed that whatever Native people had to say would be inherently of interest to the visiting public—a belief the Exhibits Department explicitly did not share. Curators did not know what the product of the exhibit process would be, but they had faith that the process would bring forward something valuable and insightful. It seemed, however, that fulfilling the mission of the museum came at a special cost to their power, prestige, and positions.

five
Authorship

I used to doubt it right at the beginning, the first year and a half. I was just thinking, "Oh my god, I'm never going to be able to do this"—working with all these communities. How am I going to put this together? How is this going to come together?... I don't know if I would say [the exhibits] are a success. I guess I'm looking at the successful part being more about the collaborative process, and I see that as separate from the actual final product.... But, certainly, I think that just in the way that I went about working with the communities and what we ended up coming up with—I think that was successful.

—Cynthia Chavez, lead curator, Our Lives, *2004*

As a community curator, you were considered *the* authority or expert. This was a very frightening idea for me. From a museum standpoint, I know that someone has to be accountable.... This concept was intimidating as I did not consider myself the ultimate authority. To say this, I don't mean that I don't stand by the information. What I do mean is that the history was shared with me, it was passed down generation to generation to the community members I talked with. It is a history that will also flow through us to future generations.

—Lindsey Martin, community curator, Listening to Our Ancestors, *from* NAASA 2005

The Construction of Native Voice

In December 2000, the development of the *Our Lives* gallery was a year behind the development of the *Our Peoples* and *Our Universes* galleries. Dormant for a year, the project had been assigned a new team of curatorial staff. Bruce Bernstein arranged a vetting session (see chapter 4) with *OL* team members and five "Native scholars" to discuss the *OL* "narrative"—a preliminary description of its thematic structure and content—that Cynthia Chavez had written based on earlier descriptions of the gallery and her own vision for its future.

The meeting was chaired by Bruce but was relatively unstructured. The group sat in executive desk chairs around the CRC's large conference room table, the room illuminated by floor-to-ceiling windows on two sides. Discussion ranged from evaluating Cynthia's narrative, to the greater goals of what an exhibit like this should be, to what the audience would or should know, to the participants' personal narratives of contemporary life in their own communities. Cynthia also took the opportunity to express some of her worries and to seek guidance concerning the process she was about to embark upon:

> Ms. CHAVEZ: Is it realistic to go into a community and ask them to articulate a communal identity? Is that something that can be achieved? That worries me.
>
> UNIDENTIFIED SPEAKER: It worries you?
>
> Ms. CHAVEZ: Yes.
>
> UNIDENTIFIED SPEAKER: Why?
>
> Ms. CHAVEZ: Because I think there's a fine line between having them communicate what they think their communal identity is and having them just talk about what's going on in the community. Do you know what I mean?
>
> UNIDENTIFIED SPEAKER: There are different negotiations as to how to present that. They would be concerned about how they [portray] their image in public.
>
> Ms. CHAVEZ: Yes, and some of these contestations and conflicts and compromises that we've been talking about, how are you going to get them to communicate some of that?[1]

In the meeting, participants warned *OL* staff against working with "Rolodex Indians"—Native people who were often enlisted as consultants with museums—and everyone considered how to make "identity" in the exhibit not look like isolated individuals, but like community identities. There were concerns about the possibility of leadership changes in a community and how that might jeopardize the project, and participants returned a number of times to the issue of sovereignty. The Native scholars emphasized that the *Our Lives* exhibition should be a challenge to visitors *and* Native people (not just a packaged message about them) and discussed public misconceptions about what it means to be "traditional." Participants discussed the inclusion of an urban Indian community—and agreed that it would be Chicago—and what it would mean for an urban community to be included in the context of more conventional ideas of community, such as a reservation or tribe.

This meeting was long and wide-ranging and included concerns, subjects, and suggestions that were beyond the scope of the exhibition. It was clear that the Native scholars were talking not just to NMAI staff but also to one another. This same dynamic had occurred in the original consultations in the early 1990s and continued throughout the dialogues with Native communities to establish the museum and to create the inaugural exhibitions. Similar meetings among Native and non-Native scholars had resulted in shifting the NMAI toward developing community-centered exhibits in the galleries and the process of community curating.[2]

Cynthia's concerns continued throughout her work on the exhibition. Her anxiety was related to her relative inexperience in curating exhibits at this scale (few curators have ever worked at this scale), the number of communities she worked with, the time allotted to complete the exhibition, and an uneasiness about representing others—a concern that also permeated the staff's and the Native co-curators' efforts, as Martin's comment in the epigraph illustrates. Cynthia's uneasiness also was due to her being Native and at the same time occupying a mediating position between the bureaucratic museum institution and Native communities (Chavez Lamar 2008).

Cynthia's emphasis on the process, illustrated in her epigraph, was a common perspective among curatorial staff. What often surfaced when I was working for the museum and later when I interviewed people about it was that the process is as important as the product (and some would say more important). This aphorism was reiterated many times in the Curatorial Department, has been emphasized in literature about museum work with Native peoples, and is common in Native discourse. For example, in *Museums and Source Communities*, a seminal book about museum-community collaborations, Laura Peers and Alison Brown (2003:9) explain: "One of the most important elements of the new way of working with source communities is that trust-building is considered integral to the process, and creating respect or healing the effects of the past is seen as being as important as co-writing labels or enhancing the database."

The *Our Lives* exhibition was simultaneously a locus for cultural production, a reflexive ethnography, and an example of collaborative knowledge production. The Native co-curators were not primarily talking about objects or ceremonies or historical events (though these were included in their exhibits); they were talking about *themselves*, their identities—what it means to be Inuit in Igloolik, Kalinago in the Carib Territory, Indian in Chicago, or Mohawk in Kahnawake. These situated identities were reflected upon and conveyed through the Native-authored texts of the exhibit, which were developed by and about "reflexive subjects."[3] Taking seriously the signing practice involved in the exhibition's text panels, I turn to authorship as a frame for understanding collaboration in exhibit content production, most notably

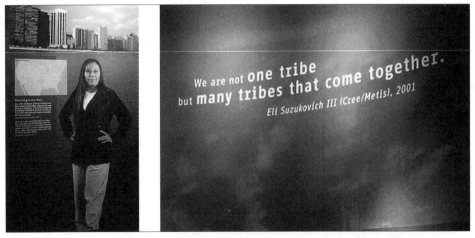

Figure 5.1. Chicago exhibit text panels. Photo by author. Reproduced with permission of the National Museum of the American Indian, Smithsonian Institution.

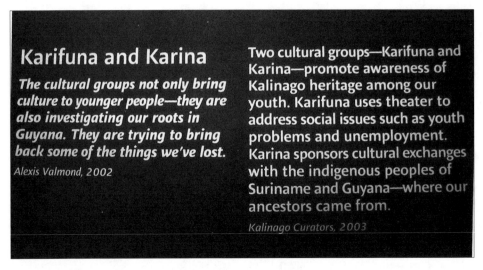

Figure 5.2. Kalinago exhibit text panel "Karifuna and Karina." Photo by author. Reproduced with permission of the National Museum of the American Indian, Smithsonian Institution.

in the construction of "Native voice," and then consider the mediation of authenticity in these panels.

The quintessential artifact of collaboration at the NMAI—an index of both Native voice and Natives' participation as reflexive subjects—was the Native-authored text panel, which was ubiquitous in the museum's exhibitions. For example, on a general introductory panel, the text is attributed to the "Kalinago Curators" as a group. For specific quotations, the speaker's name and tribal affiliation are displayed (figures 5.1, 5.2). These are products of collaboration in exhibit making at two levels: in the meetings where Native American community co-curators discussed the content of the exhibit and in the museum institution where museum specialists worked together to transform Native community discussions into exhibit text. There is a wider "circumference of authorship" (Baggioli 2006:136) than simply those named on the text panel. I begin, then, with a basic question: How were these authored panels created? or, put another way, What does authorship mean in practice?

Authorship, as Mario Baggioli (2006) explains in his analysis of bylines in scientific papers, is about credit and responsibility; in contemporary museum practice with Native communities, it is also about ethical practice and authenticity (see, for example, Peers and Brown 2003; West and NMAI 2000). So what does authorship *mean* in this context? Who is responsible for the text? And how is authenticity mediated through this form of authorial practice? The answers are located at the intersection of museum professionals and Native community members as they struggle together with how to characterize Native identities to a greater public.

An Anthropology of Mediation

Cultural anthropologist William Mazzarella (2004:346) defines a "medium" as, most broadly, "a material framework, both enabling and constraining, for a given set of social practices. In this guise a medium is also a reflexive and reifying technology. It makes society imaginable and intelligible to itself in the form of external representations." As the co-curators and NMAI staff contemplated their own cultural identities or career trajectories, they discussed and wrote and produced Native identities as built material forms in the museum exhibit. They certainly engaged in a process both reflexive and reifying. Furthermore, in calling for an anthropology of mediation, Mazzarella explains that such work "produces and reproduces...mediated self-understandings that depend on the routing of the personal through the impersonal, the near through the far, and the self through the other" (ibid.:61).[4]

Whereas Mazzarella (2004:350) asserts that the notion of agency is what is taken to extremes in media studies (a false theoretical dichotomy of agency rendered as either an overdetermined cultural imperialism or an overactive audience), Barry Dornfeld problematizes the segregation of scholarly studies into analyses of production and of reception (revealing that underlying the false theoretical dichotomy is a methodological one). Dornfeld (1998:14) insists that, in practice, production and consumption are intertwined because the anticipation of reception, or the imagined audience, is part of the production process. Assumptions about the audience, then, guide producers' creative decisions (ibid.:188). This approach goes beyond the general categories of imagined audiences in museum studies—such as children versus adults, streakers versus strollers, and rechargers versus explorers—which exhibits are often aimed at. Instead of asking theoretically who the audience should be, this approach asks whom individual culture producers imagine, sometimes unwittingly, they are talking to in the everyday practice of their work.

Bringing Dornfeld's focus on the imagined audience into conversation with

Mazzarella's definition of a medium prompted me to identify the imagined audience as (one of) the external form(s) through which exhibit makers pass their self-understanding in order to arrive at an exhibit about their own identity. Accordingly, although mediation most often is thought to occur through objects and persons, one can also consider as part of this process the assumptions about the audience that guide producers' creative decisions. The prefigured audience is another agent that influences the content of the exhibit. The analysis below shows that the characterization of the prefigured audience was another conceptual fault line separating the various cultures of expertise at work on the *Our Lives* exhibition. I borrow Dornfeld's (1998:69) concepts of the "social organization of authorship" and the "ideology of authorship"[5] to frame my discussion of the community-curating process.

The Social Organization of (Collaborative) Authorship: Community Curating

Cynthia Chavez invited the Native communities with which she worked to structure their own participation in the *Our Lives* exhibits in three important ways. First, as already mentioned, she left it to each community to determine its own appropriate method of co-curator selection, which provided insight into local practices of self-representation. Second, Cynthia gave the community curators basic guidelines according to her vision of what an *Our Lives* exhibit "should *not* be": not a history, not a tourism version, not a solely traditional view of the community. She also offered what "every community component *should* be": honest, complex, and specific. Third, she invited each co-curator committee to interpret the term "identity" in whatever way it chose for the purpose of the exhibition. These sparse guidelines for the communities indicated the high degree to which the co-curators were responsible for the content of the exhibits.

To prepare for working with the communities, NMAI curators and their research assistants did extensive library, online, and archival research about each community. The *OP* staff researched tribal histories and first-person accounts, the *OU* staff gathered information about seasonal ceremonies, and the *OL* staff researched possible "identity issues" that might be highlighted. In many instances, the co-curators did not include in their exhibit content what NMAI staff had researched and anticipated. For example, because the Kahnawake Mohawks' main message for their exhibit was focused on sovereignty, researchers included tribal membership rules, residency requirements, and the 1990 Oka crisis in the preparatory research documents, but these issues were not mentioned in the exhibit.[6]

For other topics, such as the 1924 Racial Integrity Act of Virginia and its effects on the Pamunkey tribe, no community member wanted the responsibility of authoring or crafting the words, even if it was a subject community members had discussed in co-curator meetings and felt should be part of the exhibit. In the only instance of its kind that I found in the *OL* gallery, one that highlights the twin nature of authorship that Baggioli describes, the co-curators asked the Pamunkey exhibit's field worker, Ann McMullen, to write about the Racial Integrity Act and to place *her* name as the author on the text panel.[7]

It was not necessarily the use of this background research in the exhibits, but rather the process of doing it, that was appreciated in communities. For example, on July 24, 2001, Cynthia convened a preliminary meeting with prominent American Indian community members over dinner at a restaurant near the Native American Educational Services College in Chicago to determine an appropriate process for selecting co-curators to represent them.[8] Some people asked Cynthia why they were selected over all other urban Indian communities in the United States. Cynthia's well-researched response impressed the people at the dinner and earned her a shout of "Good research!" from a future co-curator, followed by kind laughter from the group.[9]

Each community selected a "liaison," who was responsible for organizing NMAI visits with the community, presiding over independent meetings when NMAI staff were not present, gathering the objects and other items for the NMAI, and coordinating interviews for both the field workers and the media teams, among many other tasks. For Chicago, Rita Hodge was the liaison; for the Kalinagos, it was Prosper Paris. These individuals played a central role both in sustaining the interest in and momentum of the exhibition work over years of sporadic interaction with the museum and in legitimizing the project.

In "Private Politics, Public Strategies: White Advisers and Their Aboriginal Subjects," Phillip Batty discusses the relationship between government advisors and Aboriginal communities in Australia and the need for Aboriginal authorization to conduct projects in their communities. He examines how Aboriginal people must endorse these advisors, investing them with cultural capital. Through a one-on-one relationship with a particular Aboriginal person (like a community liaison in the NMAI community-curating process), the white individual's motivations, personal commitment, and alignment with the broader group would be explained and endorsed. A confirmation that a hitherto "unknown white fella" was "on side" was facilitated through a demonstrable relationship with an Aboriginal person within the group. One could say that through these arrangements, the Aboriginal partner "empowered" a non-Aboriginal outsider to work on behalf of the Aboriginal community (Batty 2005:217). Although NMAI curators were Native and non-Native, their relationship to Native communities as outside government advisors (in museum matters) can also be seen as needing endorsement by the community. Particularly in the process of interviewing or other work outside the community curator meetings, the Native liaison and co-curators were essential to NMAI staff's being introduced to and having positive working relationships with additional community members.

Building Consensus: Committee Meetings and the Thematic Approach

During the community-curating process, NMAI staff encouraged a thematic approach to exhibit making. Therefore, co-curators were largely responsible for producing

Figure 5.3. Carib Council Office, November 20, 2007. Photo by author.

knowledge about themselves based on a thematic structure; they were also tasked with creating a main message for their exhibit. I highlight two meetings in the Carib Territory as examples of dialogue and then present a more general sweep of meetings in Chicago to illustrate the progression of the community-curating process.

Kalinago: Looking Forward

Particular exhibit themes emerged, no doubt, as a result of the composition of each committee. The majority of the Kalinago co-curators were part of the first generation of Kalinagos who went on to secondary education and felt connected to indigenous communities as part of a larger, worldwide movement. They were founders of, and deeply committed to, raising Kalinago cultural consciousness in their community. It is not surprising, then, that through a series of meetings over the course of three years (2001–2003), the Kalinago committee members created the main message for their exhibit as "The Kalinago survive despite numerous challenges" and included "cultural consciousness" among the three main themes for their exhibit, along with "economic survival" and "challenges."

We can see what kind of deliberations the co-curators went through to arrive at these themes by looking at excerpts from a transcript of a Kalinago co-curator meeting during the NMAI staff's second visit to the Carib Territory. Susan Secakuku (Hopi), the assigned field worker and a Community Services staff member, led the meeting. As an *Our Lives* research assistant, I was responsible for transcribing this taped recording. The following account is from my meeting notes, Susan's notes, and session transcripts.

At the meeting on January 15, 2002, co-curators sat around a table in the Carib Council Office (figure 5.3), a hexagonal structure whose meeting room had fading

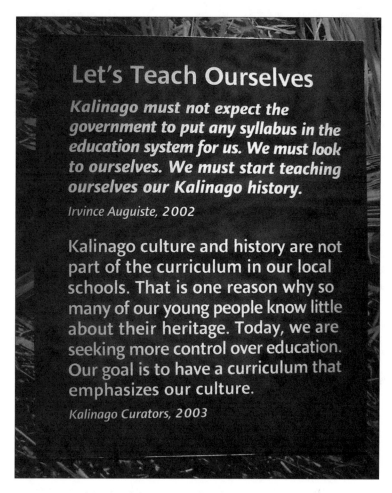

Let's Teach Ourselves

Kalinago must not expect the government to put any syllabus in the education system for us. We must look to ourselves. We must start teaching ourselves our Kalinago history.

Irvince Auguiste, 2002

Kalinago culture and history are not part of the curriculum in our local schools. That is one reason why so many of our young people know little about their heritage. Today, we are seeking more control over education. Our goal is to have a curriculum that emphasizes our culture.

Kalinago Curators, 2003

Figure 5.4. Kalinago exhibit text panel "Let's Teach Ourselves." Photo by author. Reproduced with permission of the National Museum of the American Indian, Smithsonian Institution.

yellow paint on the walls and fans turning overhead. The meeting moved forward with a fast rotation of speakers, who often finished one another's sentences, in conversation with one another as much as in explanation to Susan. Susan often spoke the NMAI's hallmark collaborative phrase—"So you're saying..."—as a commitment to accuracy and a form of guidance to the discussion. Broadly, the co-curators expressed concerns over the impact of the outside world on youth through the influence of television, the economy and education in the territory, the Dominican government, and the surrounding Afro-Dominican society (some of these themes were reflected in a text panel titled "Let's Teach Ourselves"; figure 5.4). As usual, there were many humorous asides in the meeting—something that unfortunately did not translate into the exhibition despite being an important and enjoyable part of working with communities.

The group often returned to what it would like to see happen in its community in the future. At one point in the meeting, Susan brought up the issue of "self-identity," saying that she had heard someone mention it earlier. Sylvanie Burton rephrased this as "who you are." Then Susan asked whether she heard right from community members—that it's a "conscious decision to be Carib."[10] Sylvanie replied that the co-curators would like to have the exhibit be "not just focusing on the past, but something in the future."

Later in this meeting, Susan again recalled an earlier statement to help guide the discussion to possible exhibit themes: "You said something a little earlier I want to go back to. Right now, you're an agricultural-based people, right?" She asked whether that was changing, to which Garnette Joseph replied, "Yes," and Sylvanie added, "The pressure is on to change." Garnette reiterated, "Pressure is on." When Susan asked from whom, Garnette said, "We see, well, the global system is at hand, and we are part of it.... We've seen changes begin in the tourism industry, for example. For the past five years, we find organized tours coming into the Carib Territory. And around that, we've seen changes—the craft marketing and the *possibility* of strengthening the craft industry. So, I mean, there are very serious constraints here." He then mentioned a lack of marketing and a need for increased exports of Kalinago crafts. "More can be done," he concluded, and Prosper repeated, "More can be done."

Garnette began again, "More can be done. Our heritage village is due to open soon, and there are possibilities around that as well." Susan said, "I'm listening to you and I want to make sure I heard you right: you're moving, you think, to more of a craft-based and tourism..." and the co-curators finished her sentence, agreeing, "tourism-based economy." The concerns expressed in other co-curator meetings, in interviews, and in subsequent community-wide meetings highlighted these same themes of hardship, survival, tourism, and future cultural potential (some of these themes were included in the "Kalinago Economy" text panel; figure 5.5).

It was important to the co-curators that the exhibit not be from their perspective alone, but from the community's as a whole. So they held the first community-wide meeting two days later and Prosper invited all the prominent "resource persons" of the Carib Territory.[11] The co-curators wanted to get a wider view of Kalinago identity from a broader cross section of people from the territory. The meeting again took place in the Carib Council Office, where community members were seated in rows of benches and NMAI staff sat at a table facing them.

After an elder offered a prayer to begin the meeting, Prosper gave a summary of the work conducted so far by the NMAI and the co-curators, saying, "It is a project of the Carib community." He did not want people complaining later that they did not know about it. He referred to the gallery as *Our Life and Time*. Susan then described the focus of *Our Lives*:

> [This gallery is about] the identity of indigenous peoples. Contemporary identities today. I think a lot of non-indigenous peoples believe either we're no longer around, no longer live here or exist in this world, or that we still wear feathers or,

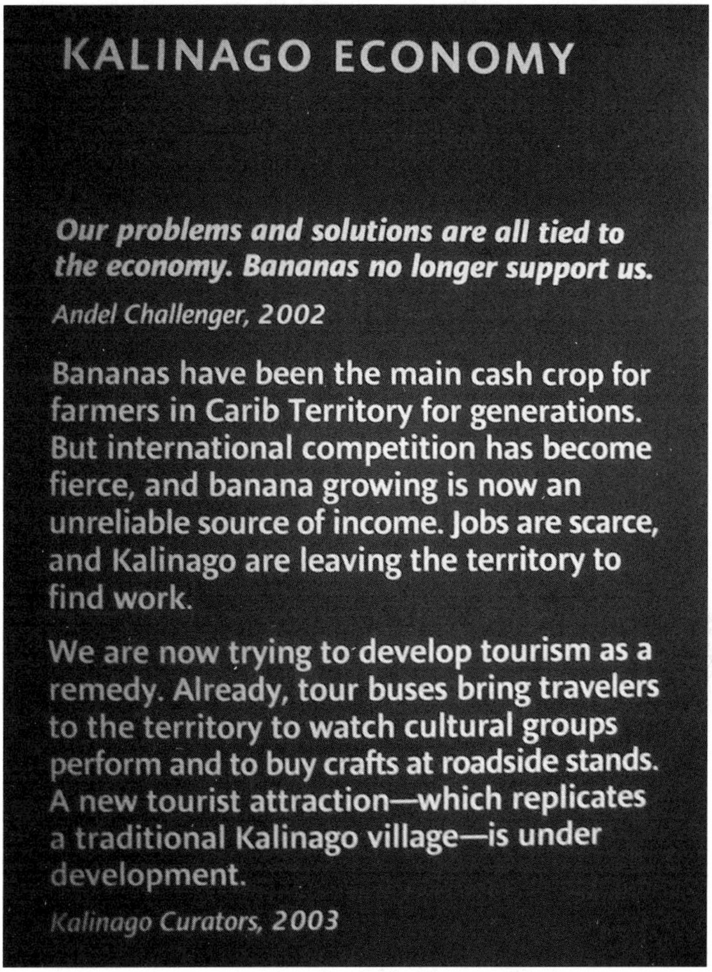

KALINAGO ECONOMY

Our problems and solutions are all tied to the economy. Bananas no longer support us.

Andel Challenger, 2002

Bananas have been the main cash crop for farmers in Carib Territory for generations. But international competition has become fierce, and banana growing is now an unreliable source of income. Jobs are scarce, and Kalinago are leaving the territory to find work.

We are now trying to develop tourism as a remedy. Already, tour buses bring travelers to the territory to watch cultural groups perform and to buy crafts at roadside stands. A new tourist attraction—which replicates a traditional Kalinago village—is under development.

Kalinago Curators, 2003

Figure 5.5. Exhibit text panel "Kalinago Economy." Photo by author. Reproduced with permission of the National Museum of the American Indian, Smithsonian Institution.

you know, live in tepees. Everybody lives in tepees, they think. And we've never lived in tepees [*laughter*], and I know that the Kalinago never lived in tepees. Our goal is to try and *demonstrate to the visitor* coming in, saying, we are still here as indigenous peoples but we live in a particular way and we have different issues today than we did way back when. But we still have the same thinking and values probably that we did, that have maintained us today.

So what we're trying to ask from you is—or get some information from you is—pretty much, what does it mean to be a Carib? How do you define your-selves as being a Kalinago?... And the other...communities we mentioned are going for the same thing.... They're all being asked, What does it mean to be a Yakama? What does it mean to be a Mohawk?... And all these will be put in the same room, and the visitor will decide, will hear from you directly, what does it mean to be a Carib.[12]

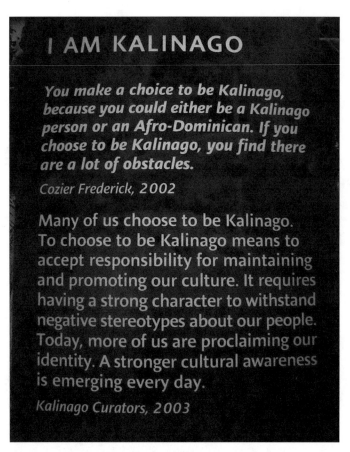

Figure 5.6. Exhibit text panel "I Am Kalinago." Photo by author. Reproduced with permission of the National Museum of the American Indian, Smithsonian Institution.

Prosper explained that we were tape-recording what people said and then opened up the floor to the community members. One by one, they stood and made a statement about what it means to be Carib, in a passionate way; some were called on specifically by Prosper, who insisted that everyone contribute. A teacher who would later manage the Carib Model Village said that an exhibit in the NMAI would be an opportunity for tourism: "I think it is a very good medium for Dominica on the whole to market itself as a tourist destination, as an eco-tourist destination, [that] showcases indigenous people."[13] Susan and I came away from this meeting impressed by the candor of the community members. Many talked of discrimination and insisted that to be a Carib, one must be, as they were, *proud* to be Carib (figure 5.6).

The second community-wide meeting, held almost two months later on March 17, 2002, was a vetting session for the main message and themes the co-curators had developed, which Susan read aloud to those gathered.[14] At this point, the main message was "The Kalinago people make a conscious choice to be Kalinago despite

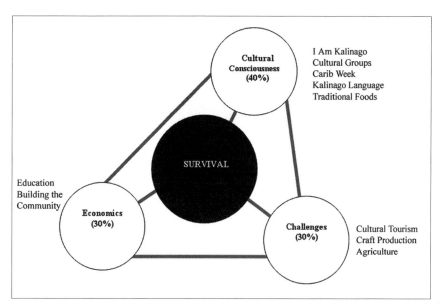

Figure 5.7. Reproduction of the Kalinago bubble diagram, showing the relative emphasis each content category should receive in the designed exhibit.

numerous difficulties." The main themes were "cultural revitalization," "cultural tourism," and "difficulties."

Prosper then called for group discussion. Some community members were concerned about the negative tone of the exhibit. Cozier Frederick, a representative for youth on the co-curator committee, suggested that they "strike a balance" in the positives and negatives of the exhibition. Co-curator Irvince Auguiste, a representative for tourism and a former chief, asserted that the museum is like an advertisement and that it is something they are not dependent on the Dominican government for: "It's now *our* business to develop and [see] how we can maximize this advertisement." Prosper indicated that the exhibit should not be too positive (perhaps keeping Cynthia's guidelines in mind), such that it does not reflect reality, because then people will not be inclined to help them.[15] In this meeting, individuals were talking more to one another than to NMAI staff, and the discussion ranged from wanting something back from the NMAI to concerns over intermarriage and that their "race will die" in the future.

During the co-curator meeting directly after this community gathering, Prosper, responding to concerns about the negative tone of the exhibition, suggested the term "challenges" instead of "difficulties" for the main message. Susan commented that perhaps "survival" could be a more positive spin, referencing another person's concerns. The co-curators agreed. The main message was finalized: "The Kalinago survive despite numerous challenges." Then the co-curators went down the list of themes, asking where particular kinds of information should be placed in the exhibit script according to the revised categories: "cultural consciousness," "economics," and "challenges" (figure 5.7). It was basically a classification exercise as they determined which community practices should go under which themes. The answer was not always obvious; for instance, "cultural groups" could have gone under "economic survival," because they earn money from performances for tourists, but the co-curators chose to include them under "cultural consciousness" instead, because they also teach youth cultural knowledge.

Chicago: Establishing a Foundation

The Chicago community held similar co-curator meetings in which it deliberated over how to represent the community in an exhibit. Whereas visits with the Kalinagos were months apart and lasted a week or more each time due to the difficulty and expense of traveling there, visits to Chicago were more frequent and shorter. The NMAI staff who participated included Cynthia Chavez and Wenona Rymond-Richmond, who was a contracted field worker and a graduate student at Northwestern.[16]

The Chicago co-curators developed their main message to be "Native peoples from different tribes come together in Chicago and maintain a supportive community network." This reflected the more than one hundred tribes represented in the Chicago area (including Lakota, Navajo/Diné, Ojibwe, Ho-Chunk, and Menominee) and the fact that the community was based on voluntary association and had no central governing body. The American Indian Center had served as a gathering spot over the years, but it was not the first place the NMAI went to find representatives to help determine the best way to put together a committee of co-curators. As mentioned, the first encounter between NMAI staff and Chicago community members was at an informal dinner the night before a more formal meeting at the Native American Educational Services (NAES) College with its director and a number of prominent community members.[17] The NAES College had been recommended as a "neutral" organization through which to contact the community, by a scholar who was well respected in the area. The group produced suggestions for who should be involved in the exhibition project, including young people.

At the July 25, 2001, meeting at NAES, each person told of his or her experience in the community and where he or she fit into the community's history: some were in Chicago because of federal relocation programs, some were born and grew up in the city, and some were passing through. This process would be repeated in meetings with the eventual co-curators. Ed Two Rivers (Ojibwe), who has since passed away, commented, "There's a history here.... The board meetings used to be a war zone at the Indian center. You would go to a board meeting and tribal people were saying, 'That's not the way it's done. Why, the Navajos would never do that!' But the Sioux would say, 'But that's the way *we* do it!' [*laughter*] ... But out of that, we...got solidified eventually. We *married* each other! [*more laughter*]" Someone added, "Now we fight at home!," which was met with even more laughter.

Ed Two Rivers also spoke about how Chicago Indians were unique—in the city because they were Indian and among other Natives because they were urban. His words would resurface as a pull-out quotation in the final exhibit (figure 5.8).

Figure 5.8. Chicago exhibit text panel "All Tribal Nations." Photo by author. Reproduced with permission of the National Museum of the American Indian, Smithsonian Institution.

Everyone agreed that the AIC provided a place for Indians to come and be welcomed when they first arrived in the city. These themes of the community being inter-tribal, its organizations and coalitions, and its welcoming spirit were reiterated by other community members and eventually became the main issues presented in the exhibit.

Three months later, on October 29, 2001, a meeting was held at the American Indian Center.[18] The AIC is on a residential block, a large multistory building that used to be a Masonic temple. The uppermost floors are mainly unused and dilapidated; the other floors house the main hall, education and computer rooms, social service offices, and AIC staff offices. The main meeting area is a large hall with rows of tables and chairs, a performance stage, and a kitchen; it hosts elders luncheons, powwows, and graduation ceremonies, as well as meetings such as this one.

By this time, the co-curators had been selected along with alternates, and almost all of them were in attendance (see appendix A). Rita Hodge began the meeting with her own main message, a suggestion to spark discussion: "Urban Natives: Weaving our circles of strength through heritage, culture, education." "Heritage" referred to the past, "culture" to the present, and "education" was a tool for the future, she added. One person said to use the term "connections" rather than "weaving," because weaving is associated with specific tribes—likely referring to the Navajos, who are known for their textile weavings, and to the fact that Rita is Diné (Navajo). The group discussed the concept, and Cynthia cautioned them not to design, but instead to create "themes" and "topics" for the exhibition. The exhibit would be designed by Design+Communication, Inc., a contracted firm based in Montreal.

Both Cynthia and Rita directed the meeting, and they each wrote lists on a board to keep track of the terms they were hearing in the course of conversation: "serving communities; cultural traditions; social gathering; connection—drum, reservation, healing; recover ID; rejuvenate, rebalance; 1970s era AIM politics; Hub. AIC is known nationwide; Native People—VOICE; extended family; role model; Native professionals; tradition v. _____; willingness to help; respect for other tradition; uniqueness; diverse within diversity; feeling of closeness; AIC powwow and beyond; identity; struggles—voice; ID—pan-Indianism inhibiting and enhancing; 1970s hindered ID—in Public School." This meeting—like the others that followed in Chicago and like the Kalinago co-curator meetings—was a mixture of educating NMAI staff, talking among themselves, brainstorming, and sharing personal narratives. This meeting was also where they formed the subcommittees mentioned in chapter 4.

At a meeting on December 17, 2001, Cynthia encouraged the Chicago co-curators to think about what is different about the urban experience, since the rest of the exhibits in the gallery would be reservation based. She asked, for example, "How do you maintain your Indian identity in an urban area?" and encouraged each person to comment from his or her own experience. So they went around the table and did so, often with other community members interjecting and asking questions about their experiences. Co-curators talked about corporate work environments, discouraging grade school experiences, what their parents were like, visiting home reservations, the importance of language and spiritual practices, and sometimes feeling—or never feeling—"ashamed" to be Native American.

At the February 8, 2002, meeting, the conversation turned to categorizing the topics that co-curators wanted to highlight in their exhibit; these had been organized on a worksheet by NMAI staff. References to the worksheet dominated the conversation: "Section I, C-1" and "3A, cross that out." The co-curators were focused on the task of properly categorizing so that items were not duplicated in more than one category (for example, NAES College could be located in the outline under "education," "community support," or "powwow"). The co-curators also worked on filling in other boxes on the worksheet, including the "media" and "objects" they wanted to accompany the various themes and subthemes of their exhibit.

Cynthia asked whether the co-curators wanted to appear in the exhibit—their images, their comments—or did they want community members not on the committee to be displayed instead? The group members said that they wanted to be included. The co-curators also debated the use of the term "pan-Indianism." They removed the word from the worksheet but kept the stories associated with it. One co-curator said that the term was a "political thing." Cynthia noted that it was an academic word from the "white perspective" and not from Native people. A young co-curator said that it made her think of assimilation. Cynthia then discussed with them what to expect for their design consultation, the upcoming meeting with the NMAI that would also include Design+Communication staff.

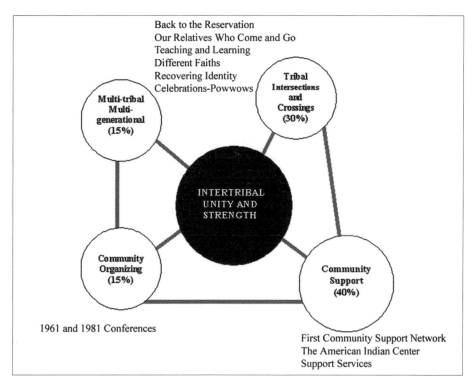

Figure 5.9. Reproduction of the Chicago bubble diagram, showing the relative emphasis each content category should receive in the designed exhibit.

The design consultation took place on April 14, 2002, at the AIC.[19] Cynthia had reorganized the worksheet and the exhibit's thematic categories according to the co-curators' suggestions, and she presented the newly organized content and guided the meeting to make sure that each subtheme supported the community's overarching theme. The group also talked about the "bubble diagram"—an illustration that shows how much relative emphasis/space each theme should get in the overall exhibit design (figure 5.9). The conversation included "So what are your thoughts on these other things: community organizing, tribal intersections?... We have to take 5 percent, or should these be moved around to these other ones?" "Community support is 40 percent." "Where did you put that 5 percent?" "Does that come out to 105 percent the way we have it now?"

A designer from D+C asked, "If you had one postcard from this exhibit, what would it be? [What] would be representing you?" He was trying to elicit what would later become the "icon," as his firm called it, for the exhibit.[20] Another member of the firm said that the exhibit, and exhibits in general, would emphasize the visitor experience over objects today. He explained, "Because we're dealing with the identity, your identity today, we won't make use of the Smithsonian collection." Later in the meeting, the design team again stressed that no "artifacts" were available from the collection. A designer emphasized that the co-curators should not try to "compete"

Figure 5.10. The Chicago exhibit's "living room." Photo by author. Reproduced with permission of the National Museum of the American Indian, Smithsonian Institution.

with the NMAI collection, explaining that the museum would instead use ordinary objects to communicate ideas. They stressed, "Testimony will be a very important part of this exhibit. With complex issues, it's the best way to deal with them, by just having people telling the stories, telling how it is. It's the best way to communicate." This emphasis on testimony came out most strongly in the Chicago exhibit in a reconstructed "living room" filled with "ordinary objects" from the homes of co-curators and other community members and a television that played videos of interviews with different families explaining their experiences of being Native in the city (figure 5.10).

A D+C designer listened and commented during a discussion about what would be a unique image for the community: "You're saying, dancing with the cityscape background?" The group settled on a "powwow in the city": "[This is] what would make us unique [in the context of the *Our Lives* exhibition]." The designer replied, "That's a good one." The group also discussed the symbolism—activity, inviting other people in—that this focus on a powwow in the city would have. When the designer asked the committee about sounds they associated with their community, one co-curator got everyone laughing with a quick response: "The el train!"

The second day of the design consultation at the AIC was April 15, and Cynthia opened the meeting with "Taxes are due!" Everyone laughed and then got down to business with Jen Miller, the NMAI project manager, leading the discussion. She systematically went through each theme, eliciting ideas for objects and explaining that they would need to give size information for each object for the design plans. The upcoming deadline for object, photo, and loan information was in June. Wenona was tasked with conducting one-on-one interviews with the co-curators and additional community members about the various themes on the worksheet.

On January 19, 2003, Cynthia visited Chicago again to update them on the status of the exhibit, telling the co-curators that the icon for the exhibit would be the Chicago skyline and the "main attraction" would be the intertribal powwow. Cynthia prepared the co-curators for the upcoming NMAI media team visit and requested suggestions for whom to interview on video and what events to cover. In an independent meeting of the co-curators on May 29, 2003, the group reviewed a "needs list" from Cynthia for the media visit (whom to interview, whom and what to photograph, and so on).

A media team composed of NMAI staff and contracted sound and camera operators visited each *Our Lives* community in 2003 to videotape and photograph individual interviews, community events, additional images, and, occasionally, scripted scenes according to the needs of the exhibit. These media visits were often the last visit by curatorial staff to the community, so they included any remaining object collection, object measurement, and final script approval by the co-curators.

The Ideology of Authorship: Reflections on the Exhibit-Making Process

During my fieldwork after the museum opened, I asked curators and co-curators to reflect on the community-curating process. Prosper Paris compared the thematic approach to writing down a title for a song and then composing lyrics according to that title; it was a familiar process to him. Prosper, like Garnette Joseph, believed this approach to be successful. Garnette said that it worked: "I think, listening to people speak and [noticing] some of the things that they spend more time [talking about], I guess, that is only because it is important to them. If people keep on saying the same thing all the time, then that is how [they] feel most of the time."[21]

Garnette's comment points to assumptions in a thematic approach that is coupled with collaborative practice and no doubt also reflects the responsibility of authorship by co-curators *on behalf of* a wider community: the more people talk about something, the more important it is, and the themes should derive from what community members talk about the most. However, it was the responsibility of the co-curators to determine which of those recurring topics were appropriate for the exhibit. Prosper noted, "I'm very satisfied that we had a good cross section of people. We had the community workers, we had people involved in tourism, in community work, farmers, boat makers, and youth, and all these people.... We can safely say that we had the *voice* of the Carib *people* on *tape*."[22]

During a tape-recorded interview with Sylvanie Burton in 2005, I asked specifi-cally who wrote the script. She talked about the NMAI "pulling" the script out from recordings, and both of us started laughing as she detailed the process I was engaging in as she was describing it. She explained that it was the community members who did the script, not the NMAI staff: "Because it's *you* who said everything anyway! It wasn't *they* [the NMAI]. [They were] just asking all the questions and throwing out the topics or whatever for us to discuss and saying, 'What do you think of this?'" She said that the script came from "meetings and discussions" and added, "Everybody's contribution was recorded. [*laughter*] And out of that, a certain script was selected, and then when [NMAI staff] came down, we had a *consensus* on…different things."[23]

The selection and visual arrangement of the quotations from transcripts and the images from the media team visits were made by NMAI staff members. Although the co-curators did not physically write the script or select the quotations that resulted from their meetings, they were responsible for making sure that these were accurate. Sylvanie said, "[The NMAI] put [this exhibit] together in a way that *we ourselves* were really happy." A Chicago co-curator said the same for their exhibit, noting that it was best the NMAI made those choices, and not they themselves, so that other community members would not think that the co-curators had placed themselves so prominently, and disproportionately with respect to other community members, on display.

Sylvanie and the other Kalinago co-curators felt strongly that the script reflected their voices. Garnette said that their job was basically to make "corrections" to the script,[24] fact-checking names and dates. He said that he didn't change the content of the script because it came from the community and that people were already famil-iar with the script because it was what they had said.[25] This ideology of authorship suggests that credit for the script was related to widespread community contribu-tions, content choice, and the oral statements and paraphrases from meetings and interviews inscribed in the text panels—not the selection of particular content or the writing of the script.

The Chicago co-curators made similar evaluations—that they revised but did not write the script—at a meeting on October 11, 2005, a year after the opening of the museum. Rita Hodge arranged the meeting at the AIC so that I could present my research to the group and they could provide feedback about their experiences creating the exhibit. During the discussion, Joe Podlasek said that, to meet a dead-line, one year the "core" co-curators were reviewing and working on the script at Rita's grandson's birthday party: "[We were] still working when we weren't supposed to be working.… We sat out there and went through scripts." They looked at all the "quotes, comments, and stories—and it was a book!" Rita added that they went through "a bunch of revisions." Joe said that all the co-curators were asked to "sign off" on the comments of theirs that were included in the script. Rita said that they revised the script but did not select which comments were used in it.

Joe said, "We had no input as to what actually was going to be put on the walls," although there were general ideas, such as beadwork would go here or pictures there. He said, for instance, that they did not know that Eli's statement was going to be in "really big letters" (see figure 5.1).[26] He added, "We had no idea this was going to happen. Or what the quote would be, whose quote it would be. So we actually saw it for the first time on that Monday [during the grand opening of the museum]." Cindy Soto felt that it was better the NMAI chose the quotations, to avoid "fighting" and to avoid the co-curators making the community "look one certain way or lean towards maybe one belief"—in other words, so that the exhibit would be more objective. Although there were some comments in the text panels that some co-curators might not have agreed with, she said, the text did reflect some community members' perspectives. Rita agreed: "We had to keep reminding ourselves, you know...it's not our exhibit. It's the community's."[27]

Like the Kalinagos, the Chicago co-curators noted that the script came from what had been gathered in their community, so they felt that they had read or previewed it. Joe added, "Something I'd be really interested in is getting some feedback from somebody that *hasn't* been to Chicago, to our community, and get an opinion of what their interpretation of our community is now. You know, maybe from a rez, from another urban Indian community, to see, did we do what we were supposed to do and represent?" This curiosity about the reception from other tribes is in stark contrast to the Kalinago co-curators' hope of speaking to tourists through their exhibit.

The Chicago co-curators also agreed that when the NMAI was working with the community, while the museum was still under construction, people did not understand the impact that the museum was going to have. One of the biggest challenges was getting community members to donate items or participate in the exhibit. Cyndee Fox-Starr described running around her home and gathering items for the exhibit because they did not get contributions of everyday items, such as unfinished beadwork, from other community members. But now that the museum is open, she said, "it's a whole different perspective": "If I asked somebody to donate something *now* to the NMAI, they'd be hustling to get it," punctuating her statement with a snap of her fingers.

Although community participation in the exhibit may not have been as widespread as the co-curators would have liked, both communities were practiced at talking about the subject matter of the exhibition. Trying to measure the impact of the museum's intervention in their community, I asked whether it was usual for them to talk about their identity. Kalinago co-curator Gerard Langlais said:

> It is an everyday topic. Every day, people talk about Kalinago, the identity, and so on. But sometimes we have that pull between who is a Kalinago and who is a half-breed or who is a negro.... So that was kind of a little bit ticklish. That talk about Kalinago identity, and so on, it's something that everybody's talking about in the Carib Territory. But, as I said, some straight-hair people and some who have the *real* features would look at the [*laughs a little, perhaps sheepishly*], you

know, half-breed and say, "Well, you're a negro, you're not a Carib, you're not a Kalinago man, you know? You [are] something else." That sort of thing. But we get over that and we all work together, and so on.[28]

I learned through fieldwork that comments like Gerard's were common in more forthright community conversations—even at the Carib Model Village task force meetings. And although broached in the community-wide *OL* meetings, the issue of race and racial mixing was not included in the exhibit.

In the Chicago community, identity was a common if sometimes difficult topic. Identity as discussed in the community was more about blood quantum and tribal enrollment or membership, however, than organizations and powwows. At one powwow meeting, the "identity police," as critical community members referred to them, had challenged publicly and raised doubts about a community member's tribal status by waving their own identity cards in the air (he was indeed an enrolled member of a tribe but did not, perhaps, "look Indian"). Other ways of talking about identity in the community revolved around reservation and city tensions and the process of "becoming Indian" or learning about one's heritage through the welcoming embrace of the AIC community. One AIC program, Enter the Circle, was dedicated to teaching community members how to sew dance clothes and dance powwow dances.

The "identities" on display in the gallery were descriptive about daily life in the community, leaving out the contentious issue of *tribal* identities. Co-curator Dave Spencer explained that the focus on the powwow was a result of trying to be "safe, universal, inclusive." The Chi Town drum was selected for display because it did not have a Native language name and was therefore not privileging one tribe above others. Dave noted at the American Association of Musems conference in 2005 that working on the NMAI exhibit was the first time the community had talked about "first voice issues" and "self-representation"; this was not common discourse in the community. He told of a debate among the co-curators about whether to include in the Chicago exhibit a bronze statue created by a non-Native person from outside the community, depicting the stereotype of an Indian on horseback with bow and arrow. Five out of nine co-curators wanted the sculpture to represent the community, but in the end, the object was not used.

Intermarriage and race in the Carib Territory, suicide in Igloolik, and pan-Indianism and organizational infighting in Chicago were three topics brought up in many meetings among community members when preparing the exhibition, but these were not incorporated into the final exhibit. Although suicide prevention was in the original Igloolik script at the co-curators' request, the NMAI scriptwriter/editor removed it from the final text. For the Kalinago and Chicago communities, it was the co-curators who decided not to incorporate the recurring conversations about intermarriage or pan-Indianism into their exhibits. Those topics were a part of the process, community members speaking to one another, more than the product, or what they felt was appropriate for the public. Exercising this choice, often absent in popular representations of Native Americans, was key to the trust-building aspect of this collaborative process.

Mediating Native Voices

As community input moved from recorded conversation to transcript to script to wall panel, it passed through what may have seemed like a "black box" to those outside the museum (and some inside, as well). Working with knowledge generated by the co-curators, many museum professionals contributed to the transformation from field recording to authored text panel.

What was unusual about this particular exhibition was that the scriptwriter/editor worked on the exhibit content with no visuals (and not having "been there") and designers determined the amount of space available for words in the exhibits—label lengths and sizes—in the graphic elevations before the text labels were created.[29] Like the construction of the building and the development of the exhibits, everything was going on at once. In the end, regulations such as the required font size from the Americans with Disabilities Act (1990) and space availability in the museum determined the (amount of) text just as much as did the content that co-curators developed. Scriptwriters and designers were working at the same time that curatorial staff members were working with the communities, all in relative isolation from one another and sometimes with little or no interaction with the communities. This was one of the more stark divisions of labor between the visual and textual tasks of the collaborative work. Although the design team did meet with each community once, the scriptwriter encountered the co-curators only as names and transcript quotes—as text.

Script Development

After the co-curators had selected their exhibit themes and finalized their subthemes, NMAI staff worked on the script structures. In general, Cynthia wrote the first draft of the scripts, and then a collaborative editing process began.[30] The back-and-forth collaboration among NMAI staff can be seen in an example from the Kalinago exhibit (figure 5.11).

After the tapes of the co-curator meetings were transcribed, curatorial staff excerpted portions of the transcripts and categorized them according to the themes and subthemes selected by the co-curators. Originally, NMAI curators assumed that they would be responsible for writing the exhibit scripts, since they had worked closely with the communities and knew what, of the hundreds of pages and hours of transcripts, was most important to include. The hiring of an NMAI scriptwriter/editor—who did not have intimate contact with the communities—was not welcomed by the Curatorial Department. This was a part of the "baton pass" that they contested, as detailed in chapter 4.

Post 11/18 curatorial revisions
Last edited by MH: 1/21/04
Reviewed by CC: 2/13/04
Edited by KM: 2/24/04

	Kalinago Curators, 2003 **#**
GRAPHIC: Map of Carib Territory with Kalinago place names G10.2.5.1 This is courtesy of Lennox Honychurch. This graphic is being recreated from a map he drew.	The Kalinago name for Dominica is Waitukubuli which means "tall is her body." Map with Kalinago place-names. Courtesy of Lennox Honychurch. ~~Waitukubuli contains several Native place-names, including Bataka and Sineku. Waitukubuli—the Kalinago name for Dominica—means, "tall is her body."~~ *Kalinago Curators, 2003* **#**
Traditional Foods **T10.2.6** Should this say "farina"? What is "farine" exactly? Taryn's note: Farine is flour made from cassava, used in different recipes	**Kalinago Cuisine** Sometimes when I give my children Kalinago food, they tell me they want store-bought bread. *Sylvie Warrington, 2002* Our young people are more interested in store-bought foods, so fewer people are making traditional foods these days. But we still consider food an important part of our heritage. Traditional foods such as farine and cassava are often served at special events, celebrations, and tourist attractions. *Kalinago Curators, 2003* **#**
PHOTO: Cooking cassava G10.2.6.1	A versatile root, cassava can be made into bread, pudding, and even beer. Here the root has been peeled, shredded, and the water extracted. People then add sugar to the meal and roast it on a hot iron, which produces cassava bread.

Figure 5.11. Kalinago script structure, showing the process of editing.

The *Our Lives* script process was opaque to me because, at the time, I was a consultant only for the Igloolik exhibit while earning my doctoral degree and I was not present at the NMAI during this phase. The script process involved a number of writers, compilers, and contributors from the Curatorial and Exhibits Departments; an outside scriptwriter was contracted early on for *OL* (some of whose work curatorial staff considered uninformed and clichéd, filled with Native stereotypes that prompted curatorial staff to rewrite the preliminary scripts), and later an NMAI scriptwriter/editor was hired. It is clear that the final scripts and text panels, including sections of text attributed to the "Kalinago co-curators" or the "Chicago Native co-curators," were in some cases written and in other cases edited by the NMAI

Figure 5.12. Preparing an exhibit sticker for installation. Dennis Doyle (facing camera) and Jeff Smith from Hadley Exhibits replace the introductory panel to the Kalinago exhibit (in rear). Photo by author. Reproduced with permission of the National Museum of the American Indian, Smithsonian Institution.

scriptwriter/editor. The co-curator and community member statements were paraphrased or summarized to introduce the main thematic sections of each exhibit. The quotations attributed to particular individuals, such as Ed Two Rivers or Eli Suzukovich, were nearly verbatim from the transcript, sometimes paraphrased or shortened or slightly changed by the scriptwriter/editor for "clarity."

However, in the view of lead curator Cynthia Chavez, curatorial work was "translated into regular museum text" by non-curatorial staff. Cynthia said that those who supported simplifying the script like this thought that visitors "won't get it." But, she asked, exasperated, "How do they know if they don't try?" She felt that her work with the communities had produced "something different." Again she asked, "How do we know that [visitors] would not have gotten it?" adding that the curators had argued with the scriptwriter/editor over these issues. They felt that the editor took all the nuances out of the script: the text was just "glossed over" and now sounded "matter-of-fact," she said, disappointed but resigned.[31]

Each final script eventually was transformed into a "sticker" for the exhibit wall (a text panel) through the creative work of designers and the material production of fabricators (figure 5.12).

Media Production and Design

It was the designers who ultimately determined how much of the script text would go in the exhibit, because they determined the label size. They also were responsible for the location and juxtaposition of media, text, and imagery in the exhibits. The technologies that media and design professionals used to create their contributions to the exhibits added to the overall feel of the gallery as busy, loud in both sound and image, lively, and colorful. The NMAI media team stood in an intermediary position between the Curatorial Department and the contracted design firm, D+C. They crafted "media sketches" of what they wanted to collect in their visits to the communities—particular photographs or video sequences—in order to complement the themes developed by the co-curators.

In June 2004, I spoke with Dan Davis, an NMAI media producer, as he sat at a desk in his office looking at a couple of monitors and a bank of knobs and buttons. He was splicing together digital footage from the Kalinago community and replaying his handiwork on a computer. Kathy Suter, the media coordinator and his supervisor, joined our discussion later. Dan explained that the Exhibits Department had wanted very short video segments, because that was what visitors "can take," and curators had wanted videos of seven or eight minutes.[32] "The visitors can't stand for eight minutes, and we can't alienate the visitors, according to Exhibits." He said that Kathy and he found themselves "in between" what the two departments wanted in terms of video length.

Dan also explained that if the media team recorded something in the community that contradicted the curator's "thesis," he did not put it in the media piece. He was responsible for editing all the *OL* videos, and the interactive computer displays were completed by a contracted firm. Dan went to a number of communities himself, and he also edited the materials from communities he did not visit, which were provided by Kathy. He lamented not being able to do preliminary visits with communities before the actual media trip but, he said, the media team would have needed "time and more money" to do so. Kathy said that she felt they were more like a "news team than a documentary team," dropping into communities unprepared. They were "doing work forced into a news format." She explained, "News tramples a place, a place you are never coming back to." You are dropped in somewhere, and you make the best of it instantly, knowing that you are never coming back. For a documentary, on the other hand, you start with a couple of "cold visits" without the camera. "We survived it," she said, "[but] the process could have been better." She liked the overall product, however; she said that the media pieces could not have been better. Between the budget, time constraints, and NMAI curators' schedules, Dan said, it "end[ed] up being lots of compromises."

Dan described the media team process as we looked at some Kalinago footage Kathy and her team had collected in Dominica. As he showed me the rough cuts that would later be displayed on monitors mounted on the walls of the Kalinago exhibit, Dan mentioned how hours of tape get edited down to minutes. Although they tried to feature everybody who was interviewed, with so little time in the pieces, it was not always possible. He said that ten hours of a community's footage would be reduced to an average of ten minutes total in the gallery.

Kathy told me that her interpretation of Native voice in the media pieces, and how she instructed Dan to edit the videos, was to not have a narrator "who helps glue it together." This meant that Dan, in the editing process, had to string clips of interviews with Native community members together, with only their own words to advance the narrative. To begin this process, Dan would start with an event. He would put together footage that explained what it was and then remove the "tangents" that people explored in the interviews. After he finished putting together all of the "talking"—the words he needed to explain the exhibit section he was working on—he would overlay pictures that corresponded with what the person was talking about. It does not change the "essence" of what the person is saying, he assured me. The problem is, he said, that he needed "sound bites" and the people on the tapes tended to be "long-winded." Again noting the required content reduction, he said that four days of interviewing needed to be condensed into a three-minute story. It's "like a crossword puzzle"; you have to be "really creative." The "rule of thumb" is "to show rather than to tell."

"It's a rewarding, and fun, challenge to work on," Dan said, "[but the] review process is hard on all of us." Each person has "passion to do a good job," yet each sees things differently. Because he did not know what would be on the wall around the videos he was creating, he relied on the NMAI curators to ensure that the tone of the media piece was appropriate. After he reviewed the video transcripts, selected clips, and completed an edited rough cut, he would have an internal review with Kathy and afterward would show it to the curator "as is," expecting to make no changes.[33] The media pieces were not reviewed by the community co-curators because "who knows how long it would take" and time was short.

Kathy noted—in a way that sounded a lot like what curators said about Native communities (see chapter 4)—that the media team needed to work on building trust with the NMAI curators. She said, "Building of trust with the curators took the entire eighteen months that we were in the field." The media team's "biggest hope" was that they would "meet communities early on" in the future. She wanted a little more "self-sufficiency so that [they could] email so and so and get more details" from Native community members—and not always have to go through the curators to contact them.

The media and design teams both contributed to what one person described as "putting words back into the exhibit"—making space for previously omitted information or text to be inserted in other places than the main text panels. Erica Denison of D+C considered the photo captions in the exhibits to be "disguised text,"[34] a way to include additional information that the restrictions on label size prohibited. Virtually every contributor to *Our Lives* acknowledged the large amount of material and information left out of the designed exhibit.

Kathy Suter explained a similar process of "adding back" information as a result of the media sketches' being made in advance of the final scripts. The media team was working with the earliest drafts of the scripts or maybe even the "script structures," which were created as outlines before the prose was drafted and the content reduced. Kathy said that, although the script labels were limited in length, the information could be included somewhere else—so the curators squeezed a lot into the media, which was collected last in the community-curating process. Kathy considered Dan and herself "the last stand." They provided a place where the information could come out. They were "turning back the clocks" on the information that had "vanished from the wall scripts."

The *OL* wall scripts were large graphic stickers, a new form of exhibit production that allowed Design+Communication to present its leading-edge display methods in a highly anticipated new museum. The design of the *Our Lives* gallery in particular was largely influenced by displays of innovative technology—most notably in the form of the "supergraphics," but also in the large reflective video walls in the entrance to the gallery. Pushing image resolution and image size to the limits, D+C's supergraphics were wall-size stickers that the design firm printed and mounted on the aluminum infrastructure of the exhibits. All of the images and text and background wall colors—anything that was not a built structure such as wall contours, glass cases, or video monitors—would be large, two-dimensional stickers with printed borders and shading to give the illusion of a three-dimensional layering of items on the walls. Until this particular year, the industry had not had the technology to do this kind of exhibit production. Therefore, newly available software and hardware drove the aesthetics of the design, along with the community consultations and content.[35]

Collaborative Authorship and the Imagined Audience

Again drawing on Mazzarella and Dornfeld and inspired by the work of Faye Ginsburg (2002[1995]), I view the exhibit as a form of mediation that is routed through the imagined audience, the "other" that all contributors—the scriptwriter/editor, the NMAI curators, the Native community curators—considered as they participated in making the exhibit. Dornfeld (1998) found that the imagined audience for the PBS documentary producers he studied closely matched their own class positions, life experiences, and values. They assumed an audience like themselves. Among those involved in community curating, this seemed to be true for the scriptwriter/editor, but not for the co-curators. One way to understand these different orientations is to examine the audience that each imagined and wanted to "speak to."

Briefly, the imagined audience of the scriptwriter/editor was the non-Native visitor. Some NMAI staff commented that the scriptwriter/editor did not know "Indians 101,"[36] but he told me that this made him a better translator for the visitor, who was "in the same boat." A CRC staff member and at least one group of co-curators involved in the *Our Lives* exhibition noted that after the scriptwriter/editor had done his work, all the exhibits seemed to have a similar "happy-go-lucky" tone. In general, the public-oriented departments like Exhibits and Education imagined their audience as "National Air and Space Museum overflow"—"streakers" in museum-speak—who they believed did not want to read a lot of text. (Streakers are seen in opposition to "scholars" or "studiers," who read everything in, say, the exhibits of the US Holocaust Memorial Museum. The in-between category is "strollers.")[37]

As lead curator, Cynthia Chavez expressed great anxiety in the course of making *Our Lives*. She worried over the proper representation of the communities, as well as what she called the "*huuuuge* and endless sort of subject" that contemporary Native identity is. She said of her early weeks on the project, "A lot of the advice I was getting was to sort of create a framework for identity. And I'm thinking, 'How can you create a framework for identity?!?'"[38] She was also concerned about *her* imagined audience, the community curators with whom she worked—a group of particular persons to whom she felt accountable.

Although the public-oriented staff insisted that their expertise was essential in translating community-produced knowledge to the museum audience, what they perhaps missed was that the communities had their own audiences in mind as they worked on the exhibits.[39] As mentioned earlier, Joe Podlasek, a co-curator and the director of the American Indian Center, was concerned about how other tribes would respond to the Chicago exhibit. This imagined audience of "other tribes" is reflected in the more "retrospective perspective"[40] of their exhibit, its emphasis on the longevity of the Chicago community, the institutional support available for maintaining Indian identities, and a demonstrated tolerance for different tribal traditions. The Chicago community appreciated being included in the NMAI as a validation and celebration of their identity, in counterpoint to the reservation-versus-city antagonism about who is a "real Indian." (Although over half of all Native Americans live in cities, this was the first time I know of that an urban community was treated and displayed equally alongside reservation communities in a single exhibition.)

The Chicago co-curators were aware that many of their community members—members of many tribes, like them—would eventually visit and see their work in the NMAI, unlike the Kalinago co-curators, whose prefigured audience was not like themselves. The Kalinagos imagined their audience to be potential tourists as they constructed their exhibit. Prosper said that people in his community felt they were "talking to the world."[41] Their exhibit maintained a future perspective, a hope that their audience, after seeing the exhibit, would visit and participate in their local economy. This perspective was also reflected in their highlighting a model village, which did not open until 2006, and Carib Week and cultural groups—all having the potential for a greater awakening of cultural consciousness in their community.

This hope for tourists to visit was fulfilled in one particular instance while I was in Dominica in 2005. I was invited to a cultural performance by the Karifuna Cultural Group at the Sineku Resource Center. Two busloads of white-haired, older American tourists arrived from a cruise ship. They had come as part of a Carib

Indian Tour (as opposed to the Rainforest Tour). As they wound their way to the upper level of the resource center, where the performance would take place, I noticed a woman wearing a Pamunkey Indian Tribe T-shirt. It turned out that not only was she Pamunkey but she also was carrying around two photos from the *Our Lives* Pamunkey exhibit in a plastic bag: one of her two grandchildren and the other of the text panel with the name of the tribe and its introduction. She had seen the Kalinago exhibit while at the NMAI and told her friends from California that they should all take this tour to see the Carib people. After the performance, she met Sylvanie Burton and showed her the photos. Sylvanie told me later she felt encouraged that the exhibit really was having an impact, that people were seeing it and coming to visit her people.

For the Kalinagos, reaching consensus on the exhibit content was not so much the challenge as doing the exhibit the right way. Perhaps this was because the Kalinagos were practiced at defining themselves to outside audiences; Garnette once said, "I've been representing people half my life."[42] It seemed that the most difficult task for the Kalinagos was the local politics of representation: who would be on the committee, where the money from the museum would go, how the co-curators were perceived as benefiting from the process, and how to stave off jealousies, apathy, or false accusations from others. The most important aspects of the exhibit making, according to the Kalinago co-curators, were to ensure that a wide swath of the community was represented on the co-curator committee, that the wider community was involved in producing the exhibit content, and that the community felt ownership over the project.

In contrast, for the Chicago community, the co-curators said that consensus building around a concept of identity for a multitribal community—the substance of the exhibit—was the most difficult. Few co-curators were practiced at representing this community as a multitribal whole, and the greatest challenge of the co-curator meetings—beyond getting people to come, as Rita Hodge told me—was respecting one another's very different tribal traditions in the course of making an exhibit about identity. This struggle and ethical commitment within the Chicago committee, in the end, became the main message about the community as a whole. And rather than focus on specific tribes, the exhibit presented the main institutions of support for all tribal peoples in the area.

Through the exhibit, the Kalinagos made a case for economic need and called for tourist engagement; they promised that a renewed cultural product would be waiting for visitors (figure 5.13).[43] The Chicago community made a case for longevity and for the support of tribal identities despite living in a city (figure 5.14). Their imagined audiences were present in other activities in each community as well. The future tourist was discussed in Carib Model Village task force meetings, and the Chicago community produced a major annual powwow that was attended by many different tribes and nations. Both of these usually marginalized communities, often discussed by academics or considered by surrounding societies as somehow "less"

Figure 5.13. Kalinago exhibit "craft house" photo collage. Photo by author. Reproduced with permission of the National Museum of the American Indian, Smithsonian Institution.

Native than others—through assimilation due to a devastating history, racial mixing, or greater contact with the dominant society—felt "honored" to participate in the inaugural exhibitions partially because they appreciated the validation and symbolic capital gained through their representation at the NMAI alongside the more familiar museum representations and forms of Native identity and life.

In *Museums and Source Communities*, Peers and Brown (2003:9) explain that "for many source communities, collaboration means full and equal partnership in all stages of a project; it is a recognition of their expertise and their attachment to objects that are central to their culture, and their participation will often be based upon expectations of community benefit." Expecting reciprocity blended with taking control over representation has by some theorists been considered a form of "mediating identities" (Ginsburg 2002[1995]), the approach I prefer. Elsewhere, it has been characterized as "tactical museology," in which groups take advantage of the symbolic capital of the museum or employ it for legitimizing a group identity, particularly in community museums (Buntinx and Karp 2006). Corinne Kratz and Ivan Karp (2006:8) write in the introduction to *Museum Frictions: Public Cultures/Global Transformations* about the tensions in contemporary museums, which are striving to be simultaneously "community-based, national, regional and global." They explain that communities have "sought the legitimacy conferred by museums for themselves, not necessarily to display themselves for others" (ibid.:11).

Figure 5.14. Chicago exhibit facade of AIC entrance. Photo by author.
Reproduced with permission of the National Museum of the American Indian,
Smithsonian Institution.

Because NMAI director Rick West described the NMAI as more like a community museum than a national one, it would seem that this idea of tactical museology could apply to what I present here—especially with respect to the Kalinagos and their imagined audience. But I would caution against this simple explanation. For state-subsidized cultural institutions, Georgina Born (1995:27) explains, in the "absence of validation through market, legitimation is the primary concern" in "subsidized spheres." Born discusses how IRCAM "continually legitimates itself" (ibid.:4). The NMAI does so as well, and this is observable in and accomplished by its rhetoric of collaboration and thus ethical museum practice, most notable in the co-curating process and the emphasis on Native voice.

I want to emphasize that the NMAI *as an institution* also gains symbolic capital here. It is a two-way street. The artifacts selected for exhibits—the faces, the signed text panels—are indexes of community participation and evidence of collaboration.

These give the *museum* legitimacy in the eyes of both its audience and its constituency. Native communities often express that the process is as important as or more important than the product. I argue that the process *was* the product in regard to establishing this legitimacy.

Conclusion

Native community participation in museum displays is a way to access a wider public sphere in which a struggle over what it means to be Native has all too often been controlled and defined by non-Native people. The *Our Lives* gallery is in many ways eight autoethnographies assembled by museum and Native community experts. Patricia Erikson describes "autoethnography" as Native communities' "representations of themselves that engage with dominant cultural systems yet still have a degree of local control" (Erikson et al. 2002:66). But the exhibits were not exactly or only autoethnography. By exploring how authorship was produced in *Our Lives*, we see that the artifacts of collaboration elided a number of producers involved in their making.

Although the exhibits are about the Kalinagos and the American Indians of Chicago, their everyday lives and identities were far less defined by (interactions with) the museum than were the lives and identities of those who worked at the NMAI. Whereas the communities experienced exhibit making sporadically for a number of days every few months, when NMAI staff visited them, exhibit production was an ongoing and frenetic experience at the museum. The researchers' and curators' lives and sense of identity revolved around working on this exhibit. In other words, the exhibition was not just about the lives of the co-curators, but also about the lives of the NMAI curators: their competence, their ingenuity, and the future of their careers.

We have seen that the Native communities and the museum professionals struggled with issues of representation, with how to present and display Native identities and lives to the public. The credit and responsibility for the content of the exhibits did indeed reside with the co-curators: they developed the themes, their names were on the panels. In contemporary museum practice with Native communities, authorship—particularly, collaborative authorship—is especially about ethical practice and authenticity. Like the NMAI itself, the co-curators had both a constituency (their neighbors, families, and friends) and an audience (other tribes or potential tourists). And just as the museum felt that collaboration with Native peoples was the best practice for making exhibits about them, the co-curators emphasized collaboration within their own communities in order to arrive at an "authentic" exhibit about themselves.

Rick West's (2000:7) promise of authenticity has always been located in the concept of Native voice. At a senior management retreat, he acknowledged, "We have had a great debate from time to time about what [Native voice] is." From his point of view, Native voice "is authoritative Native people speaking in an unfiltered way":

"I do not want an unsigned label in sight." Because if it is unsigned and one cannot attribute a statement to an individual, then it has likely been "filtered."[44] Through the mediation of Native voice—from tape recording to edited script to text panel—there was, of course, filtering going on, as curators and others noted. However, the community curators recognized their own voices, concerns, and decisions about content in the final text and thus signed it as their own.

As Anna Tsing (2007:39) writes, only when one speaks "in a publicly recognized genre" can one "gain voice." By exploring the social practice of authorship in the *Our Lives* gallery, we see how the artifacts created through this form of knowledge production—about the self, in relation to another—were both constructed by and recognized as Native voice. For NMAI staff, the term "Native voice" is intended to displace authority from the museum to the communities. And by extending the category of "expert" to Native community curators, NMAI staff attempted to subvert entrenched conceptions of Native peoples and their knowledges—as an ethical act intended to both recognize and correct the inherent and historical imbalance of power and authority between museums and Native peoples.[45]

In later chapters, I address how attempts such as these to rebalance power are not always successful and how the critique of Native voice can be seen as a form of what Alison Wylie (2008) calls "misrecognized expertise." At this point, it is important to note that the individual community curators with whom I spoke felt empowered by the collaborative process and appreciated the work of the NMAI curators and researchers to elicit and organize their discussions and to respect their wishes in the course of exhibit development. In this respect, the museum was successful in building trust relations with these communities.

Although the process was praised (specifically for its ethics and intentions), the product was often highly criticized. The goal had been to exhibit Native identities through the medium of Native voice, but neither the content nor the form had been predetermined or agreed upon within the institution. There is a particular parallel here with Sally Price's account in *Paris Primitive* (2007): both museums sought through their particular form of ethics to elevate "the Native" in a particular way. The Musée du quai Branly intended to elevate Native "objects" to the status of art through its methods of dramatic, sparse display and lack of contextual labeling. The NMAI sought to elevate Native "subjects" by giving them control over the contextualization of their objects and naming them as authorities in the labeling. The Musée du quai Branly sought to increase and recognize the value of Native objects as art; the NMAI sought to increase and recognize the value of Native knowledge as expertise.[46] The former was criticized by Native people and praised by art critics; the latter, quite the opposite (see chapter 7). This seems to get at the crux of collaboration as ethical practice: even though the process may be considered ethical and consequently be praised, the product—shorthanded as Native voice—is not necessarily appreciated equally beyond those who were involved.

Plate 1. Installation in progress, August 18, 2004. Photo by author. Reproduced with permission of the National Museum of the American Indian, Smithsonian Institution.

Plate 2. Installing objects in the Kahnawake Mohawk exhibit, September 2, 2004. From left: curator Cynthia Chavez, contracted mount maker Abby Krause, registrar Maria McWilliams, and research assistant Arwen Nuttall. Photo by author. Reproduced with permission of the National Museum of the American Indian, Smithsonian Institution.

Plate 3. Dance demonstration in the Potomac area inside the main entrance to the museum. Photo by author. Reproduced with permission of the National Museum of the American Indian, Smithsonian Institution.

Plates 4a, 4b. First-floor gift shop. Photos by author. Reproduced with permission of the National Museum of the American Indian, Smithsonian Institution.

Plates 5a, 5b. Native Modernism was the inaugural exhibition in the changing gallery. Photos by author. Reproduced with permission of the National Museum of the American Indian, Smithsonian Institution.

Plate 6. Beadwork exhibit in Window on Collections. *Photo by author. Reproduced with permission of the National Museum of the American Indian, Smithsonian Institution.*

Plate 7. Our Lives *gallery entry. Photo by author. Reproduced with permission of the National Museum of the American Indian, Smithsonian Institution.*

Plate 8. *Our Lives gallery introduction (detail). Photo by Walter Larrimore. Reproduced with permission of the National Museum of the American Indian, Smithsonian Institution (no object number).*

Plate 9. Yakama exhibit with sacred mountain as icon. Photo by author. Reproduced with permission of the National Museum of the American Indian, Smithsonian Institution.

Plate 10. Igloolik exhibit showing "media inuksuk" detail. Photo by author. Reproduced with permission of the National Museum of the American Indian, Smithsonian Institution.

Plate 11. At the center of the Kalinago exhibit is an image of a rock staircase leading to the ocean, with Prosper Paris on video telling the tale of the boa constrictor that created it. Photo by author. Reproduced with permission of the National Museum of the American Indian, Smithsonian Institution.

Plates 12a, 12b. Kalinago exhibit photographic collages. Photos by author. Reproduced with permission of the National Museum of the American Indian, Smithsonian Institution.

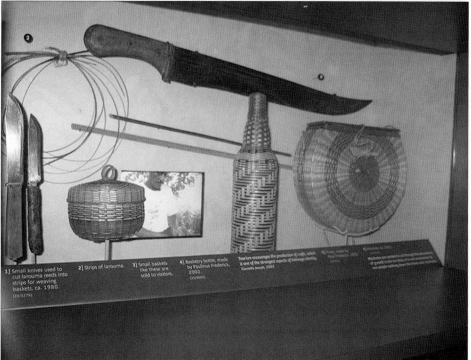

Plates 13a, 13b. Objects in the Kalinago exhibit. Photos by author. Reproduced with permission of the National Museum of the American Indian, Smithsonian Institution.

Plate 14. Chicago exhibit features. Photo by author. Reproduced with permission of the National Museum of the American Indian, Smithsonian Institution.

Plate 15. Chicago exhibit features. Photo by author. Reproduced with permission of the National Museum of the American Indian, Smithsonian Institution.

1] American Indian Center
T-shirt, 2002.
(25/8413)

Honoring the A.I.C. Community

Plate 16. AIC T-shirt in Chicago exhibit. Photo by author. Reproduced with permission of the National Museum of the American Indian, Smithsonian Institution.

Plate 17. AIC princess crown (upper left) in Chicago exhibit. Photo by author. Reproduced with permission of the National Museum of the American Indian, Smithsonian Institution.

Plate 18. Native Nations Procession, September 21, 2004. Photo by author.

s i x
Exhibition

Figure 6.1. Countdown timer at Aerospace Building, June 21, 2004. One month later, the installation of Our Lives *began. Photo by author. Reproduced with permission of the National Museum of the American Indian, Smithsonian Institution.*

The physical space for the *Our Lives* gallery did not exist until 2004. Between July and September of that year, I traveled between the CRC and the mall museum to observe and help out with the installation process for *Our Lives*. There were speculations that the building and even parts of the galleries would not be finished on time, and this turned out to be the case. The building was not completed by the opening, and some portions of the galleries had yet to be installed, particularly in *Our Peoples*, but staff considered these omissions to be unnoticeable to visitors.

Counting Down

One of the unique factors in the process of making the inaugural exhibitions was that the community curators and NMAI staff were creating the plans without having seen the space in which these would be displayed. This was a voiced frustration for community curators, who did not have a clear idea of the size or shape of the space their exhibits would occupy. It also meant that the exhibits were being installed as the building was being completed (plates 1, 2): both were literally (mostly) finished mere hours before the opening of the museum.

Before the downtown staff had relocated their offices to the mall museum, they had hung a countdown timer in the reception area in the Aerospace Building (figure 6.1). It embodied the feeling of time speeding up and the hectic race to finish before opening day. As the day drew nearer, an employee taped a blank sheet of paper over the seconds column; seeing the numbers soaring by was apparently too much for people to confront each time they passed through the office. The image of this countdown timer was replicated in cyberspace, where museum employees saw it every time they visited the front page of the NMAI's internal website.

In contrast to this image of time flying by, recall the installation scene in chapter 3, in which museum experts gathered around object cases and patiently awaited their turn to perform their specific tasks. But while this small and usually quiet group worked with the objects, a large group of fabricators—men wearing tool belts, occasionally joking as they constructed wall panels and built the exhibition's infrastructure, music playing in the background—constantly worked away throughout the *OL* gallery, with occasional visits from electricians and audiovisual specialists as well. As the opening drew nearer, the amount of activity and the number of specialists at work in the space increased.

For years, the *Our Lives* gallery was an amalgam of documents and images, seen by different experts through their own particular renderings of the gallery space: for the designers, bubble diagrams and elevations; for the fabricators, a thick book with line drawings and precise measurements; for the project manager, a large compendium of graphic elevations with colorful layouts of each exhibit; for the Curatorial Department and the co-curators, scripts, worksheets, and object lists; and for the media team, video clips and three-ring binders of video transcripts. Whether it was "the Kalinago exhibit" to curatorial staff or "Exhibit Area 10" to the fabricators, the physical manifestation and coordination of all these experts' contributions finally began to materialize in space in the summer of 2004.

The physical outcomes represented mostly faithful, although sometimes compromised, translations of the documented plans. They exposed fissures in communication within and among departments, as well as the budget, time, and resource constraints on the process. In June 2004, a month before the installation of the *Our Lives* exhibition began and three months before the museum opened, I talked with Erica Denison of Design+Communication. When I told her that I was interested in understanding and documenting the process of making *OL*, she said, "I'm just as curious as you are."

She presented the "Campo tree" as an example. For the Campo Band of Kumeyaay Indians, the oak tree is an important part of who they are and where they come from—and it was translated by D+C into the icon, or main design feature, for their exhibit. For the Kahnawake Mohawks, the icon was a large ironwork structure. For the Saint-Laurent Métis, it was a large vehicle used for ice fishing. For the Chicago community, it was the city skyline. For the Campo Band, it was the oak tree.

Erica explained that the tree started as a three-dimensional, abstract form with photographs of community members hanging off the tree like leaves. This element went from evocative, she explained, to more and more literal, like a "diorama." The tree was "too expensive," however, so they reformatted it to be less costly. It was "reduced" to a "cutout," she said: a picture of a tree with images collaged onto it. However, when the design firm approached the Campo community to collect images of people for the tree, no one was available to do it. So then it was just a tree with no images. To make matters worse, they took a photograph of a tree at the Campo reservation and adjusted it proportionally to the space provided in the gallery. Erica said, "Now we have a cardboard cutout of a bush."[1]

When the "Campo tree" was installed in the gallery space in August 2004, Erica's prediction of what it would look like was spot-on. When the fabrication team's project leader saw it, he said that it looked like a "bush." Arwen Nuttall said that it looked like a "shrub." When Cynthia Chavez saw it, her face dropped. She said that this was the kind of thing she was afraid of and looked disappointed and nervous. Arwen, Cynthia, and I went over and looked at the Campo tree together. Cynthia asked me to take a photo she could email to the co-curators so that they would not be shocked when they came for the opening (figure 6.2). This was her first concern— that the Campo co-curators would dislike it. She lost sleep worrying about it. Then Cynthia saw the Polaroid photographs taped on the wall to the right of the "Campo bush": mock-ups of the tree and rocks, created months before to ensure that the installation was properly done onsite. She realized that the project manager from the Exhibits Department had seen the bush in Buffalo, New York, where the exhibit materials were prefabricated. But no one had told Cynthia about the changes in design; they were certainly not on the last design layouts, which the firm had sent in July 2003. Cynthia had been neither included in the decision making nor informed of the change. Worried that this could ruin visitor and Campo co-curator impressions of the exhibit, she talked to the project manager, who replied that she would make D+C fix it. But no plans were made to fix the bush, and it remained.

Conflict over the reduction of exhibit content was something to which many departments contributed. The process of exhibit making was a process of distillation,

Figure 6.2. Cynthia Chavez in front of the Campo exhibit, August 12, 2004. Photo by author. Reproduced with permission of the National Museum of the American Indian, Smithsonian Institution.

from hundreds of pages of interviews to a seventy-word statement, from a rich, three-dimensional, abstract tree to a flat, minimized, and less comprehensible bush. In addition, there were bureaucratic constraints. Costs and deadlines influenced design, and design shaped content.

The bush incident occurred early in the installation process as the framework of the gallery was being constructed. Toward the end of the summer, Cynthia and the designers were more focused on object placement. They often arranged objects in groups, rather than one object per glass case, as one would expect in a "traditional" display. As I watched the installation unfold, I noted the extreme care and steward-ship that staff from the Collections, Conservation, and Registration Departments demonstrated for the objects. They followed strict protocols for lighting, dusting, and mounting objects, as well as for watching over them at all times. Objects were never left alone without an NMAI staff member at their side; at times, someone would stay behind with a cart of objects during the lunch break so that the cart would not have to be moved and locked away. In addition, staff members treated the props as seriously as the collection objects; a bar-coding system was specifically created for the props and maintained separately from the one developed to track objects in the museum collection. This was a demonstration of respect, since the loans that museum staff classified as "props" were important objects to the community members who provided them for use in the exhibition. The ways in which NMAI staff showed great care for the objects, not just in the museum but also in the communities, helped to cultivate and maintain trust relations during the community-curating process. For example, Cynthia made a special trip to Chicago to pick up a scrapbook from Susan Power. It was filled with archival documents about the Chicago community and the American Indian Center. Cynthia insured it and personally vouched for the safety of this precious record of memories of the Chicago Indian community.

Museum Tour, 2004

As you walk into the museum, you enter the Potomac—a rotunda area designed for group gatherings, live demonstrations, and performances (plate 3). The first floor also includes a main theater, a cafeteria that serves Native foods such as salmon and wild rice, and a gift shop that some describe as another exhibition space (plates 4a, 4b). A less expensive gift shop takes up most of the second floor. The third floor includes the *Our Lives* gallery, the Resource Center, and the changing gallery. *Native Modernism: The Art of George Morrison and Allan Houser*, curated by Truman Lowe, was the inaugural exhibition in the changing gallery. With its boldly colored and curved walls, minimal text, and sparsely displayed artworks, this gallery is a calm respite for many visitors after the overwhelming amount of information, imagery, and sound in the other galleries (plates 5a, 5b). The Lelawi Theater and the *Our Peoples* and *Our Universes* galleries are on the fourth floor, and the entire fifth floor is dedicated to staff offices. Along the hallways of the various floors are additional glass-cased exhibits; most prominent is the *Window on Collections: Many Hands, Many Voices* exhibition of objects organized according to type, such as beads, containers, and arrowheads (plate 6).

When you approach the *Our Lives* gallery from the hallway, the motion of passersby in the entryway to the exhibition catches your attention. It is a short hallway flanked by large video screens that show people walking by, with a reflective glass intended to give visitors a view of themselves walking alongside various Native people (plate 7). The message is that the people in the videos are Native people—whether dressed in a naval uniform, in plain clothes, with dark skin, with light skin—and that anyone walking beside you anywhere in America could be a Native person.

Greeting you as you pass through the entryway is a sea of Native faces, close-up photographs accompanied by a video on a loop that bisects and divides a single face through a myriad of colors, shapes, and features. The pictures were taken by NMAI photographer Cindy Frankenburg, and the display was referred to as the "Face Wall" by staff. Most are photos of NMAI staff members and their families (plate 8). It was not planned this way. The photographer put out a call for Native people to come in and be photographed on a particular day, and visitors at the CRC participating in consultations and various staff members answered the call. On each photo is a notation of the person's name and tribal affiliation(s). On the reverse of this wall is a description of the various ways in which Native identity has been defined through time by outsiders, such as the US government and anthropologists.

The Face Wall and other central portions of the exhibition were "NMAI curated" by guest curator Jolene Rickard (Tuscarora) and the NMAI's Gabi Tayac (Piscataway). They blended academic terms, such as Native scholar Gerald Vizenor's "survivance," and sociological and historical research with imagery and contemporary Native art to convey the various legal and political constraints and the historical milestones of activism and organization that impact the lives and identities of contemporary Native peoples. Other aspects of the NMAI-curated sections include land rights among South American tribes, the "hard choices" tribes have had to make about mining and casinos for economic survival, the American Indian Movement in the 1970s, the United Nations and indigenous organizations, and the importance of the maintenance and survival of Native languages in contemporary communities.

The NMAI-curated exhibits occupy the central area of the gallery, with the circular community-curated exhibits positioned along the exterior walls. The community-curated exhibits are designed in a realistic manner that evokes the feeling of "being there." Each community exhibit is essentially a flat surface with huge graphics that re-create some part of that community's local environment.[2] Larger-than-life images of co-curators and other community members cover the walls (plates 9, 10). Although there are eight community-curated exhibits in the *Our Lives* gallery, in this book, I focus on Kalinago and Chicago.

The Kalinago exhibit is the only one to have a more abstract approach to its imagery—a famous waterfall and a craft shop are not single images, but collages of many photographs (plates 11, 12a, 12b). The designers developed this aesthetic for the exhibit, explaining that it was reminiscent of postcards or tourism photos. The Kalinago exhibit also has the least prominent objects—and some are even hidden behind camouflaged cabinet doors that, due to a design flaw, are difficult to open. Baskets, a cricket bat and ball, DVDs, brochures, and books are on display (plates 13a, 13b). The bulk of the visual impact comes from the various videos in the exhibit, which the co-curators liked very much. They told me, however, that they were disappointed that a number of objects they had provided and expected to be on display—such as bigger, more impressive baskets and a canoe—were not present.

Unlike the Kalinago exhibit, the Chicago exhibit has many built-in architectural features that add more depth to the display (plates 14, 15): a replica facade of the American Indian Center, a full-size and three-dimensional living room, and powwow and graduation ceremony videos playing on a huge three-by-three bank of monitors. There are beaded items, flyers, and everyday household objects in cases. The exhibit includes a contemporary AIC cotton T-shirt folded neatly and presented alone in a glass case with a label (plate 16), as well as commissioned beadwork. Cyndee Fox-Starr said that the most challenging part of being a co-curator was making the princess crown featured in this exhibit (plate 17). She was tasked with creating a replica of the original princess crown, which had been lost. She duplicated it from a picture, but she had "wanted to make it more elaborate looking": "[Keeping to the design in the photograph] was more challenging to me than to do something real bright and shiny and flashy, how I'd like to do it. I had a hard time sitting down to do that.... I kept thinking, 'This isn't what I want to sew. But I'll do it like it says in the picture.'"

Whether a casino mug, a T-shirt, an archival photograph, a clay pot, a fiddle, or a pair of sealskin pants, each prop and object was selected by the co-curators to communicate something about their life today. The item most talked about was a large ice-fishing vehicle, called a bombardier, in the Saint-Laurent Métis exhibit. The size of a car, this object is neither exclusively made nor exclusively used by this community or the Métis more generally, but it is important to the community's lifeways. It is this blend of props and objects, everyday things and handcrafted artworks, items visitors recognize and others that are unfamiliar—what is often glossed as the "traditional" and the "modern"—that creates the unique character of the *Our Lives* gallery.

Conclusion

Seeing the gallery in photographs, or even in person, is not the same as walking through it with its makers. As I went through the exhibition landscape with NMAI staff members during the *OL* installation in the summer of 2004, the curators seemed to measure it in relation to the imagined landscape they had conjured in their minds over the years. Keith Basso's *Wisdom Sits in Places* (1996), which is about Apache place making, came to mind. The gallery was a more literal form of place making, but it still evoked the same sense of walking through space and remembering histories and the tales of how the NMAI came to be. Within this landscape, people recounted stories of meaningful relationships; decisions about objects, cases, color choices, attributions, photographs, and text panels; budget constraints and deadlines; and compromises and personality conflicts, usurpations and triumphs.

As NMAI staff members passed through the gallery space, each object, wall, and text panel had a story behind it, stories that went beyond the subject matter and evident content of the exhibits to a shared and contentious history. And like the Apaches in Basso's account, the stories people told about the past that resided in the exhibit landscape were not *only* about remembering the past but also about communicating something in the present. The conclusion of these stories was often "This is not how we wanted it to be."

One curator said that, as she was walking through the *Our Peoples* gallery with her supervisor, he asked, "Why did they put a rock there?" She replied to him, "We fought it for one and a half years."[3] Later, she summarized this experience: "You walk in and see specific physical features [in the gallery]. Each one represent[s] a hard-won compromise or a battle lost."[4] As Sharon Macdonald puts it (2002:203), "the gallery presents a face cleansed of the struggles to achieve it." For curators, the images on the walls and in the videos recall meaningful—sometimes enjoyable, sometimes tense—interactions with Native community members, NMAI staff, and designers. Each image, object, rock, and bush in the exhibits represents embedded social relations, shared histories, and particular kinds of social practices to those who collaborated in their making; the gallery is a landscape whose history can be read in this way only by those who participated in the process. This includes not only how the co-curators read the "cultural biographies" (Kopytoff 1986) of the things in the exhibits—Cyndee's recollections of running around her house to collect half-finished beadwork for the living room scene in the Chicago exhibit and working diligently to create an outdated beaded design—but also how the NMAI staff viewed the exhibition in which these objects were encased.

The images of Native people on the walls are symbols of Natives (their voices, perspectives, differences) to visitors and other NMAI staff. But for those of us who worked directly with the people in the photos, they are individuals with their own life histories. Without this intimate knowledge of the gallery landscape—its history and creation stories—the experience might seem like watching someone's "wedding videos," one curator worried. If you do not know the people who are represented, is something lost? Co-curators and curatorial staff, on the other hand, were delighted to see the familiar faces of individuals they knew.

One scholar who worked regularly with the Chicago Indian community emailed me what amounted to a wedding-video reaction after a visit to the NMAI. She wrote about her "wonderful experience" at the exhibit and enjoyment seeing the graduation ceremony she had attended. To her "delight," a community member she knew appeared on the screen and waved; she felt as though he was waving to her. "It made my day!" she wrote.[5] But at least one curator was concerned that, for visitors and for NMAI staff who were not involved in the community-curating process, like people not invited to the wedding, the exhibits might include too much information or be boring or tedious to view.[6] Many curators and NMAI staff made comments reflecting their trepidation over the reception of their labors and a desire to anticipate the critiques, so they spoke of what might have been.

In some ways, this apprehension was a recognition of the constraints and problems of collaborative exhibit making. A shift in museum practice and authority from the institution to source communities, as reflected in the *Our Lives* exhibition, is often portrayed as a rupture or break from past exhibition practices. By 2004, however, these "new" practices had already been embraced by a number of museums, although not at this scale. But there were also some enduring continuities with past representational practices, including a commitment to realism and to the concept of culture. In regard to the latter, Miriam Kahn describes the collaborative process of the *Pacific Voices* (1997) exhibit:

> While working with community advisors, I was continually reminded of a contemporary paradox. Just when anthropologists are questioning the concept of culture, especially as a bounded, integrated whole, those same groups who have been invited into museums are clinging passionately to it, conscious of its power as a marker of modern identity. While anthropologists are deconstructing, destroying, and discarding the concept, community groups are invoking, embracing, and deploying it....
>
> Whereas curators and academics wanted the museum to portray the dynamics of such things as inter-generational tensions, competition between local and central forces, and intra-community variability...many advisors wanted to focus instead on an idealized, unified, "frozen moment." (Kahn 2000:71)[7]

The *Our Lives* gallery both embodied and resisted these concepts. The manner in which the exhibition was produced—through committee work and consensus-based knowledge production—resulted in exhibits with an authoritative voice that claims to represent each community as a whole. The resulting impression is that Native community members are homogeneous in their thinking. This is clearly not the case, as details of co-curator meetings in chapter 5 show. However, for public presentation, each community often did have a well-known and somewhat well-defined narrative about its identity distinct from the surrounding society. This is often a burden of being Native: having to assert one's identity in the face of forces that constantly—through law, popular culture, federal policy, or other means—attempt to define, erode, or undermine it.

The display of each community as a self-contained, curved space separate from its neighbors reinforces the notion of bounded cultures,[8] but the communities' emphases on the changing circumstances of their contemporary lives work against the idea of a "frozen moment" and certainly against the common and outdated conceptions of indigenous culture as static or valuable only as an idealized past. Through the exhibits, the co-curators speak directly to the audience, in first-person voice, in the present tense, communicating the message "We are still here." This message would become even more palpable when throngs of indigenous people came to the US National Mall for the opening of the new museum.

s e v e n
Reception

There's always been a feeling, for me, that we're kind of invisible. I can't tell you how often I've felt invisible in my lifetime.... It was almost like something every one of us had been waiting for our whole lives, and [we] couldn't really believe it was happening. Just the basic gathering of all these Indian people in one place, to be honored, was such a fantastic thing for us. It has never happened before—ever—in this country and it was wonderful.

—*Valerie Wilson (Nitmuck), AIC board member, 2005*

Some of [the co-curators] were asking, are they going to be required to give a speech? You know, they didn't realize how big the opening was going to be. I don't think anyone realized how big the opening was going to be. And it was all about giving of ourselves, to make [the co-curators] feel a little more welcome.

—*Teresa Tate, NMAI research assistant, 2004*

Indians are Everywhere

At the opening of the National Museum of the American Indian, over twenty-five thousand indigenous people marched in the procession and over eighty thousand onlookers were present on the National Mall to celebrate the Native peoples of the western hemisphere (Evelyn and Hirsch 2006:90). The gathering was a main topic of the news for about a week—on television, in newspapers, on the radio, and online. Everywhere you looked in DC, there were Native people, their presence affirming the museum's message: Indians are still here. Whereas this message was widely celebrated and well received, the content and design of the exhibitions provoked more varied responses.

"Reception," as I use it here, includes several different aspects. First, it suggests how the community curators were received at the grand opening. They were treated as objects (images, words on the wall) and as subjects (living, breathing persons attending the opening). They were seen both as symbols (diverse "Indians" marching on the National Mall) and as experts (co-curators of the exhibitions, yet they received no formal recognition from the museum during the opening celebrations). Second, this approach highlights the ways in which critiques and praise of the museum circulated among staff and how they responded to those reviews. Finally, I examine how participating in the exhibitions affected the communities with which I worked. The politics of expertise comes to the forefront here, where both exhibition and reception can be seen as performance. I use the term "performance" to highlight intentionality, an awareness of audience, and a practice-oriented analysis, not to suggest something disingenuous or inauthentic about individual presentations.

I present the performance of cultural identities at two levels: popular notions of culture and cultures of expertise. I expand the concepts of "exhibition" and "reception" beyond a built gallery and visitor responses. "Exhibition" also references the display of Native people more generally, and "reception" includes how Native people were received both as museum exhibits and as culture producers in the NMAI and in their communities. For museum professionals, art critics, and academics, the performance of expertise is also a politics of critique, since the way in which they write about the museum influences and discloses their own professional commitments and aspirations (and I am no exception).

In the anthropology of museums, analysis usually focuses on the content and design of exhibitions and, more recently, on the methods of their makers, which I have already documented. In this chapter, however, I also detail the co-curators' experience of exhibition—in the procession and in the gallery space. In museology and the anthropology of media, reception studies typically consider the agency of the audience in its interpretation of media, as opposed to the culture producers' intentions (Ang 1996:64; Mankekar 1999, 2002). I go one step further and consider the agency of the culture producers to frame and reproduce audience responses in their own fields of expertise.

By viewing all the knowledge practices of the various cultures of expertise involved in the making of the NMAI through the lens of performance, I show how the politics and performance of expertise can be an alternative to the predictable and problematic characterizations of identity politics when considering Native participation and discourse in public cultural and legal spheres. At stake in the exhibition and reception of the products of community curating were whether, according to visitors, scholars, and critics, Native knowledge can be seen as expert knowledge and whether Native voice can be seen as an authoritative voice that belongs in the museum.

Preparing the Way

The staff of the NMAI planned for a tremendous number of guests at both the museum opening and the concurrent First Americans Festival, sponsored by the Smithsonian Center for Folklife and Cultural Heritage. The invited guests were associated with different departments in the museum and included dignitaries and diplomats, members of Congress, tribal delegations, and donors to the museum. However, there were some people missing. Smithsonian Folklife and downtown staff had invited "bigwigs" and tribal people from all over the world but never thought to include the Native community members who had worked on the community-curated exhibits. At a steering committee meeting, a curatorial research assistant told me, a senior NMAI staff member apologized to the Curatorial Department for "forgetting" about the co-curators.

Curatorial staff members were concerned because they had no budget to cover the costs of bringing the co-curators to the opening: "One of the things that NMAI and especially Curatorial have always tried to make at the forefront of our work here is hospitality and care towards our co-curators, who are giving us so much for our exhibits. And it's painful that we can't treat them the way we want to and [how] they deserve to be treated."[1] Curatorial staff lobbied for travel money and received it, but instead of Smithsonian Institution travel agents or Folklife staff, who had experience doing mass travel arrangements, the curatorial research assistants (RAs) had to manage the travel for more than 140 community curators and guests. Because of the limited budget, only a certain number of co-curators from each community would be paid for. This resulted in, for example, only enough funds for six of the eight Kalinago co-curators to attend the opening, forcing their committee to decide who had to stay behind. A couple of CRC staff members noted that the amount of money provided for bringing the co-curators to the opening—$150,000—was the same amount budgeted to the National Park Service for the anticipated destruction to the National Mall's grassy area due to the First Americans Festival. One person quipped that the co-curators "were literally treated like dirt."

As the RAs prepared the travel arrangements and schedules for the co-curators' visits, making phone calls to consulates and communities, restaurants and hotels, Cynthia and the rest of the *OL* team were at the mall museum placing the objects selected by the co-curators into glass cases. But just as the *OL* gallery was coming together before my eyes, just as the opening was nearing and I could feel the staff's mounting anticipation, I had to leave DC. I was scheduled to be in Dominica September 10–16 to ask for permission from the Carib Council to conduct research in the Carib Territory. It was an abrupt change from the loud, bustling city to the lush, rugged, and isolated countryside. Dominica was plagued with heavy rains that soon became Hurricane Ivan. Between the rain and the cancellation of Carib Week—a major reason I had visited at that particular time—the hours passed slowly. Meanwhile, I missed the museum's "soft opening,"[2] after which reporters and art critics would write their reviews.

On my last evening in the territory, Prosper Paris talked about his concerns for the Carib Territory, including the still unopened Carib Model Village. He said that he was on every single board regarding the model village and it was "all red tape, red tape, red tape." When the government and tour operators "do Carib tourism," he said, "we are the product." He tried to get people in the territory to understand that, but there was not "a lot of consciousness" there. Prosper also made what would be a recurring request, which went unanswered by the museum despite my and Cynthia's efforts: he wanted a video from the NMAI that included the Kalinago exhibit so that he could show it to other people in the Carib Territory, who surely would never see it otherwise (more on this concern below).

Back in DC, Curatorial Department staff were trying to "scrounge" for tickets to a preview reception for distinguished guests and to plan a dinner reception. While chatting with an RA after I returned from Dominica, I was shocked to learn that the preview reception I had heard about before I left was *not* for the community curators. It was for the "important people," she said, correcting my false assumption. That was why the research assistants and Ann McMullen were "scrambling" for tickets—to get the co-curators added to the guest list. Curatorial insisted that the co-curators be invited, because no special museum-related events had been planned for them otherwise.

Exhibition

On the morning of Friday, September 17, I made a brief visit to the *Our Lives* gallery, which was filled with a riot of sound and color. I then went to the CRC, where RAs were preparing for the arrival of the community curators the next day. One RA mentioned that Rick West had emailed the staff his opening day speech; she was annoyed that he was not planning to thank the co-curators. This sentiment—that the community curators were being ignored—would only grow stronger as the week proceeded. For my volunteer work, the RAs provided a schedule (a stapled packet of eleven-by-seventeen spreadsheets) that included the days and times I would meet different co-curator groups at the various DC area airports, my "welcome desk" duties at the hotel where the co-curators were staying, and my scheduled times to visit the *Our Lives* exhibition with the Chicago, Kalinago, and Igloolik co-curators.

At 6:30 p.m., I went to Dulles Airport to meet the Igloolik co-curators. When they saw me, big smiles spread across their faces, and I was happy to see them again too. We rode back to the hotel through a torrential downpour. Because of weather associated with Hurricane Ivan, the Dulles Airport had been closed and then reopened just before their flight landed. The hurricane had also delayed the

Kalinago co-curators' flight, which finally arrived around 1:00 a.m. They had experienced a lot of turbulence and were noticeably relieved to be on the ground. Everyone was tired, and I brought them straight to the hotel. I got home around 2:00 a.m., exhausted—much like the "bleary-eyed" RAs, I noted in my field notes that day—knowing I was scheduled to be at the hotel "NMAI Welcome Desk" the next morning. The days that followed were just as hectic and long and wonderful as this one.

Visiting the Exhibits

On September 19, the co-curators were invited to visit their exhibits on their own. The Curatorial Department had insisted on and "fought for" this privilege, and it almost did not happen. Curatorial felt strongly about this symbolic gesture—that the co-curators should be able to see their exhibits for the first time alone and before the visiting public viewed them. A number of the co-curators later told me that this portion of their visit was their favorite and most meaningful experience of the week.[3]

In the first week of September, there had been a flurry of emails among the curatorial RAs, Ann McMullen, Bruce Bernstein, and me to plan for these visits. Teresa Tate assigned everyone to specific communities and suggested in an email, "Please ask your [assigned] communities if they want to do a blessing, what supplies they will need, how many people will be there, should it be indoors at their exhibit space or outdoors, do they have a preference to the time of day?" She then scheduled CRC staff (and me) to accompany the communities for their "quiet time" in the exhibits on particular days and times.

I was assigned to accompany the Igloolik co-curators Arsene Ivalu, Madeline Auksak, Leah Otak, and Zipporah Inuksuk for their scheduled time with their exhibit, 9:00 a.m. on September 19. (Theo Ikummaq, Terri Iyerak, and John MacDonald were unable to travel to the opening.) We went straight to the Igloolik exhibit, and they liked the "media inuksuk"[4] of stacked television monitors, but the video and sound were not operating. They spent about ten minutes in the space and seemed uninterested. This would change a couple of days later, however, when they returned and the video was running; then, they were pleased and patiently watched the entire presentation, spending more time now that the exhibit had come to life with the voices and moving images of family and friends.

When the Kalinago co-curators Garnette Joseph, Sylvanie Burton, Gerard Langlais, Cozier Frederick, Prosper Paris, and Jacinta Bruney entered the *Our Lives* gallery later that morning, they immediately noticed and talked about some spelling errors in the videos on display (for example, Sylvanie's name was spelled "Sylvie Nbutu"). They gathered next to the craft-shop graphic in the exhibit to do a blessing, lighting a tuft of sweet grass in a bowl (Bruce had made sure that fire alarms would be turned off during blessing times). A plume of smoke flowed steadily to the ceiling, and they circled in, close together, as Gerard led the blessing. Cynthia and I respectfully gave them privacy. After the blessing, she explained to the co-curators that, during the exhibit-making process, the media team stopped sending scripts to her and instead sent them to the scriptwriter/editor; that was why what would have been a glaring spelling error to her was overlooked and not corrected ahead of time (we reported the error to the media coordinator the same day, and it was corrected soon after). Cynthia soon went downstairs to a "donors brunch" while I gave a quick tour of the rest of the gallery to the Kalinago co-curators. On our way out, we passed the brunch, a fancy affair in the Potomac rotunda, with china and cloth-draped tables and an army of caterers laboring behind a privacy screen.

The Chicago co-curators' blessing time was scheduled for the following day, Monday, September 20—also during a catered event. As additional Chicago community members arrived at the museum to meet up with the co-curators, NMAI staff told them not to "stray" on their way to the *OL* gallery, because the preview reception was in progress. The Chicago co-curators were pleased with what they saw in the exhibit, except that the largest feature—a three-by-three stack of television monitors—was not operating. After they were all gathered within the curving walls of the exhibit, the community members formed a circle around the Chi Town drum encased in glass at its center. They had brought a videographer and a photographer to record the event; the video was later distributed as *From Wilson Ave. to Washington, DC*. The group passed tobacco, said a prayer, and took turns speaking. They asked Cynthia to join their circle, and one of her comments was included in the edited film: "Thank you for lending your expertise to this project."

Preview Reception and Co-Curator Dinner

Some of the co-curators of the inaugural exhibitions had expected to be honored for their contributions to the museum: perhaps they would give a speech or receive some sort of ceremonial appreciation. Many recognized upon their arrival that the scale of the event was far beyond their imagining and even their contribution, but curatorial staff were more critical of the lack of acknowledgment. Staff did manage to secure tickets for the co-curators (but not additional family members) to the preview reception. The Kalinago co-curators watched the spectacle for a while and then gravitated to the *Our Lives* gallery to talk with visitors in their exhibit (figure 7.1).

The only event that was planned specifically for the co-curators was a dinner reception at a Vie de France chain restaurant across from the museum; meanwhile, donors and dignitaries were wined and dined nightly in the museum itself. The co-curator dinner was a poorly lit, lukewarm buffet; it felt like a slapped-together affair, set under a canopy in an open-air cement area between office buildings. The Kalinago co-curators had actually lost their way trying to find this in-between space. And due to budget constraints again, only co-curators and one guest could come to this dinner; if more family members were in town, they had to find food elsewhere. Those who attended were polite about the circumstances, and people enjoyed finally

Figure 7.1. Cozier Frederick and Sylvanie Burton talk with a visitor during the preview reception; at the same time, their voices are heard in nearby exhibit videos. Photo by author. Reproduced with permission of the National Museum of the American Indian, Smithsonian Institution.

having a moment to visit with one another. But there were no speeches of appreciation and no visits from senior NMAI staff, except Bruce Bernstein—just the co-curators, some family members, and CRC staff.

It was an awkward experience for curatorial staff and all of us who represented the NMAI at the dinner. We made the best of the situation, but we were embarrassed at the banality of it and the obvious under-recognition of the attendees; it was all that the allocated money could afford after the travel arrangements had been made. But despite the dim light and the so-so food, NMAI staff members and co-curators enjoyed one another's company and took advantage of the opportunity to speak with people whose names they knew but whom they had never met.

Months later when I was in the Carib Territory, Prosper expressed his disappointment at never meeting any "higher-ups" when he was at the NMAI, although he knew that the curatorial staff ("you guys") had very little power:

> One of the difficulties…we had is that we only dealt with co-curators. We never got a chance to [meet] the director of the museum, for example, [or] some people [who] could take decision[s] for anything that would be a follow-up to what we have done. I thought that was bad. We had no communication with anybody—director, deputy director—anybody doing programs directly…[someone who

could say,] "Yeah, I'm a program manager for this, and we can help you in that area here." We saw some brochures…but that was all. I think that was a big gap between us and the museum [as far as continuing the relationship]. I mean, you guys were there, the co-curators were there, but you couldn't make decisions on behalf of the museum. As far as I know, if you didn't come back here, if Cynthia didn't come back and say anything, the linkage is closed. There's no link.[5]

Prosper had wanted to network, to find a way to have Kalinago crafts sold in the museum, or to get an invitation for the Karifuna Cultural Group to dance in the rotunda. Instead, the co-curators were limited to interacting with the NMAI staff they already knew. The rest of the museum staff were too busy or were uninterested in meeting the co-curators who had co-produced the exhibits or were simply unaware of the co-curators' presence.

But the co-curators were greeted with much pomp and circumstance the next day, even if they experienced it as part of a much larger group of Native Americans being honored more generally on the National Mall.

Grand Opening

Finally, September 21, 2004, the long-awaited day, arrived. To celebrate the opening of the museum, there was a procession of Native people along the National Mall, an opening ceremony with speeches by dignitaries and museum staff, and the launching of the First Americans Festival. The opening procession was a joyous and emotional experience for many who worked at the NMAI as they witnessed thousands of Native people arriving and the museum ready to receive them. They could finally exhale and enjoy the result of so many years of preparation.

The Native Nations Procession began at 8:00 a.m. and lasted four hours (plate 18). Picture taking was the most notable activity on the mall during the procession—by observers and by participants. Everyone was filming, snapping photos, recording the experience for friends and families back home—to document being a part of history or to record the exotic Others who had descended on the capital. The Chicago co-curators had a videographer, and the Kalinagos a disposable camera, to document their experience of walking in the procession.

The day was very hot under a bright sun, and many people waved fans in front of their faces or held them over their heads for shade. NMAI associate director Jim Pepper Henry (Kaw/Muscogee) was in full regalia and led the procession of tens of thousands of Native people from all over the world who were singing, drumming, and walking proud. There were young men in full regalia; other participants were in everyday clothes; some people wore buckskin hides; others were in elaborately colored cloth dresses. Some people marched with their nations (the Kalinago co-curators and Chicago co-curator Susan Power); others, with Native organizations (such as the AIC). Many Native people watched from the sidelines, calling out in solidarity with particular tribes and greeting old friends. Later, many people recalled chance meetings and unexpected familiar faces in the crowd—some of whom they had not seen since they participated in the activism of the 1970s. When the procession ended, all of the curatorial RAs and Native co-curators gathered to sit in folding chairs under a tree near the main stage to watch the opening ceremonies together.

At noon, the opening ceremonies began, and the first person to speak at length was Alejandro Toledo (Quechua), the president of Peru and an indigenous leader. Senator Ben Nighthorse Campbell (Northern Cheyenne) and Senator Daniel Inouye also spoke. Described by Campbell as the person most responsible for the creation of the museum, Inouye called the NMAI a "monument to the first American."[6] Then Inouye introduced Rick West, who, he said, "walks with mastery in both worlds"— the Native one and the world of law, politics, and museums. Everyone was clapping and standing when Rick took the podium.

Rick began, "For a decade and a half, I have thought about what I would say in the next seven minutes. I realize that no reflections of mine can possibly match in significance what we celebrate today on America's National Mall. But once in a great while, something so important and so powerful occurs that, just for a moment, history seems to stand still—and silent—in honor." The museum "uses the voice of Native people themselves to tell their stories," and it is a "symbol for the hope that the hearts and minds of Americans will welcome Native American people in their history and their contemporary lives." He spoke of colonization: "We are not its victims.... From a cultural standpoint...we have survived...triumphed." The museum is a "true cultural reconciliation." He declared, "To all here, welcome to Native America," and the applause was deafening. He continued after a pause, "To all Native Americans, welcome home!" And the crowd again went wild. West then spoke in Cheyenne about the great mystery, and, with everyone standing, the drums began to play as he exited the stage. He and the other speakers then went to the mall museum for a private ceremony inside.

With that, the First Americans Festival was officially under way; it would continue until the closing ceremonies on September 26. That afternoon, an Andean pan flute band played at the Potomac stage while the National Congress of American Indians hosted a "social dance circle" and a young Nakota man who was an award-winning hoop dancer. He was accompanied by his father, who sang and played a drum. Later, a Tlingit storyteller presented a commentary on Indians in the contemporary prison system through a story about how mosquitoes came to be. A performance by singer Buffy Sainte-Marie (Cree) capped the first day; her opening remark was "A dream should come true—and it did today!" This diversity of performers would only increase in the days to come, including scissor dancers and throat singers, and there were countless celebrations of humor, tradition, art, and athleticism.

There were Native people, in plain clothes and dance clothes, throughout the city—on the sidewalks, in the restaurants, and in the museums. This was a rare occasion, because most visitors in the NMAI were Native American. At the RAs' makeshift "welcome desk" in the Holiday Inn Capitol Hill later on opening day, some co-curators gave feedback to NMAI staff about the museum: "Outstanding! You all did an outstanding job!" By the next day, most of them were on their way home.

That night, I went to the hotel bar, which was a lively gathering place at the end of each day for the community curators and other Native individuals staying in the hotel. I sat with Igloolik co-curators Leah Otak and Arsene Ivalu. Leah, ever concerned about and dedicated to Inuktitut language preservation and learning, was telling me about her upcoming visit to an Inuit immersion school in Greenland the following week. During our conversation, a woman came up to our table and asked whether she could take a picture with Leah. Leah looked at her somewhat uneasily. I asked, "Where are you from?" The woman replied, "Kansas." I said that I was from Chicago; Leah said that she was from Canada. The woman asked her friend to take a picture of her with Leah and Arsene. The woman then explained, "I'm Dakota Sioux, and *you* were in the exhibit. That's why I want to take a picture of you." Leah replied, "Oh, okay." The woman continued, addressing Leah and announcing loudly to all who were sitting in the bar, "I'm Dakota Sioux. You did justice to your people. We're real proud of you. We have a lot of respect for you." Leah quietly said thank you with a smile. After the woman left, I told Leah, "You're a celebrity now!" and we laughed.

At the Cultural Resources Center in Suitland, Maryland, the final NMAI event of the opening week took place on September 24. This open house was an opportunity for the museum to show off its innovative collections space, as well as for visitors and Native people to visit with some of the objects. Big buses arrived each hour, and NMAI collections manager Pat Nietfeld gave each group of visitors an introduction in the rotunda. She talked about the building and its connection to the outside, the large windows in the collection space, as being "different." "It's not a warehouse," she said, like the collection's previous home at the NMAI Research Branch in the Bronx. She introduced the various departments at the CRC and then left people to explore on their own. They could go into the Conservation, Photo Services, or Collections Departments. Most people went into the collections area first. Pat pointed out the signs on the shelves saying "Don't Touch the Objects." But she added in typical CRC fashion, "That doesn't mean Native people can't touch their objects."

Even though the opening was an exhilarating experience for them, everyone working at the CRC open house was waiting for noon, when the event would be over. When the whole week would be over. They all wanted to go home, and everyone was looking forward to the weekend and to finally getting some sleep. It sounded as though they had not slept for years.

Intervention

"Before" is an ubiquitous word in the Carib Territory, as in "Before, we used to work together, but now we are selfish." Or "Before, we used to eat healthy," or wear a *waicou* (loin cloth), or walk days to get to market to sell crafts. This vague reference, "before," is never followed by a qualifier—not before Columbus, not before the road was built, not before the British invaded, not before the killing of 90 percent of the Carib people. Just "before." But it is clearly understood as the time when Kalinago cultural knowledge and practices were still "intact," without the influence of *neg* culture ("neg" is patois for "black man"). Similarly, though the term is far less pervasive, one elder in Chicago noted as she critiqued contemporary powwow attire, "Before, you could tell by the dress someone was wearing where they were from, but not any more." Now, everyone wants to wear jingle dresses, she added, because they like the way they look. But the Jingle Dress Dance is specifically associated with Ojibwe people.[7]

These fieldwork experiences helped me see that the opening day of the museum was a first encounter, a first contact, between the NMAI staff and the visiting public. It, too, signified a rupture between what the museum was "before"—a promise to an imagined public, its makers' hope for a paradigm change—and what the museum forever would be: a material reality traversed by, and responsible to, an outside public. Public culture was now in contact with the NMAI community—directly influencing the museum's practices and defining the museum through discourse. Although the audience, however defined, had always been present as an imaginative force influencing the work of the various cultures of expertise, the audience now inhabited the museum space. The comments of reviewers and the responses on visitor surveys would from now on influence the established philosophies and practices of the culture and knowledge producers in the museum. They would also show that, although the NMAI recognized and presented Native communities as experts, the public was not necessarily of the same mind.

During the exhibit-making process and after the museum opening, the NMAI was an intervention on two levels, public and private: in published articles and personal conversations, in the national media and around the water cooler, in the museum and in the social lives of its makers. As noted earlier, I am using a wider notion of "reception" than is generally put forward in media and museum studies. I have shown how the exhibit makers as subjects and objects were received in and by the museum. Now, I present the reverse perspective: the ways in which the exhibits were received and evaluated by insiders and outsiders and how, after the museum opened, the exhibition process affected those involved in its making.

Reception

The reception of the Native people in Washington, DC, was overwhelmingly positive and encouraging—for procession participants and observers alike. However, the response to the exhibitions was far more varied. Amid all the transitions occurring at the time of the opening—a shift in focus from the CRC to the mall museum, the loss of CRC staff, the hiring of new staff at the mall museum, and the radical change from a private to public existence—the long-awaited reviews from critics, scholars, community members, and visitors about the museum and its exhibitions began to enter into correspondence and talk around the office.

I do not provide here a summary of visitor surveys or newspaper reviews.[8] Instead, I focus on the details that can be accessed only through ethnography and an attention to everyday practice: which reviews circulated and were talked about most among staff (and were later represented in their written work), what the community curators said about the exhibits after seeing them, and how working on the exhibits affected the three communities with which I worked.

During the opening week and afterward, specific press reviews sparked a lot of discussion among the staff. The most common phrase I heard in response to these reviews was "They just don't get it." This was also the reaction of a visitor I encountered outside the museum on opening day, who told me that he had read the newspaper reviews. This sentiment was repeated in more formal settings, including in a memo to staff, in a museum-wide meeting, and in interviews I did with CRC and downtown staff. The first formal acknowledgment of the negative press, and an attempt to put it in context, came one week after the NMAI's grand opening. George Horse Capture (A'aninin [Gros Ventre]), a former curator, the special assistant for cultural resources, and a senior counselor to the director, emailed a heartfelt memo:

To: NMAI Administration and Staff
From: George P. Horse Capture

As we enjoy the long sought peaceful rest we can be proud and honored that we had the privilege to build the National Museum of the American Indian. Soon the elation and fatigue will give way to melancholy as this part of the circle closes and we see many of our friends, some of whom we worked with for years, begin to leave. The binding force that will keep memories alive over the years is that we shared an incredible historic experience together that will forever change, not only Indian country, but far beyond.

Some reviews have been critical of the exhibits, but that shouldn't dampen our joy, because we did something no one else has ever done and may never do again—build a national museum for the Indian people. Remember the tribes came from everywhere in unprecedented numbers to take part in the procession, their faces filled with great joy. I have never seen such a thing before and they made me feel proud to be an Indian. I had almost forgotten how pretty and proud we are. As we walked, I looked at the museum and felt the emotions of the Indian people around me and knew we had succeeded in our quest. Here are the people and there is their museum. Good and solid. Nothing can change that. Improvements are always made later, but now the buffalo has his nose firmly in the tipi—before we didn't even have a tipi. So those long hours, weekends and years of work [were] well worth it, you have helped to build a legacy. Celebrate in it, you all did a great job and now you have bragging rights.

Thanks, we all appreciate it.
George P. Horse Capture

This memo was greatly appreciated. Staff pride, staff exhaustion, the loss of staff, and the negative reviews were recurring themes as I spoke with people in my remaining few months in DC; these were also the main focus of the "all-hands" meeting the next day.

The morning after the memo was distributed, people gathered in the main theater of the mall museum, where Jim Volkert convened the first general staff meeting after the opening. I noticed that none of the curators were there; the meeting was being broadcast to the CRC by webcam. Most of the downtown staff and more recent hires like the mall museum's cultural interpreters were present. People settled down as Jim welcomed everyone back after their first week of working at a "truly world-class museum." He listed some statistics for the week: 112,310 people came through the museum, 161 memberships were made, the shops did $970,400 in sales, 8,640 rolls of toilet paper were used, 3,000 buffalo burgers were sold, and 54,000 glasses of wine were consumed. It had been an "extraordinary week," he said. "We got wonderful press."

Elaine Heumann Gurian, whom Doug Evelyn called "a guiding force in the background through the years," gave an emotional pep talk of sorts. She was a consultant who had been hired to help the museum get to the opening and as part of her work also contributed to the reorganization of the museum's departmental structure. But many staff members were not aware of the earlier role Elaine had played at the NMAI. She began, "For those of you who don't know me, I had the privilege of being in the first staff here, the staff *before* Rick, the staff that was seconded from other parts of the museum. And I left from here and went to the Holocaust Museum, and then ten years ago, I became a consultant who works with museums around the world as they build and then open. You are probably somewhere in the neighborhood of my twenty-fifth museum."[9] She compared her experience at the NMAI with her experience at the opening of the US Holocaust Memorial Museum and described the NMAI as a metaphor for "all the inspiration and hopes of the Native people of our land" and as a place that is "more than a museum," explaining that it is also "a civic space that talks about the ways...we need to treat each other and talk to each other." She became choked up and said, "*You* did it," and praised the work of the staff.

Elaine also addressed the negative reviews, framing them in a way that would later be reiterated by Rick West:

> The critics of this museum judged it as a museum. And I would venture to say that they thought your exhibitions were the reason you were in business and the Potomac was only a very large, quite outsized entrance foyer. *But the reality is, your exhibitions are 30 percent of your land mass* and the Potomac is where the heartland is.[10] So they didn't *get* it. But they are a small percentage—do not get fussed about the critics who didn't get it. Not that they were necessarily wrong. The exhibitions are not perfect. That's okay. The exhibitions were a direct conversation between the people who lived someplace who wanted to talk to others. And they do exactly what they're supposed to do.

Each time I heard Rick or Elaine say things like this, their tone implied *"only 30 percent,"* as though one should not judge the whole museum by something that *minor*. One interesting aspect of these twin responses—"They didn't get it" and only "30 percent"—is that the first phrase traveled among all groups inside and outside the museum but the latter was mainly associated with Elaine, Rick, and Jim, and it was sometimes shocking and at other times disappointing or depressing to NMAI staff.

Later that evening, I dropped into Cynthia's office to say hi. She brought up the *New York Times* September 21 article (Rothstein 2004a) and called it one of the few she had seen that was critical; she wished that there were more that provided such feedback. She also showed me photos of her family and her in the procession and talked about what a wonderful experience it was. She reiterated a common complaint among CRC staff at this time about all the "fancy" dinners for donors and dignitaries at the museum but nothing like that for the co-curators during the opening. Perhaps their being omitted from the acknowledgments in any formal or informal talks by senior management during and since the opening—including at the all-hands meeting—was a reason it surfaced again on this particular day.

"They Just Don't Get It"

The response that critics "just don't get it" is not unprecedented among culture producers. In Dornfeld's study (1998:170), the producers of the television series responded to critics by saying, "Our audience wasn't ready for us." In Macdonald's study (2002:209–210), the curators were surprised at the amount of criticism the exhibit received, declaring that reviewers "missed the point."

In general, I found that when people were talking or writing about the museum as a whole or critiquing the exhibitions in general, they were often referring to *OP*. The *Our Peoples* gallery was a controversial exhibition in its making and in its content both within the museum and without. In a study conducted in 2006, most visitor complaints were about *OP*, and *Our Lives* was not mentioned.[11]

The *Washington Post* did a number of articles on its front pages and in its Style and Metro sections prior to and during the week of the NMAI opening; the articles covered everything from the architecture and landscaping, to the dates and times for the procession and festival events, to reviews of the exhibits, cafeteria, and gift shops. Some of the articles were celebratory, others more critical. In one piece published before the opening, "In Tonto, the Museum Comes Face to Face with Its Biggest Faux," Hank Stuever (2004:C2) contended that the museum "doesn't unpack" stereo-types but rather "serves...an altogether new flavor of tourist Kool-Aid, redefined concepts of history, cosmology, spirituality, and diversity." But two articles in particular—often referred to as "the *Washington Post*" and "the *New York Times*" articles— were most often mentioned in staff discussions about reactions to the new museum.

"The Studious Avoidance of Scholarship"

Edward Rothstein's *New York Times* (2004a) article was the source of a particular phrase that traveled like wildfire in the museum as staff discussed his criticism that there was a lack of scholarship at the NMAI: "The studious avoidance of scholarship makes one wish that the National Museum of Natural History's American Indian Program, with its scholarly staff (directed by an anthropologist, JoAllyn Archambault, herself a Standing Rock Sioux), could have proceeded with its once-planned revision of its aging exhibits instead of having to close them down, scuttle hopes of renewal and slink into insignificance in response to its new competition."

Rothstein (2004a) concluded his essay: "The museum...seems satisfied with serving a sociological function for Indians of the Americas. It may indeed succeed, because it has packaged a self-celebratory romance. Understanding, though, requires something more. It is not a matter of whose voice is heard. It is a matter of detail, qualification, nuance and context. It is a matter of scholarship." Three months later, in an article that praised the work of Chicago's Field Museum, Rothstein (2004b) again touched upon the issue of scholarship at the NMAI: "Since almost no tribes had a written culture and oral traditions were disrupted by disease, massacre, government policy and assimilation, the tribal curators often seem to know less about their history than do scholars. Yet, scholars' assessments are ignored in favor of self-promotional platitudes."

Staff reactions were often incredulous. In response to the reviews, Gabi Tayac said, "The level of checking was extremely high." She asked in exasperated disbelief, "Not scholarly?"[12] The charge of a lack of scholarship seemed tragic to those who espoused a collaborative ethic and the ethos of advocacy, whose knowledge of history, museology, and anthropology informed and prompted their commitment to Native voice and its authority and expression in the museum. Casey MacPherson, the lead RA for the *Our Universes* gallery, said, "You know, all the criticisms—I've seen the paper talking about our lack of scholarship and stuff. And I think, what a bunch of hooey." He insisted that NMAI staff "know exactly what it means to achieve a high standard of scholarship and research." He saw the NMAI's work as "push[ing] the envelope": "We wanted to have these people from these communities tell their story. Why is that somehow less academically stringent? It blows my mind." He dismissed the review as "an old-fashioned way of looking at the world," a "case of sour grapes in some other institution," or a result of talking "about philosophy," for example, in the case of *Our Universes*, "to people who don't have a philosophy" (meaning, the reviewers). "Have we fallen down?" he asked. "Yeah, most certainly. But there's a lot to be learned from *that* [*banging the desk with his hand*] aspect as much [as] from the things that we felt like we succeeded, too.... We've never made any bones about what we were doing, and we went out and did it and kept going forward, you know? Pretty fantastic."[13]

Anthropologists Ann McMullen and Bruce Bernstein responded directly to the "lack of scholarship" critique in a document they wrote for the Research Committee of the NMAI board of trustees in an attempt to contextualize the unexpectedly negative response to the exhibitions and to foster discussion among the board members. Their view was that the museum's philosophy, as it was carried out in the displays, was not persuasive in establishing Native voice as authoritative:

> What is clear from the reviews is that NMAI's dependence on Native voices—without "conceptual rigor" and without integration with other sources, versions, or voices—makes the exhibits and their content distinctly unpersuasive. The direct question posed is "Why should visitors believe what the museum says, including what Native people say?" This suggests that NMAI has failed to make a case for Native voice as an authentic source by not providing visitors a foundation in the essential subjectivity of all sources—Native or non-Native—and failed to explain its own epistemology in bringing forward Native voices and depending on them for the authority of the exhibits. (McMullen and Bernstein 2004:4)

Ann and Bruce felt that there needed to be more contextual information about the methods, processes, and underlying theory for creating the exhibits. But Rick West, one staff member told me, did not let the board talk openly about the critiques. Rick, "in top form," as one person recounted, steered the discussion by saying that the exhibits reflect the next phase in museology, intimating that the reviewers were unprepared for what they saw. He also told the board not to judge the museum on its exhibitions alone, that exhibits are just *one* thing they do. The staff member remarked on this, "But museums *are* judged by their exhibits."[14] According to the curators, one of the more poignant comments by a board member at the meeting was, now that the museum is open and "We are still here" has been established, what message does the museum want to convey next?

"Skin-Deep"

The second critique that most often circulated among staff was represented in an article by Marc Fisher that came out the day of the opening, "Indian Museum's Appeal, Sadly, Only Skin-Deep" (2004). This article contended that the museum's form was beautiful but its content was disappointing. I see this criticism as linked with senior managers and consultants' emphasizing that the exhibitions are only a small portion of the overall institution. Fisher touched on both "the lack of scholarship" (the museum not giving the audience the tools to "judge" Native stories as accurate) and the "30 percent" (a beautiful building with disappointing exhibitions) critiques, but Paul Richard, the *Washington Post* critic, was more infamous among NMAI staff.

Richard (2004) had a more positive view of *Our Lives* than did Fisher: "The 'Our Lives' exhibit, in which various tribes suggest the various ways they live, is more coherent, and more poignant." But it was embedded in a similar review of the museum as "skin-deep": "The new museum that opens to the public today is better from the outside than it is from the in." Like Rick West, Richard contended that "what's best about the building is that it isn't just a museum. It's a reparation, and a reconciliation." But, at the same time, he raised the specter of a lack of scholarship, a missing expertise: "One of the museum's problems is the extent to which it *does not discriminate*. Are ancient painted bowls made before the white man came and those thrown for the gift shop equally authentic?" (emphasis added). He recognized and affirmed that Native Americans have survived and their stories deserve to be presented, but he contended that this was not done "with enough precision and discrimination so that they are believed."

I met with Rick West in November 2004 to talk about his reflections on the opening of the museum. We sat in his office, a bright, sparse space with floor-to-ceiling windows along one wall that led to a balcony, on the fifth floor of the mall museum. The office was tucked away in a corner off a curving corridor, which made it quiet and peaceful in comparison with the sea of cubicles, desks, and chatter on the other side of the floor. Rick first commented on what George Horse Capture and others had noted: the museum was "a kind of symbol." Rick felt that it indicated "a *shift* in the cultural consciousness…in this hemisphere, about the *place* of Native peoples in the history of the hemisphere, [and] their role right now."[15]

When I asked specifically about his "personal response" to the exhibitions, he answered first with the "30 percent" line of reasoning before he brought up the reviews that staff had been talking about. He noted the almost *"obsessed* quality on the part of people who look at museums and talk about what they do," assessing *only* the exhibitions. He called the museum a "cultural center" and emphatically insisted that it "is *not* just the objects, but it's about the people who made the objects": "I want people to understand that in terms of how I would fundamentally *define* this place…. I *don't* look just at exhibitions." He went on to talk about the reviews, separating what he considered to be "the intellectual wheat from the chatty chaff." His comments reiterated what he had said in board and staff meetings and in his conference papers. He also mentioned the notorious articles: "the *New York Times* review, the [*Washington*] *Post* review, and then derivatively the thing that showed up on the electronic magazine or whatever it was, *Slate*—which really kind of came from both of those."

The *Slate* article, "The National Museum of Ben Nighthorse Campbell: The Smithsonian's New Travesty" (2004), was less frequently mentioned by name, but Timothy Noah's point did become a topic of discussion (and some staff agreed with his assessment): Campbell was a US senator who had helped to implement the NMAI, and having a temporary exhibit about his jewelry crafting in the museum at its opening constituted a conflict of interest. But Noah was also critical of the "museum's botched debut" and of West, a former lawyer who was not an "experienced museum director." He suggested that an experienced director would "seek legitimacy among scholars, and we can probably expect quiet changes in that direction over the next few years." Noah also predicted that "Native Americans, too, will likely chafe over the museum's amateurishness—if not now, then after the achievement of getting it built fades into memory. But why should we have to wait? The Smithsonian should have gotten it right the first time."

Rick appreciated some of the critics but dismissed others as not understanding "what they were bumping up against": "*This* institution, in a very, very fundamental way, has turned the museological paradigm...*on its head*." Before, "the *influence*, the *expertise*, the exposition all sat *inside* the institution"—and now it rests in Native communities. Then he cited Claire Smith (2005), whose review inspired his "2005 major speech topic" ("Journeys in a Post-colonial World"), noting that although he can talk about theory, how staff members "spin it" on the exhibit floor is more challenging. He hoped that future exhibits would not "involve a departure in principle from letting these voices *speak* in as unfiltered a way as is possible." Clearly, Rick felt that Smith was on the right track, that she "got it."

As he walked me to the door, Rick noted that when Native people come to the museum, they "get it"—they understand it as a place for Native communities. He asked, "Do you think Paul Richard would understand that? No way." Non-Natives, if you pull someone off the street, "they get it too." He surmised that non-Natives "get it *inversely proportionate to their expertise*." But others have "just enough museological expertise to be dangerous," each approaching the museum with a particular set of expectations.

Ruth Phillips (2006:79), in an article comparing the Canadian Museum of Civilization and the NMAI, referenced the *Times* and *Post* articles and commented that "the reviewers missed the point." Kyle MacMillan's "DC Indian Museum Keeps Dialogue Alive" (2004) was an article that I heard Rick West appreciated. MacMillan wrote, "Notions among critics, curators and members of the public about what museums are and should be remain very much in flux. This became clear during recent heated disagreements over the new National Museum of the American Indian in Washington, DC"; he specifically referred to Noah's *Slate* piece and Rothstein's first *New York Times* article. He then quoted Nancy Blomberg, the curator of Native arts at the Denver Art Museum, who emphasized that the NMAI's "stated mission is to give voice to native communities in their museum" and that it had accomplished this. She said, "For centuries, there has been enormous mistrust between museums and Indian Country.... And they have worked very hard to overcome that mistrust and to make Indian people...feel a sense of ownership and pride in this museum. That's no small accomplishment." MacMillan concluded, "Who's right in this debate? Who's to say?"

Scholars circulated, and often took issue with, these notorious reviews in their work (see, for example, Berlo and Jonaitis 2005; Reinhardt 2005). Scholars in museum anthropology specifically praised the community-curating process and the intention of the NMAI to "disrupt past paradigms," as Phillips (2006) put it. However, as the work of Amy Lonetree (Ho-Chunk) suggests, some Native scholars felt that the museum "missed an opportunity" to highlight the colonial encounter and genocide in the Americas (2006, 2012; see also Lonetree and Cobb 2008). For both Native and non-Native scholars, although the emphasis on Native voice and the community-curating process was generally commended, the content of the exhibits left many dissatisfied.

At the NMAI Scholar Symposium on September 20, 2004, the day before the museum opened, Rick W. Hill Sr. (Tuscarora), a former NMAI assistant director of public programs when the main facility was in New York, reminded the audience that, regardless of the work that goes on in museums, work in the communities is more important and needed. He had quit most museums he had worked for, his "disgruntled" departure from the NMAI included. He added that "Native people speak with their feet," which he did when he left, but that thousands would come tomorrow to celebrate the opening of the museum. "Despite the spotted history of the museum," he said, "[they still] hope this museum might do better than the other museums." It is this "sense of hope" that would bring them. "But we're also realists." Hill emphasized that the money spent, millions of dollars, would not go to change communities; the NMAI "is still a museum," a "federal facility." He challenged the notion that it is a "Native space," as a sign outside proclaimed. At one point, he noted dryly that they spent "$150 million on the museum" but "they forgot to buy a remote," as he called out for someone to advance to the next slide, adding, "Maybe this *is* an Indian place after all!" and everyone laughed.

Hill's presentation recounted the changes that have occurred in Native life, including boarding schools, alcohol abuse, and museums' theft of objects from their communities. He showed Native artwork—both contemporary and hundreds of years old—that either represented or provided the opportunity to evoke discussion about these changes. He also talked about how the saying used to be "The only good Indian is a dead Indian" but nowadays seems to be "The only good Indian is a dancing Indian.... We feel we have to perform for you to get you to listen to us."

Hill emphasized that the museum is not the "real stuff." He talked about the "commodification" of Indian cultures through museums and the commodification of Indians through the collection of DNA samples. He asserted that tobacco (for prayer and ceremony) is more useful in preserving Native culture than is the museum: the "real stuff" is tied to their beliefs. In the end, he said, "My search for the good museum is a foolish search." But, he acknowledged, there is an "awful lot that holds true to the original vision" of the NMAI: there is "Native voice there, and some objects *do* sing."

Visitor responses were also mixed, and a 2005 NMAI visitor survey of the *OL* gallery concluded, "Though it was not what they expected, most people enjoyed the *Our Lives* exhibit. They liked the personal accounts and media usage; they liked seeing things they knew and learning new things. They understood the central themes of the exhibit: identity, survivance, community, and modernity. The complaints include[d] way-finding within the exhibit..., being overwhelmed, not finding specific tribes/communities, and a lack of history."[16]

According to Carolyn Rapkievian, most visitors were disappointed because they "want[ed] a history lesson," something "chronological" (as opposed to cyclical or thematic). She said that visitors did get the message that Native people are here today and that they are diverse: "We are getting that across." They also "get" that the "museum is from the Native perspective." Those are the three things "that visitors are getting," but, she added, "beyond that," they are not getting "some of the deeper messages."[17]

Impact of Exhibits (and Their Making) on Communities

In addition to the negative press reviews, positive reviews traveled among staff—some from the press but most from Native community members. The general vibe in Indian country was a positive one, but that was in part related to the fact that the museum existed at all. The Native community members who participated in making the exhibits mostly liked the galleries and felt that their work and voices were accurately represented in the museum. But the impact within their own communities that participating in exhibit making has on collaborators—during the process and after the exhibition is completed—is a particular kind of reception that often gets overlooked in projects with originating communities, such as *Our Lives*. Here, I compare the effects of the NMAI intervention on communities both in and at a distance from Washington.

Generally, in places that are more remote and not in the United States, such as Igloolik in the Arctic and the Carib Territory in the Caribbean, participating in community curating had little community-wide impact. The people in Igloolik had worked with museums before and were quite blasé about it until they saw the final product and were beaming at the familiar faces in the videos on display. For the Saint-Laurent Métis of Manitoba, the experience sparked a cultural center project in their community because they had won awards for their exhibit and were recognized in Canada for their contributions to the NMAI. Meanwhile, for the museum professionals community—the curatorial staff—working on the exhibitions created tensions with their colleagues and further destabilized their role in the museum and in future exhibit-making processes.

Curatorial Department: Increasing Uncertainty

During the development of the inaugural exhibitions, participating in community curating had profound effects on curatorial staff, who were more trusted by Native communities but acquired a reputation for being "obstructionist" within the museum. The "lack of scholarship" and "30 percent" critiques were particularly harsh blows to curatorial staff, who had not only paid a great amount of scholarly attention to their work but also dedicated years of their lives and in part staked their professional identities on the exhibits.[18] They felt underappreciated and that other departments did not really understand what they had done, how they had achieved these exhibits, and why. One researcher told me, "I don't think [the mall museum staff] have the *feeling* that we've all put into it. I think that's the hardest thing to get over."[19] Cynthia told me, "[But] you don't do it because it's a job. You do it because you *believe in something.*"

I discovered during my fieldwork that behind Rick West's comments about the exhibits being 30 percent of the museum's real estate was another, less publicized but nonetheless acted-upon, conclusion. Elaine Gurian told me that she had written a letter to Rick that made two points after the opening: exhibits are not all the museum does (Rick had clearly taken up this point), and the NMAI had to "break [the] hold of curators as translators," to remove the "arrogant curators" and the Ph.D.'s from the process. She said that the curators just would not "give content over," which was a problem.[20] Elaine added that part of the "worldview" of Indians is that they "don't trust Ph.D.'s."[21] She suggested that Native artists—she gave the examples of Truman Lowe, Gerald McMaster, and Rena Swentzell—would make better "guides" or "translators" for exhibits than curators do.

The poor reviews—or at least the impression that they were overwhelmingly poor, which resulted from a focus on art and museum critics rather than on Natives and academics—provided some after-the-fact justification for the weakening of the Curatorial Department's role in the museum. As described in chapter 3, the department was basically gutted: researchers were let go, curators were reassigned to other departments, and project managers were put in control of future exhibits. The reorganization was not a direct result of the reviews, however, and was a long time coming: the result of consultants' recommendations, a shift in museum practice to an exhibit-developer model, and a stated desire to make the bureaucracy more efficient and businesslike. The lack of appreciation for the curators and co-curators, along with the widely discussed, negative reviews and the loss of research assistants, seemed to cause NMAI curators to further retreat into their own projects after the opening.

Chicago: Making the Most of National Exposure

Joe Podlasek estimated that about 10 percent of American Indian Center members had visited the NMAI. The Chicago urban Indian community, through its exposure in the museum, experienced recognition on a personal scale. At powwows, Chicago co-curators would be greeted by other Native individuals with "I saw you in the exhibit!" Participation in the *Our Lives* exhibition also afforded the multitribal group a more public recognition as a Native *community*; community members mentioned their inclusion in the NMAI in everything from grant applications to public gatherings. As already mentioned, the Chicago group recorded their experience attending the opening in *From Wilson Ave. to Washington, DC*. The video won an award and was later sold in the AIC gift shop and in the NMAI.

The community was also made more visible regionally; for example, a *Chicago Tribune* reporter (Kilian 2004) used the occasion of the NMAI opening to recount the history of scientific racism in the Smithsonian, to highlight Chicago's participation in the *OL* exhibit, and to notify his readers that there are more than thirty thousand Indians in the Chicago area. The article even quoted Ed Two Rivers from a text panel in the Chicago exhibit (see figure 5.8).

There was also a sense of revitalized energy in the Chicago community as a result of participating in *Our Lives*. Eli Suzukovich was working at NAES College as an archivist in the early days of the exhibit-making process, and he was at the first meetings between the NMAI and Chicago community members. We spoke in January 2005, a few months after the opening of the museum. "Had the Smithsonian exhibit not come about," he said, the community would not have realized how "unique" it is. "Because a lot of people were really shocked that Indians from across the United States picked *Chicago* [instead of a different city].... It brought back some pride" and advanced his own goals of highlighting the community's history and encouraging people to reflect on the community's impact on "modern attitudes."[22] Cyndee Fox-Starr corroborated Eli's observation: "I think I value things a lot more than I did before"; she had not realized that many everyday things she did, like her beadwork, were valuable and appreciated.[23]

Participating in the exhibition lit a "fire under their asses," one AIC member said with humor about the community. It was directly responsible for their being offered a property in the suburb of Schaumburg to open the Trickster Gallery, dedicated to displaying and supporting the work of contemporary Native artists. *OL* co-curator Dave Spencer was the first arts director for the gallery. Working on the exhibition also empowered some community members to expect more reciprocity from the institutions with which they worked. One co-curator told me that she had been invited to sit on a committee as a consultant for the Field Museum, which was working on a new exhibition about Native North Americans. When the museum refused to consider a relationship like community curating with its Native consultants, she chose not to participate.

Kalinagos: Struggling to Share Their Experience

For the Kalinagos in the Carib Territory, there was a sense of pride in being selected, but it was realized only in the few people who participated directly in the exhibit and traveled to Washington, DC, for the opening. In Dominica, there was little acknowledgment or knowledge of the opening of the NMAI or the Kalinago exhibit, although Sylvanie said that, when she returned to the Carib Territory, some people did tell her they were looking for the co-curators in the television coverage of the Native Nations Procession on opening day.

The Kalinago co-curators desperately wanted to share their experience—not just to show the community what they accomplished but also to allay particular suspicions and to demonstrate the opportunity the community had in participating in the exhibit. In all the community meetings, co-curator meetings, and even individual interviews, community members wanted to know what they would get back from the museum. The Kalinago co-curators had requested from the museum a video of the NMAI and their exhibit in order to show their community what they had done in DC and how their community was portrayed in a major international museum.[24]

The museum never provided the video, however, so instead I prepared a slide presentation of photographs of *Our Lives*, which the co-curators offered in each hamlet of the Carib Territory. On the evening of June 6, 2005, at the Sineku preschool, Cozier presented the slides. At the end of the meeting, a well-recognized resource person from the hamlet thanked us and asked what the community would get back from this experience. Cozier mentioned two possible benefits: Kalinago crafts might be sold in the museum, and a tour company from Canada had expressed interest in the Carib Territory (by way of a Saint-Laurent Métis co-curator). But neither of these possibilities came to pass, despite our efforts.[25]

A week later, Sylvanie gave a presentation in the Carib Council Office to people living in the Salybia hamlet. As I was taping to the walls copies of some text from the exhibit, which featured many names familiar to the gathered community members, Sylvanie said, "You know, Jen, we get so many people coming to the Carib Territory who take information, and we never see them again. I never expected this would happen, but the NMAI kept coming back." She said that it was a real surprise. Sylvanie introduced her presentation by sharing this same sentiment with the audience—that in the Carib Territory, it is frustrating the way things end up not happening. The co-curators did not know whether it was really going to work out, despite spending so much time at these meetings. But the NMAI kept coming back. She said that the museum "collected exhibits" (objects or artifacts) but quite a bit was not used because there was little space in the museum. "We sent a canoe, but you do not see it in the exhibit," she explained. And then she showed them the images of their exhibit.

Like Cozier, Sylvanie anticipated the community's primary concern: "You might ask about the benefits." She, too, mentioned possible craft sales but added, "We are seeing some benefits already." She then recounted the story about the Pamunkey woman who came to visit the Carib Territory (see chapter 5). So, Sylvanie concluded, another benefit is that people will see the exhibit and come to the Carib Territory. And at the least, they will "know we are not extinct." That, too, is a benefit, she said. In the five years the exhibit will be up, at four million a year, that will be twenty million people attending—"Learning about us," she said.

It was important for these co-curators to discuss openly their work with the NMAI because there was suspicion from community members and from the recently elected chief about their involvement in making the *Our Lives* exhibition—not so much for being selected to co-curate it, but because they were paid to travel to Washington, DC. For example, Chief Charles Williams had written a letter to the NMAI demanding an explanation for why a former chief (co-curator Garnette Joseph) and other individuals, rather than the current chief, were invited and paid to go to the museum opening. This played into existing tensions between the current and former chiefs. Williams's email was passed along from department to department until it finally reached Curatorial just prior to my visit to Dominica in September 2004. The museum never responded in writing, so it was left to me to explain in a one-on-one meeting with Chief Williams that the museum's arrangement was to provide funds for community curators and not heads of state. It was important to the co-curators to validate that their travel was legitimate, that they earned it, and that it was not a mishandling of funds or for personal gain.

Furthermore, as mentioned earlier, because of the tight budget provided to the Curatorial Department for co-curator travel, only six of the eight co-curators were given travel funds. The Kalinago co-curators selected the six who attended the most meetings; Alexis Valmond and Irvince Auguiste were unable to go. Being left behind for such a momentous occasion fostered resentment, as I learned when I reviewed the exhibit-making process with the co-curators. In the Chicago community, some individuals paid their own way to attend, many traveled by plane or bus to see the work of the co-curators and to participate in the procession, and still others would see it later at NMAI powwows. But the Kalinagos did not have the means to visit the museum, nor did they have access to the same amount of media coverage to feel connected to the opening events and the exhibition.

Conclusion

A CRC staff member said that many people at the NMAI felt "brain-dead" after the opening.[26] There had been immense pressure to complete their work in time, and the overwhelming response from Indian country was a heady and exhausting experience. Many commented that they felt they were witnessing "history in the making." The spectacle of the procession was unprecedented, and its purpose a simple one: to celebrate the lives of Native people and to make visible their continuing presence in this hemisphere.

What has become clear is that performance does not concern only Native people and expertise is not held only by museum professionals. The dual interpretations of the co-curators—who were seen as both symbol and expert, as both Indians in the procession and exhibit makers—were responded to differently by the museum and the public. In the procession, the public was quite comfortable with Indians as (recognizable) signs of themselves, through song, dance, regalia, and difference. And this more general form was the only specific recognition arranged by the museum for the co-curators. They were praised in the museum's rhetoric as symbols, as "Native voice." However, the exhibitions failed to persuade many reviewers that Native voice constituted legitimate expert knowledge for a museum. Although most visitors and reviewers considered community curation and the exhibitions authentic representations of Native peoples, they did not necessarily think that these represented good museum practice—contrary to the perspective of the NMAI curators and the co-curators.

Although the Native co-curators were essential to producing the symbols and content that represented Native voice and Native identities in the museum, when the community curators arrived in person at the institution, they were not honored or recognized in a way that was expected by some NMAI staff.[27] Despite co-curators' prominence as symbols and objects on the walls of the museum, they were barely acknowledged as experts or creative subjects outside the confines of the gallery. They were visible as symbols but not formally recognized as creative agents by the museum—not through events, speeches, or interactions with upper-level staff. Native voice was publicly praised as a concept, but those who provided its substance were not celebrated by name or as individuals.

The juxtaposition of the "tribal donors brunch" and the dinner "reception" for the co-curators made a stark contrast that led some CRC staff to comment bitingly that the museum cared more about money than about Native communities. The museum lavishly feted and honored donors of material capital, but not donors of symbolic capital. Cynthia articulated what a number of other curatorial staff members told me: "The co-curators weren't really recognized or really identified for their contributions to the exhibits."[28] Her reaction to this neglect was to facilitate their perspectives' being heard, by inviting them to speak at conferences with her. I, too, tried to remedy the situation, by creating slide shows and doing other follow-up with the communities I had worked with. But after the inaugural projects were completed, there was little formal contact on behalf of the museum with the co-curator communities.

According to NMAI intern Meg Birney's visitor research study, carried out under the direction of Carolyn Rapkievian in October 2004 and titled "NMAI Visitor Study: Memories of the NMAI," "the two most memorable things at NMAI are the building, and the Lelawi Theater." Not the exhibitions. Despite the best efforts and wishes of both NMAI staff and Native Americans, the exhibitions made only a brief intervention in local, national, and international media and political discourses. However, the media coverage did bring to the fore a fundamental debate about scholarship—including who defines it and what constitutes it—in public and academic discourse. This debate over the legitimacy, content, and review of collaborative exhibitions is also about the status of Native voices as expert knowledge.

From the perspective of the politics of expertise, the writing of reviews is also performance, as much as walking in a procession or crafting an exhibition area. As a scholar from the Smithsonian noted at the American Anthropology Association meetings in 2005, the NMAI is a "political statement...not a museum." How one evaluates, writes, or speaks about the NMAI, then, can be a political matter and have professional consequences. In this sense, there is a "performance of expertise" in which a reviewer's article can also be seen as a political statement. Museum professionals who work with Native people appreciated the NMAI as a feat, as a model for contemporary practice, and as a necessary methodology for Native American–museum relations. They celebrated the presentation of Native voices, which likely aided in their building trust relations with other Native communities. But art critics and press reviews clearly wanted to see some scholarly "facts" from "Ph.D.s" up on the walls as well. They wanted more direction in judging which objects and which community self-representations were more or less authentic and accurate. These views are quite divergent and polarizing: either Native voice lacks scholarship and thus requires a particular kind of "expert" substantiation or interpretation, or Native voice is finally being validated *as* expert knowledge, a long-awaited and ethical commitment to self-representation.

Similarly, the main NMAI responses to the negative reviews can be viewed through the lens of the departmental ideologies, and they illustrate staff performing their expertise. Those who espoused an ideology of advocacy said, "They just don't get it." Those who espoused an ideology of translation said, "Exhibits are only 30 percent of our real estate." To put it bluntly, the former asserted the changing paradigm and wanted to maintain the integrity and value of the community-created content (consequently responding through greater contextualization and transparency about the *process*); the latter contended that this is what happens when museums rely on amateurs and wanted to rewrite or reframe the content (consequently contextualizing the *product*).

In *Being Ourselves for You*, Nick Stanley (1998:63) notes the "stubborn resistance of an audience to revise its stereotype" of indigenous people. Meeting the goals of the NMAI and the co-curators required evoking a particular kind of reception in the audience and critics alike. But as we know from media studies, audiences are "active" in making their own interpretations, and as we know from museum studies, audience members walk into the museum with their own past experience and knowledge, which influence how they interpret what is on display. Although the NMAI endeavored to present Native co-curators as experts, audiences did not always respond favorably to this refiguring of an object (the American Indian) as a speaking subject (expert knowledge producer).

Stanley (1998:168) also provides a provocative question to consider with respect to the reception of the NMAI, its exhibitions, and its practices: "Is it going to be judged in terms of performance or representation?" My answer is that it has been judged as both. This is in part why the reviews were so disparate, and it is also at the heart of the dichotomy between process and product, advocacy and translation. When the NMAI was judged as a performance—a process—of equating Native voice to other experts in museological discourse, it was praised; when it was judged as a representation—the product of this process—of Native people, it was criticized.

It seems, then, that collaboration is considered ethical practice in the museum and is appreciated and celebrated but its product has yet to be widely accepted as authoritative. The critique that there was a "lack of scholarship" in the exhibitions could be based on two aspects: the exhibitions' organization and content and the knowledge form in which that content was communicated. Collaborative knowledge production, particularly the community-curating process, placed certain constraints on the NMAI curators. They alone did not direct the content of the exhibits, and even if they had particular ideas they wanted to convey, they could not do so through the community-curated exhibits, except perhaps at the widest level, through the gallery themes and organization. Perhaps the NMAI curators, more accustomed to museum exhibition and academic discourse than were most of the community curators, could have created an exhibit crafted to avoid particular kinds of critique. Instead, they shared authority and considered the infusion of different perspectives from community curators in the exhibit making to be instructive, meaningful, and valuable. In response to those who might consequently think that collaboration leads to forms of censorship, Patricia Erikson (2004) discusses the tension between what she calls "academic freedom" and scholarship in collaborative ethnography and auto-ethnography. Academic freedom is not compromised, she insists, but rather accounts are made more accurate and new forms of theory and insight are produced through such collaborative work (see also Kreps 2003b:155; Wylie 2008:3).

Community curating, as a form of collaborative knowledge production, incorporates different cultures of expertise in its authorial practice and challenges conventional notions of scholarship. Its product, "Native voice," was at the heart of the museum's philosophy and ethics, regardless of where one sat in the organization. Native voice is a form of knowledge that is presented as first person, plural (we), possessive (our), narrative, and descriptive. It speaks directly to the visitor in a conversational tone. The paradigm change that NMAI staff desired requires recognizing this form as expert knowledge, as more or at least equally legitimate and informative as the literature of credentialed scholars who have studied Native communities. Public resistance may in part be due to the fact that "voice" itself, as a medium of representation, is usually associated with activism, protest, and performance rather than with scholarship. It is associated with oral history and personal perspective rather than with written history and "facts." Native voice may be a publicly recognizable genre, but it is not always recognized as an expert one.

Whereas the political and ethical reasons for collaboration are often discussed in museum anthropology, an epistemological reasoning is cogently argued by the philosopher of social science Alison Wylie. The criticism of the NMAI's inaugural exhibitions can be read, in part, as what Wylie (2008) calls a "misrecognition of expertise." Through this concept, Wylie offers a possible explanation for why the genre of Native voice was not seen by many as a source of authoritative knowledge (see also L. T. Smith 1999:174–175). She explains that "socially marginalized communities are not credited with knowledge or expertise they actually have even if it lies in areas that are intelligible on, and valued in terms of, dominant norms" (Wylie 2008:11).[29] There is also a "double misrecognition" when marginalized communities "have cultivated distinctive forms of knowledge that are, to varying degrees, unintelligible in terms of the norms of credibility...in dominant culture" (ibid.). The benefits of knowledge produced at the margins is that it can help us all to think outside the box. Accordingly, including alternative expertise and ways of knowing can contribute to a "critical standpoint on knowledge production" itself (ibid.:11–13). Therefore, "the rationale for collaboration arises not only from moral obligations to descendent and affected communities"; it is not only the right thing to do, but it also has "epistemic payoff" (ibid.:3).

Wylie's rationale is based on the notion of situated knowledge (Haraway 1991), in which our subject position influences what we know and what we determine to be legitimate knowledge. "Epistemic injustice," then, arises when our situated knowledge, our standpoint, causes us to give too much or not enough credibility to particular ways of knowing or particular kinds of knowledge (Wylie 2008:11, citing Fricker 2007). Making space for these other ways of knowing is a part of what decolonizing the museum entails. Therefore, the paradigm shift must include not just a recognition of Native knowledge as expert knowledge but also a recognition of the value and legitimacy of the various forms in which this knowledge is conveyed. Rather than describe this form of knowledge production as collaboration with underrepresented peoples, perhaps it is more accurate to say that it is a form of knowledge produced through collaboration with people who are overrepresented *by others*, including various media, scholars, and institutions. The dominant culture's expectations then disrupt the reception of Native voices if those voices do not reinforce those expectations.

The hope among the staff and co-curators was that the collaboratively produced exhibits about Native Americans would replace the stereotypes and assumptions about them in the popular imagination with more accurate representations. The preliminary reception of the museum in the public sphere, however, suggests that, although museum professionals were willing to recognize Native people as experts, the new paradigm butted up against popular conceptions and attitudes to the point that some people—one education staff member said, about half of the visitors—were unwilling to accept Native voice as authoritative in the museum. Perhaps as the museum ages, and through the personal experiences of its millions of visitors each year, there will be a cumulative impact that will continue to work toward achieving the goals of the museum, its staff, and the Native communities featured inside.

e i g h t
Reflection

The Honor Wall, Gift of Reconciliation: Help us keep our promise to Native peoples by inscribing for posterity on our Honor Wall. When the museum opens, it will signify more than a commitment kept by the Smithsonian. It will be a historic act of reconciliation and cultural justice, an act to which you can add your name.... As millions of visitors to the Museum walk along the balconies overlooking the central public welcoming space called the Potomac, they will see your name and thousands of others who have helped us keep our promise.

—*NMAI appeal for donations, 2004*

For as much drama as there was, [the NMAI is] very successful.

—*CRC staff member, 2006*

I said to my husband, "This is the best thing I've ever done. It's the best thing I've ever done with my life."

—*Downtown staff member, 2004*

As Paul Chaat Smith (Comanche) has noted, "Indians are everywhere and nowhere at the same time."[1] In the United States, Native Americans are largely invisible in public and political spheres, except in towns situated near reservations. And when

Native people *are* made visible, they are often the object of hateful and misinformed speech, like the road signs along Highway 81 in upstate New York, posted by angry non-Native locals near the Onondaga Nation. In 2008, one billboard read, "ONON-DAGA NATION WHERE TRADTORS, RAPISTS AND MURDER'S RULE" (spelling per origi-nal).[2] Many pass these vitriolic signs near Syracuse with little understanding of what they mean or what the conflict is about.

Today, many non-Natives think of casinos when they think about Native Ameri-cans—yet the people who run the casinos are somehow not considered "real Indians" (see Cattelino 2008). The centuries-old, stereotypical image of the Plains Indian figure wearing a feather warbonnet and living in a tepee or the New Age image of an environmental steward or a shaman are ubiquitous in popular culture.[3] Beyond these popular fantasies, the contemporary lives of Native people are relatively unknown, and some non-Natives think that they no longer exist. This changed on September 21, 2004, if only for a brief moment, with the widespread publicity about tens of thousands of Native people attending the opening of the National Museum of the American Indian.

When the NMAI was being planned and imagined by its makers, it embodied hope for its constituency and the promise of authenticity for its audience. Once open, the museum celebrated its collaboration with Native people: telling their stories and privileging their voices in the telling. The NMAI's staff and supporters—in academic conferences and in publicity materials—insisted that its work and presen-tation embodied a paradigm shift in the representation of Native people and their relationships with museums.[4] The work of the museum to drive this paradigm shift was part of what motivated staff to participate in conferences and to work long and hard at their jobs, sometimes in the face of adversity. For the *Our Lives* gallery in particular, part of the challenge was to complete the exhibition in one-third the time and with half the money, compared with the other exhibitions. Many believed that the gallery would become a Day 2 project; its completion for the opening was considered a triumph of will, hard work, and overtime.[5]

Both NMAI staff and community curators felt that the long journey to open the museum was difficult—for different reasons—but most saw the work as rewarding nonetheless. As the third epigraph above shows, many staff members felt that working on the inaugural exhibitions was a major highlight, if not the pinnacle, of their career. In the political and power center of the United States, from "drama" they had forged a dramatic display of Native peoples' diversity and vitality. This journey was guided by a mission that insisted on collaboration. Although the museum's mission was inter-preted differently over time, by 2000, the instituted methodology to fulfill this com-mitment to work in collaboration with Native peoples was community curating.

By focusing on the collaborative process, we have seen how the *OL* exhibit acquired its "thingness" and how text and imagery became "Native voice," and we have examined the responses of different groups as to whether these constructions satisfied the museum's promises of authenticity and authority. The discourses, practices, and ethics of advocacy and translation entailed different ways of knowing and different relations with the reflexive subjects of the museum's exhibitions. Native voice was constructed not only through material representations but also through the social relations of its producers: the originating communities and the museum staff. Native voice was not just the authored text in the exhibit. It also included the anxiety, commitment, and advocacy that NMAI staff *and* Native co-curators brought to the process—interacting with one another and being responsible for one another within their own communities.[6]

Instead of a multivocal exhibit—created through community curating, collaborative authorship, and reliance on the committee form, all of which would engender a consensus approach to knowledge production—the result was artifacts that presented an authoritative group voice and a unified thematic content for each community. This was far from what the NMAI staff had envisioned in 2000 during the vetting session for the gallery's premise. The collaborative knowledge production employed to create the *Our Lives* exhibits did not just invoke particular forms of agency in the bureaucratic structure of the museum but also relied on the committee as a particular form of social relations and decision making. This generated exhibits that were bounded (community centered) but not static, with the "community" as agent and author in each exhibit. Factors like technology, hierarchical structure, budget, and time also affected the content. And the collaborative form of exhibit making put on display particular forms of bureaucratic sociality: committees, compromises, consensus, division of expert labor, and specialized knowledges.

"Identity" began as a neutral category and was filled in through the contributions of co-curators and the (para-)ethnographic work of NMAI curatorial staff. Similar to Annelise Riles's (2006b) account of "gender" between brackets in a United Nations document, "identity" was a debated term that on the exhibit floor seemed always already settled.[7] The production of identity for display, then, was a social, material, and self-conscious process crafted for a particular audience. These exhibits of Native life held the promise and ideals of authenticity and of a more inclusive conceptualization of expertise, authority, and authorship; they embodied hope for a new way of doing things. In practice, the conceptual ideals were subverted at times by well-established institutional practices, hierarchies, and ways of thinking about and responding to Native identities and museum displays.

Visitors may assume that museum exhibits are displayed as they were always meant to be. But each exhibition, through its multiple authors and multiple specialists and through its architectural, budget, and design requirements, represents instead a series of compromises among competing commitments, interests, and visions. As a museum staff member in 1999, I had anticipated a uniquely successful intersection of postmodern engagement and authoritative representation in the museum (Shannon 2009). However, I found during my fieldwork that the authority of the Native communities that provided the content of these collaborative exhibits, while not overtly contested, did not satisfy many reviewers both within and outside the museum. Although the NMAI staff was not able to construct Native voice as an authoritative voice in the museum, the staff did create trust-based relationships with *Our Lives* contributors and accurate representations, according to those who worked closely with the co-curators. This was essential to establishing the NMAI as a Native place.

When the museum opened, non-Native and Native people, the US government and the tribes, and the museum and its constituencies were all looking to see whether each group had kept its promise to the others through the vehicle of the museum. The NMAI staff hoped that it would generate and reinforce a paradigm shift, that it would radically alter how people viewed Native American identities, histories, and worldviews. An unpredictable product of ethical injunctions, the museum was an experiment and a risk. Some found it lacking, only partially living up to its promise. Others, like George Horse Capture, felt that the opening and the reception by Native people indicated a process that had "come full circle" and was a modest beginning of a larger sea change—a first step into the mainstream of US public culture.

Mainstream culture did not provide, however, the necessary resources to enact director Rick West's original vision of the museum as a symbol of reconciliation. In addition, this rhetoric faded over time, and his later formulation emphasized the museum as a "civic space" (West 2005). These two views of the NMAI—as reconciliation and as civic space—map onto the advocacy-versus-translation conceptualizations of the museum's purpose. It is not surprising that the rhetoric of reconciliation did not take hold, because it is not a common term in the United States, compared with Australia, for example. The US public in general knows little about the insidiousness of settler colonialism and the US government's history of systematic campaigns to destroy cultural knowledge, social ties, spiritual and family practices, sovereign rights, and access to resources. There is no general or institutionalized recognition of the genocide against Native peoples in the founding of the United States, nor any sustained discourse about the boarding school era, nor are American Indians prominent in the contemporary life and politics of the country. This history is much more complex than what is generally taught in our schools today. Perhaps, as time goes on and more people visit the museum and the museum matures, these issues will become part of a broader public conversation and be included in public education in the United States.

Politics of Expertise

The main themes in the *Our Lives* exhibition—collaboration, Native identities, and representations of indigenous peoples—have been widely discussed, theorized, and critiqued in anthropology and museum studies. My approach has been to present the story of an exhibition in the making, rather than a critique of a completed exhibit, in order to better understand what collaboration entails in everyday practice, to understand what it means beyond simply an indication of ethical practice. Ultimately, my account of the making of the NMAI inaugural exhibitions is about the politics of expertise, the rise of representational experts,[8] the exhibition of and by reflexive subjects, and the shift of the locus of authenticity from object to subject. At the heart of the matter is a concerted effort—one that encompasses debate and resistance—to redefine the boundaries of scholarship and expert knowledge to include a particular, and collaboratively produced, form of Native knowledge.

As I have discussed throughout this book, "collaboration" was a ubiquitous term in NMAI discourse and has become common in museum and cultural anthropology more generally.[9] It is most often invoked to indicate ethical practices, more equal power relations, and unfiltered representations in cultural production. These aspects were evident not only in the term's central place in the mission statement of the museum but also in the staff's reiteration of the value of collaboration in their conferences and presentations. And all of these aspects were challenged from inside and outside the museum.

By viewing exhibition making through the politics and cultures of expertise, it is clear that collaboration is a process fraught with conflict and contestation, consensus and compromise. The contestation is obscured and the compromise is embodied in the final exhibit text and display in *Our Lives*. Using the lens of the politics of expertise, we have seen the ways in which various experts attempted to frame, and to justify, their work and its significance to their colleagues and a wider public. We have also seen that some genealogies—such as anthropological theory and practice—were antagonized or silenced in NMAI discourse.[10]

Each culture of expertise—Curatorial, Exhibits, Kalinago, and Chicago—had its own shared language, speech networks, common conceptions of its identity, recognized specialists for the tasks at hand, imagined audience, motivations for participating in exhibition development, and ideology for how best to represent or work with Native people in the museum. All of these cultures interacted with or through the bureaucratic structure of the museum, which did make sincere attempts to accommodate its constituencies. However, notions for how best to make these accommodations varied according to where a person sat in the organizational structure and the physical locations of the NMAI bureaucracy.

The complexities of the museum bureaucracy were most apparent in the epic battle between two major cultures of expertise: the Exhibits and Curatorial Departments. Virtually every staff member commented on this dynamic within the NMAI (and within many other museums). At the heart of this conflict were two opposing ethics, forms of agency, and notions of best practice. Curatorial staff stood in a unique mediating role: they worked on behalf of the museum in the Native communities, and they worked on behalf of the Native communities in the museum bureaucracy, often in what was perceived as an antagonistic relation with other departments. Exhibits staff, on the other hand, insisted that translation was necessary and believed that they would make better exhibits by mediating between the communities and museum visitors. When we look at the division of labor represented by these cultures of expertise, we see a set of dichotomies inherent in museum structure and practice, including process versus product, form versus content, and textual versus visual. But these are false dichotomies. Content is constrained and enabled through the movement from two dimensions to three, the transformation from ideas to documents to fabrication, the winnowing and reduction of collected conversations and objects, and the juxtaposition of objects, text, and audiovisual media. All of these factors and more affect both process *and* product.

Perhaps the struggle within the museum between the Exhibits and Curatorial Departments was in part due to the outsourcing of some of their most central and traditional roles in exhibition making. The development of the *OL* gallery's visual and structural form was contracted to design firms; the development of the gallery's text and content was largely the responsibility of co-curators and, later, hired scriptwriters/editors. The former was intended, but the latter was considered by some to be a usurpation. Each department struggled to assert its jurisdictional boundaries and control the quality of the work, essentially becoming information and people managers in the process: curatorial staff became facilitators of content produced by groups outside the institution, and exhibits staff became project managers within the institution.[11] These developments were due both to the new paradigm the NMAI espoused and to circumstances in the wider field of museum practice, where control over exhibitions has shifted away from curators and toward exhibit developers in a team approach and a museum's primary role is now considered to be service to its audience more than to its collections. The 2005 departmental reorganization was described by some NMAI staff as the "triumph" of Exhibits' philosophy over Curatorial's.

By 2011, the NMAI had gone through several more reorganizations and was no longer practicing community curating as it had for the inaugural exhibitions (C. Turner 2011). However, the process through which the NMAI developed its inaugural exhibitions was crucial to its portrayal of Native voice and thus to its legitimacy in Indian country. To establish a positive relationship with Native communities and with the individuals displayed on the gallery's walls, an interpersonally driven sharing of authority was crucial. But as the museum's changing exhibit-making practices and bureaucratic structure suggest, the museum is a reflexive institution that is continually adapting as it receives feedback.[12] This openness to critique and change can be seen as both promising and troubling. For example, an excellent response to an internal critique at the NMAI—that no African American–Native people were represented in the inaugural exhibitions—was provided by Gabi Tayac, who curated the exhibition *IndiVisible: African–Native American Lives in the Americas*, which opened at the mall museum on November 10, 2009 (see Tayac 2009). This responsiveness can be seen as striving to be better, to be at the leading edge of museum practice, or to correct oversights, but also, as one former staff member commented, it can leave staff feeling no stability, no sense of direction.

Addressing Michael Ames's question about whether changing representations of indigenous peoples in museums are "challenging the curatorial prerogative," multisited research revealed that the curatorial prerogative *was* challenged from within the museum and at the same time was invigorated through work with Native partners on the outside. Traditionally, as Ames (1999:42) explains, the curatorial team was considered the authority in exhibit making, but the curatorial prerogative has been challenged for quite some time in museums (Terrell 1991; Witcomb 2003).[13] In the case of the NMAI, this challenge was complicated, even facilitated, by curators' willingness to relinquish content authority to Native people. This allowed other cultures of expertise within the museum to shrink the jurisdictional boundaries of the Curatorial Department and push curators to the periphery.

On the one hand, curators were criticized for not asserting their expertise, and on the other hand, they were accused of hoarding knowledge and being too protective of it. The exhibits staff's main criticism of curators who labored on the inaugural exhibitions was that they failed to employ sufficient museological expertise when working with Native communities, that they just did whatever the communities told them to do. This was not the case, as demonstrated by the subsequent *Listening to Our Ancestors* exhibition, which used a community curator model in which no NMAI curator was assigned to work with the communities; there was a publications representative, a scriptwriter, an education representative, a project manager, and a conservator. In the postmortem for *Listening to Our Ancestors* (see epilogue), the NMAI faulted some community curators for not having enough museum expertise and thus requiring staff at the NMAI to assist or write for them. This internal review also noted, "The curatorial role needs to be actively filled" (Mogel 2006:9), though who should fill that role is open to interpretation. Perhaps the special skills the *OL* curators brought to the table—as mediators and facilitators—could have been useful. It seems that, in trying to kill the *idea* of the curator/anthropologist so entrenched in the museum and Native communities, an understanding of the value of the Curatorial Department, which championed the sharing of authority between them, was lost.

I would argue that the substance of the curatorial prerogative, when collaborating with originating communities and particularly at the scale of the NMAI, has changed over time, from a specialization in content to methodology. Although curators are no longer necessarily assigned to particular projects according to their specific area or subject specialty, the methods they use and the training they have undergone to achieve that specialty are what is most important to collaborative exhibit making. Anthropological and social science training matters in this new era of collaborative work, and it is different from—though complementary to— museum training. As curatorial practice moves out of the institution and into communities and as museums more accurately represent Native peoples—which is paramount—I hope that the antiquated stereotypes of curators and anthropologists will also be reconsidered. Unfortunately, these stereotypes persist despite the role of anthropological theory and critique in the crafting of community-centered and collaborative methods of museum curation.

(In)Visible Genealogies

The *Our Lives* gallery could be seen as the epitome of the neo-Boasian approach in that it illustrated a history of each community's present, told through that community's own texts. The gallery was also a demonstration of how Native communities themselves were perceiving and grappling with an emergent world. Curatorial staff, with their ideology of advocacy and their belief in the intrinsic value of Native voices, mediated between the bureaucracy and the communities, exemplifying the Americanist tradition. The ethical imperative of collaboration (in the form of community curating) can be seen as both a derivative of the Americanist tradition of anthropology and a result of working with and responding to the demands of Native people.

Regna Darnell discusses the nature of the relationship between Americanists and their audiences, as well as issues of authorship in ethnographic relations. She writes that, as Americanists, "[we] are more accustomed to worrying about the reactions of the Native people who read what we write and impose their ethical and political agendas on us than are colleagues who work in distant areas" (Darnell 2001:18). This was a main curatorial concern at the NMAI and continues to be mine as well. It seems that this was also the NMAI leadership's stance, at least, early in the process.[14] Darnell explains that many texts by Native producers were recorded under the names of the anthropologists who collected them. But, more recently, there has been a "transfer of ownership of the words back to the language community of the original speakers. Appropriation of knowledge expressed in words is just as significant, in local terms, as appropriation of materials or skeletal remains" (ibid.:17). This "transfer" was directly evidenced in the NMAI's insistence on text panels authored by Native community members involved in the community-curating process, rather than anonymous curatorial texts. Similarly, Darnell notes that "Americanist texts have always resulted from consultation and collaboration": "They are not 'our' words but 'theirs'" (ibid.:15). One of the reasons Boas felt strongly about working with Native collaborators like George Hunt was his belief that Native people are the experts on their own traditions and it is important to have full command of the language to understand the meaning of what they think and say (Boas 1911:62). This sentiment is reflected in the NMAI's commitment to Native co-curators as experts on what it means to be Native and to their telling their stories in their own terms.

Despite all the indicators that the methodology and philosophy underpinning the very mission of the museum can be traced in part to the Americanist tradition in anthropology, along with the Native American rights movement, the NMAI has tended to conceal its own genealogies and epistemology. It is ironic that this museum, with methods shaped by Native interlocutors, informed by anthropological critiques of representation, and reflected in the changing nature of relations between anthropologists and Native people, has such an anti-anthropology bent—especially considering West's praise for the changes in the discipline of anthropology over time.[15] Not only has the institution been described to me, both positively and negatively, as "anti-Ph.D.," "anti-curator," and "anti-anthropology," but it has also been described as "anti-intellectual" by Native intellectuals who have worked on behalf of the museum.

Much of this attitude was revealed in public discourse. For example, associate director Jim Pepper Henry told one reporter, "We're not an anthropology museum. We're a museum of living cultures" (Achenbach 2004:R1); he said that the museum's authoritative voice has been replaced by many Native voices. The same news article quotes Gerald McMaster saying, "Anthropology as a science is not practiced here" (ibid.:R7). To be fair, the "anthropology" to which they refer is likely the archaeology of long ago and the stereotyped extractive "anthros." In contrast, the work of the curators reflected a humanistic if not scientific anthropology, one that included understandings of postcolonialism, human subjects protocol, and collaborative and reciprocal research relations. The NMAI curators practiced a contemporary Americanist anthropology.

In the same piece, Rick West contrasts the NMAI with what a "straight anthropologist" might do: the NMAI puts "Native peoples, in their first person voices, at the table of conversation about Native peoples and Native communities, past and present. That is a distinction compared [with] what straight anthropologists might be doing." The reporter commented that "such words are declared without harshness or bitterness, but there is a long history behind them, one that Natives find painful. 'Anthropology' and 'archaeology' are very close to pejorative terms in Indian country" (Achenbach 2004:R7). Distancing themselves from the field of anthropology seemed to be a rhetorical device and an act of political positioning by some museum personnel, and praising or panning the NMAI was doing similar labor among reviewers.

Anthropologist Bruce Bernstein, one of the architects of the community-curating process, said, "The gist is that this place isn't designed for the entertainment of tourists—despite the museum's hope that it will attract 4 million to 6 million visitors a year. It's meant to be 'useful' to Natives" (Achenbach 2004:R7). Bruce described the museum as providing an "inside-outward view." The reporter comments that the inaugural exhibits were "carefully created...visually striking, but not spectacular" and concludes his article by stating that the NMAI was "an artifact of a nation trying to understand itself circa 2004" (ibid.). I would suggest that the museum was an artifact of collaboration in which Native communities were trying to get a nation to understand *them*, their lives and cosmologies and histories, circa 2004.

Mediating Identities

In addition to responding to indigenous people's critiques of museums, a commitment to collaboration and Native voice seeks to address the anthropological critique of representation. Collaboration provides an opportunity for communities to engage in what Faye Ginsburg (2002[1995]:228) calls "mediating identities," or the various ways indigenous people attempt to "gain visibility and cultural control over their own images" (see also Myers 2006:504–505). The NMAI in this sense *co-produced* Native voice, as opposed to the problematic notion of *giving* voice. However, as Kahn

(2000:71) suggests, although collaboration establishes productive and ongoing relationships with Native communities, it does not correct past problems of representation: "Although the recent changes are a step in the right direction, museums cannot simply add multiple voices, itself a response to an academic—and, specifically, postmodern—critique." The main issue in presenting Native identities to the public, then, is not just about creating better representations. It is about who has authority and control over representations to create more equal relations between communities and museums (ibid.:72). This is a main tenet of decolonizing the museum.

One main reason that Native people became involved in the NMAI was to take control of their own images on this national scale, particularly in relation to the silences and distortions in US public culture and education. This desire is a part of indigenous media production more generally—to tell the world how they "truly are," as a Kayapo leader says in the introduction to a Kayapo-authored video (T. Turner 1992:8), or as Rick West states in an introductory panel about the NMAI, "[To tell] who we are, and to use our own voices in the telling" (National Museum of the American Indian 2004; see also American Indian College Fund 2001). The NMAI is, as Ginsburg's model suggests, an institution that mediates Native identities, and this is exactly what making the *Our Lives* gallery entailed. Although the NMAI was not alone in making it so, in a commentary in *Museum Anthropology*, Nicholas Thomas suggests that the paradigm has indeed shifted:

> Critics, including indigenous activists, have become curators, and the newer generation of curators has been trained by critics. A postcolonial understanding of the ethnographic museum has entered the mindset, not of the whole of the museum profession but of most of those who deal with ethnographic material and contemporary native art. Hence, in many institutions, though certainly not universally, it is anticipated that originating communities are consulted around exhibition or research projects, and they are indeed increasingly full collaborators. If this has become business as usual, then it is surely positive, but it is perhaps also a sign that the issue of representation is no longer the right place to start from. (Thomas 2010:6)

I hope that, by our focusing on the politics and performance of expertise and on the mediation of identities, the concept of Native identity can be unmoored from being analyzed solely as a form of political maneuvering (or identity politics) and instead be situated within a wider global recognition and misrecognition, expectation and rejection, of specific forms of knowledge in the public sphere.

Decolonizing Practice and the Ethics of Collaboration

The NMAI inaugural exhibitions were an experiment in collaborative representation and a sincere effort toward decolonizing the museum. No doubt some form of commitment to Native voice will continue at the NMAI. Although community curating was originally a process unfettered by buildings or publics or codified rules and was accountable mainly to the Native people with whom the museum worked, it and its product are now being confronted by the demands of the Smithsonian bureaucracy and the visiting public. Exhibit-making processes continue to evolve, and the future of community curating is uncertain, but it is likely to continue in some manner.

The NMAI was not the first, but it certainly was the most widely publicized institution to make the commitment to decolonizing methods through collaboration in the museum. The sheer scale of the endeavor provided visibility to and increased scrutiny of the products of collaboration, although less so its processes. The high profile of the museum provided the impetus for debate and dialogue not just in academia and museums but also in the popular media. The public and scholarly debates centered on whether Native voice should count as expertise and scholarship and whether the NMAI was, indeed, a decolonized museum. As noted earlier, if we embrace ethnography's focus on a Native point of view, what matters here is that the museum professionals interpreted their work on the exhibitions as decolonizing practice—whether or not they spoke of it in those specific terms (by 2005, the director had publicly adopted this term).

Although decolonizing the museum is an important goal to guide our endeavors, I do not believe that any nontribal museum can ever be completely decolonized when housing the objects or knowledges of Native peoples. I do, however, think that museums are useful, meaningful, and worthwhile for Native and non-Native people alike. And decolonizing the museum is not just about how a museum represents Native people or whether it makes its collections and resources available to originating communities. Decolonizing is also about how Native people unsettle researchers and curators, such as when a First Nations community member challenged one of my museum studies students by saying that there should be *no* objects in museums and that all objects should be returned. Decolonization is a rebalancing of historical relationships (which is never complete) in the present interactions between people, not just the big-picture ideas of how representation is changing or whether a display adequately represents genocide and colonialism.

In April 2012, I attended an event at the Denver Museum of Nature and Science that featured a video titled *Everything Was Carved*, in which participants in a collaboration between the Pitt Rivers Museum and the Haida Nation reflected on their experiences together.[16] Afterward, freelance curator Vince Collison (Haida), who was featured in the film, told a few of us in informal conversation that it was clear to the Haidas that the museum had coached its staff in preparation for the consultation (for example, to allow extensive object handling by tribal members). But, he added, "We also had to coach our community members." He encouraged them not to get angry if they saw something offensive, but to understand that the museum staff were doing their best. And if someone did get angry at something, he added, then everyone needed to be debriefed so that all parties would understand why. This two-way coaching is happening more and more as Native peoples and museums endeavor to work together. And the more we can provide evidence like this video to the public about the motivations and processes of collaboration, the better.

Much of the work toward decolonizing the museum goes on behind the scenes and away from the public eye. But it is important, as Sue Rowley of the University of British Columbia Museum of Anthropology told a class of aspiring museum professionals, to tell the public why. If we do not explain the process and how and why this is part of a commitment to restorative justice and decolonizing the museum, a great opportunity is lost. By sharing with the public how and why we engage in collaborative practices with Native people in the museum, we highlight the colonial situation and model ethical relations in working with, representing, and talking about Native people. For example, if a museum simply omits an object from a display because a tribe considers its public viewing inappropriate, the visitor never sees the item and assumes that the display is whole. However, if we place the object in the case, if appropriate, but have it wrapped and concealed from view, with a label to explain why, the visitor comes away understanding that the museum and the tribe are in conversation, that not all items are appropriate for all viewers, and that the museum made a choice to honor the tribe's request.[17]

The practice of decolonizing the museum occurs in interpersonal relationships and institutional commitments, as well as in the content and subject matter on display. In my work at the NMAI and since, I have come to realize that decolonization is not just something the museum does; it is what tribal members do as well. Decolonization occurs in the dynamic social relations and interpersonal moments of unease and uncertainty during the processes of museum and community work, in the experience of anxiety and concern, whether you fit in the "anthropologist slot" or work on behalf of others, whether you are a researcher or a community member, whether you are Native or non-Native.

How do we craft productive and respectful partnerships between originating communities and museums? As Chip Colwell-Chanthaphonh at the Denver Museum of Nature and Science has argued, a set of rules is not the most effective way to guide the interactions of those dedicated to collaborative work with Native communities. His argument for "virtue ethics" in many ways explains why the ethical injunctions, or the CRC's "right way" of working with Native people, were so successful in creating positive relations with the communities featured in *Our Lives*. Colwell-Chanthaphonh suggests that collaboration should be guided by a "broad and deep-rooted commitment to virtues such as respect and trust...[and] entails the cultivation of sincere relationships guided by virtuous ideals—civility, tactfulness, patience, thoughtfulness, tolerance, and honesty" (2009:7; see also Colwell-Chanthaphonh and Ferguson 2004, 2006).

"We often agonize about trying to do the right thing," Colwell-Chanthaphonh (2009:9) writes. "There often are not obvious right answers.... Historically, ethics have worked in productive conjunction with political and historical analyses to raise important questions of privilege, ownership, authorship, and participation. Not only is there little evidence that we should reverse this course now, but there is ample evidence that now more than ever we must think about the ethics of our work."

Effective collaboration is driven in part by this agonizing. Morality, ethics, and value making are key aspects of contemporary museum practice and representation, particularly in the framework of decolonization. The values of respect, reciprocity, and open dialogue can help us continue to teach each other how best to work together in light of the troubled history between museums and Native peoples (Colwell-Chanthaphonh et al. 2010:10–11).

Decolonizing practice also insists that our language matters. How we refer to the people we work with—as informants or as interlocutors or as partners—matters. Whether we call them advisors or consultants or co-curators matters. The language used in museums is certainly changing, and collaboration and its associated terminology have become normalized when working with Native peoples. Today, museum staff are more often referring to what are legally termed "human remains" as "individuals" or "Native ancestors"; in the past, they were called "specimens." We now say that a collection is "housed," not "stored." These changes, being based on consultation with Native peoples and acknowledging their values, reflect and shape our practice. NAGPRA consultations and digital catalog projects are additional areas in which museums and Native communities are working together. Native knowledge is now explicitly sought in addition to other forms of expertise to better understand, document, and care for collections.

Collaboration is always a negotiation among research and museological goals; commitments to the scholarly community; Native community desires and responsibilities to community members; and, the social and institutional constraints under which we work together. But these are not mutually exclusive interests: many scholars and community members, from museums and tribes and academic anthropology, support collaborative work. Today, there are many examples of collaborative museum projects with Native peoples, but none so large—twenty-four tribes at once from the entire western hemisphere—or so prominent as the inaugural exhibitions of the National Museum of the American Indian. Because of its scope and visibility, the NMAI brought decolonizing practice and the ethics of collaboration to the fore in public and academic discourse. Now that this institution has established that Native Americans are "still here," the next message it chooses to communicate, and how it will do so, remains to be seen. But there is no doubt that the NMAI is now a highly visible space in which Native Americans can communicate to the world.

Epilogue

Listening to Our Ancestors

While I was in Dominica in 2005, I called Ann McMullen, who updated me on what had gone on at the museum since I left. Staff were starting to talk about what she and I had talked about, including "What is community curation?" and whether they wanted to continue doing things that way.[1] In 2006, I returned to the museum for three months to see what NMAI employees were working on, what they had learned from the inaugural exhibitions, and how that experience had influenced later projects. *Our Lives* team members Cynthia Chavez (now Chavez Lamar), Taryn Salinas, and Arwen Nuttall were no longer at the Cultural Resources Center. I spent more time at the mall museum as a volunteer during this period, conducting visitor surveys for the Education Department and interviewing people about *Listening to Our Ancestors: The Art of Native Life along the North Pacific Coast*. It was the most recently opened community-curated exhibition and provided some clues as to the future of community curating at the NMAI.

In the preface, I ask the question "Who killed Curatorial?" There were many possible "suspects," including the staff of the Exhibits Department and their competing exhibition philosophy, the consultants hired to make the museum run more efficiently, the exhibits that failed in the eyes of some reviewers, the "abdication" of content authority from NMAI staff to Native communities, the prevailing model of exhibition development, which invested more control in project managers and put more emphasis on the visitor, and the devalued role of anthropology in the Native museum. Like what killed the electric car, it was not any one thing; a web of factors, persons, things, and attitudes led to the demise of Curatorial. The department had functioned precisely the way it was directed to work on the inaugural exhibitions. However, by the time of the museum's opening, the principles that had led the NMAI to select and define the community-curating model that Curatorial implemented were being questioned.

The museum used a very different model of community curating for the *Listening to Our Ancestors* exhibition (see chapter 3). It relied on contracts with cultural institutions in Native communities, worked mainly with established professional culture producers and curators in those communities, returned object selection to the start of the exhibit-making process, and did not include an NMAI curator on the exhibition team. In addition, the community curators were responsible for physically writing the script, which was then edited by an NMAI scriptwriter/editor. This did not always work out well, as community curator Lindsey Martin's concerns make clear: she wondered what "Native voice" was after it was mediated through the institution of the NMAI, and she felt that what was on the exhibit walls did not represent her voice. Meanwhile, the project manager for *Listening to Our Ancestors* sought more, and more formalized, staff feedback on the exhibit-making process. The absence of the Curatorial Department after the reorganization and the lack of an NMAI curator working on the new exhibit indicated a significant shift in protocol and practice at the museum.

Although there was no official debriefing after the inaugural exhibitions opened, some lessons learned from them were embedded in project manager Barbara Mogel's (2006) postmortem document about *Listening to Our Ancestors*. Some relevant highlights: the museum preferred partnering with institutions; the tight schedule was not a good model for future efforts; too many researchers were let go after the opening; there should be two exhibit opening events—"one for and guided by the communities…and the other…a reception style event for NMAI donors, political constituents, etc."; and "community curators need to be engaged in a more accountable contractual process" (Mogel 2006:2, 4, 12).

On the one hand, it is reiterated a number of times in different ways throughout the document that staff wanted more access to the communities; on the other hand, it recommends that NMAI staff learn more about the communities and community curators before working with them. In addition, in what appears to indicate the possible demise of community-directed content development, in a section titled "Quality Control," the review states, "NMAI assumed that the person chosen by the [contracted] institution was mutually agreed upon by the community: this was not always a correct assumption. There were conflicts of authority that NMAI should avoid in the future…. How NMAI picks who we partner with is still a problem…. *No matter how content is developed*, we still need object care and consultations with the community(s)" (Mogel 2006:10, emphasis added).

The *Listening to Our Ancestors* postmortem also indicates the following:

> The consultation with the community curators needs to be in the form of "roles" presented as job descriptions (for example, Tribal Historian, Museum Director, Hereditary Chief, etc.), that clearly identifies for each "role" the unique responsibilities for NMAI and the community curator, and specific deliverables appropriate to that "role." All expectations need to be clearly defined from the beginning, *but always focused on the final product—the exhibit.* The individuals in the communities can then pick which job description best meets their expertise, and NMAI can better understand the staff resources needed to execute the project. (Mogel 2006:10, emphasis added)

And there were "new rules" the team felt should be put in place: after a step or "deliverable" is completed, it cannot be revised or changed by an individual; each team member must meet deadlines "or be willing to be removed from the team"; and "those who miss deadlines cannot expect the rest of the team to make up for the missed deliverables" (ibid.:13). In these prescriptions, contrary to the assumptions and practices of the inaugural exhibitions, the intent is to codify the process and to render it inflexible in practice and content; consequently, the product, rather than the process, appears to be of the utmost importance.

Finally, in a section titled "Future Work with the Communities," the document states, "NMAI's and the communities' outcomes did not match for the Washington, DC, exhibit. This will be evidenced when the objects return to the communities in 'Phase II' as possible changes in object selections, and text." Rachel Griffin, an anthropologist and a curatorial research assistant during the making of the *Listening to Our Ancestors* exhibition, provided some insight into how these outcomes did not match.[2] She noted in particular the disjuncture between Native curators' emphasis on the beauty of objects and their insistence that these are not (just) art. In the end, this point was not successfully made due to the "limited budget and schedule" and the perception of "audience." For *Listening to Our Ancestors*, Rachel explained, the publications staff focused more on Native objects as "art," and "the determining factor in publication decisions [was], how will the product be received by the purchasing public?" (Griffin 2005:16). In her essay, Rachel advocates on behalf of Native communities whose wishes, she felt, were not honored as directly as they should have been. She restates her faith in collaboration between Native communities and museums to "advance our understanding of Native American objects beyond that of simply art, anthropology, aesthetics and authenticity, towards a more informed and accurate—although complex—consideration of the material" (ibid.:19–20). And she seeks more accurate representations through partnerships with Native communities.

Collaborative projects are, as this book has shown, full of logistical and technical challenges and meaningful relationships, and the debates over how to represent and who can represent, what to share and what to keep private, are ongoing. Meanwhile, the NMAI's inaugural exhibit-making process and collaborative model continue to influence many of us who worked there. For example, as director of the Indian Arts Research Center at the School for Advanced Research in Santa Fe, Cynthia is creating "collaborative catalogs" through a partnership with the A:shiwi A:wan Museum and Heritage Center at Zuni Pueblo, New Mexico. She has also co-edited a book called *Art in Our Lives: Native Women Artists in Dialogue* (Chavez Lamar et al. 2010) and worked with Native artists on a collaborative, traveling banner exhibition about moccasins, *To Feel the Earth: Moccasins in the Southwest.*

Three interrelated principles guide my research today: (1) the recognition of Native communities' sovereignty and self-determination; (2) a commitment to a collaboration that relies on relationships built through sincerity, reciprocity, and trust; and (3) the maintaining of a professional-to-professional relationship with the community members with whom I work. For example, I participated in *iShare: Connecting Museums and Communities East and West*, a project funded in 2010 by a Museums and Community Collaborations Abroad grant from the American Association of Museums (see Shannon n.d.). The National Taiwan Museum and the University of Colorado Museum of Natural History, in partnership with the Navajo Nation Museum and the Paiwan people's Laiyi Indigenous Museum in southern Taiwan, worked together to document tangible and intangible culture in local archives, network among distant indigenous peoples, share different continental traditions of museum practice, and provide originating communities with equipment and greater access to museum collections and wider publics. The project produced educational kits for local schools in the four partner locations, a web application to host community digital archives, and a public website with collection items and audiovisual materials that were deemed appropriate for public viewing by the communities.

One central tenet of the project was that you cannot build an online partnership without establishing an in-person one, so four international trips were scheduled over the course of the grant period to build a foundation for and an investment in participation. We designed the project to be reflexive and its process to be as transparent as possible as we addressed a number of broad questions, including How can museums engage in reciprocity and sharing of authority with indigenous communities? What models of collaboration and technological tools can we develop to work productively with indigenous communities? How can social networking and online collaborative spaces facilitate and create new ways of communicating with, representing, and serving indigenous communities, as well as museum visitors?

The use of online and digital technology seems to be the current trend in facilitating collaboration (see, for example, Christen 2011; Great Lakes Research Alliance for the Study of Aboriginal Arts and Cultures 2008; Intellectual Property Issues in Cultural Heritage 2012; Powell 2007; Rowley et al. 2010; Srinivasan 2006; Srinivasan et al. 2008; Turin 2011), but there are challenges and cautions as well (Hennessy 2009). A web application may not be the best way to facilitate collaboration and access to museum collections because it depends on computer literacy and access to the Internet and computers. But given the resources of the *iShare* indigenous partners and the equipment and training we could provide through the grant, this was an appropriate choice for our work together.

It is important to respect different knowledge systems and to allow partners to "structure their own participation" (Rowley et al. 2010:6). At our first meeting with our Navajo Nation partners, we learned that the Navajo Nation Museum staff wanted one outcome of the project to be teaching kits for reservation schools. Our Navajo partners also raised concerns about sensitive topics that might arise in the course of the collaboration, such as the Bering Strait theory or possible Navajo antagonism toward anthropologists.[3] In response, Manuelito Wheeler, the director of the Navajo Nation Museum, suggested, "We should have some sort of safe word like...'Popcorn!'" We all laughed as he explained his reference to the television show *Saturday Night Live*. Although there has been a troubled history between anthropology, museums, and Native Americans, ethnographic practice in and of the museum enables us to acknowledge this history, engage and work with originating communities, and move forward in new and exciting directions, with humor and humility. Flexibility and sensitivity to issues of knowledge sharing were key to this process. And like all collaborative efforts, the project was a learning process for everyone involved—learning not just about the Paiwan and Navajo peoples but also how best to work together and incorporate technology as a productive means, but not an end, of our collaboration.

It is important that we listen to some of the "ancestors" of community curating, including the co-curators and the NMAI staff who worked on *Our Lives* and subsequent exhibits. Their experiences and analyses provide important insights for the future of relations between museums and originating communities, and this is a role that Chicago co-curators told me they wanted to take on. They are ready to share what they learned from the collaboration and to introduce and explain the community-curating process—to other Native groups so that they are better prepared for the enormous responsibility of representing their communities in the museum and on the world stage and to museum professionals so that they are better prepared for their work with Native communities.

Appendix A
Who's Who: The People in This Book

Chicago

Jayne Wapahnok Blacker (Menominee/Potawatomi), student, University of Illinois at Chicago

Ansel Deon (Sioux/Navajo), AIC cultural coordinator

Cyndee Fox-Starr (Omaha/Odawa), community health worker, American Indian Health Service of Chicago, Inc.

Rita Hodge (Diné), executive director Native American Support Program, University of Illinois at Chicago

Mavis Neconish (Menominee/Potawatomi), collection management assistant, Field Museum

Joe Podlasek (Ojibwe/Polish), AIC executive director

Susan Power (Dakota/Yanktonai), founding member of AIC, historian, elder

Cynthia Soto (Sicangu Lakota/Puerto Rican), Citywide American Indian Education Council member

David Spencer (Chata/Diné), AIC fundraising developer

Eli Suzukovich III (Cree/Serbian), archivist, NAES College

Ed Two Rivers (Ojibwe), activist, author

Valerie Wilson (Nitmuck), AIC board member

Patricia Xerikos (Anishnaabe/Colombian), AIC advisory board member

Igloolik

Madeline Auksak (Iglulingmiut), Inullariit Elders Society member

Theo Ikummaq (Iglulingmiut), hunter

Zipporah Inuksuk (Iglulingmiut), Inullariit Elders Society member

Arsene Ivalu (Iglulingmiut), Inullariit Elders Society member

Terri Iyerak (Iglulingmiut), policy analyst, Department of Culture, Language, Elders, and Youth

John MacDonald, director, Igloolik Research Center

Leah Otak (Iglulingmiut), Director of Culture and Heritage, Department of Culture, Language, Elders and Youth

Dominica

Irvince Auguiste (Kalinago), tour operator

Jacinta Bruney (Kalinago), craftmaker

Sylvanie Burton (Kalinago), community development worker

Cozier Frederick (Kalinago), teacher

Lennox Honychurch, anthropologist and historian

Garnette Joseph (Kalinago), chief

Gerard Langlais (Kalinago), Karina Cultural Group manager

Prosper Paris (Kalinago), Karifuna Cultural Group artistic director

Alexis Valmond (Kalinago), Carib Council member

NMAI

Staff

Bruce Bernstein, head, CRC

Fran Biehl, Museum Specialist/Collections Coordinator, Collections Department

Duane Blue Spruce (Laguna/San Juan Pueblo), architect

Kerry Boyd, head, Exhibits Department (after Jim Volkert)

Liz Brown, *OL* conservator

Theresa Burchett, research assistant

Cynthia Chavez (Lamar) (San Felipe Pueblo/Hopi/Tewa/Navajo), *OL* lead curator

Dan Davis, media producer

Zahava Doering, Senior Social Science Analyst, Smithsonian Office of Policy and Analysis (OP&A)

Doug Evelyn, deputy director, NMAI

Cécile Ganteaume, curator

Kevin Gover (Pawnee), new director, NMAI

Suzan Shown Harjo (Cheyenne/Hodulgee Muscogee), NMAI board member

Jim Pepper Henry (Kaw/Muscogee), associate director, NMAI

Emil Her Many Horses (Oglala Lakota), curator

Rick W. Hill Sr. (Tuscarora), former assistant director, Public Programs

Mark Hirsch, scriptwriter/editor, Exhibits Department

George Horse Capture (A'aninin [Gros Ventre]), special assistant, Cultural Resources, senior counselor to the director

Craig Howe (Oglala Lakota), deputy assistant director, Cultural Resources

Tim Johnson (Mohawk), associate director, NMAI

Casey MacPherson, *OU* lead research assistant

Ramiro Matos, curator

Gerald McMaster (Plains Cree/Siksika First Nation), deputy director, CRC

Ann McMullen, head, Curatorial Department

Jennifer Miller, *OL* project manager

Barbara Mogel, program manager, Exhibits Department
Pat Nietfeld, collections manager
Arwen Nuttall (Cherokee), research assistant
Sharyl Pahe (San Carlos Apache/Navajo), cultural interpreter
Andrew Pekarik, Program Analyst, OP&A
Carolyn Rapkievian, Assistant Director for Education and Museum Programs,
    Education Department
Jolene Rickard (Tuscarora), guest curator
Wenona Rymond-Richmond, Chicago field worker
Taryn Costanzo Salinas, research assistant
Susan Secakuku (Hopi), Kalinago field worker, Community Services Department
Jane Sledge, associate director, Museum Assets and Operations Group
Paul Chaat Smith (Comanche), curator
Terry Snowball (Ho-Chunk/Prairie Band Potawatomi), Repatriation Program
    Specialist, Repatriation Department
Kathy Suter, media coordinator
Teresa Tate, *OP* lead researcher
Gabi Tayac (Piscataway), curator, Education Department
Tanya Thrasher (Cherokee Nation of Oklahoma), Mall Transition Team member
Jennifer Tozer, *OL* exhibit manager
Jim Volkert, head, Exhibits Department
W. Richard West Jr. (Southern Cheyenne), director, NMAI

Consultants
Ken Gorbey
Elaine Heumann Gurian

D+C Design Team
André Bilodeau, *OL* project manager, designer
Erica Denison, junior project manager, NMAI–D+C liaison
Jean St. Cyr, president, designer

Appendix B
Main Messages of the Our Lives Gallery

Overall Gallery

Despite many challenges, we continue to exist as distinct communities, determining our own lives.

Community-Curated Exhibits

Campo

Campo Kumeyaay strategically manage and maintain their resources to assure their future as a people.

Chicago

Native peoples from different tribes come together in Chicago and maintain a supportive community network.

Igloolik

Iglulingmiut strive to maintain Inuit language and culture through traditional and innovative ways in the face of rapid change.

Kahnawake

Kahnawakehro:non assert their sovereignty in all aspects of their lives.

Kalinago

The Kalinago survive despite numerous challenges.

Pamunkey

The Pamunkey proudly serve the Creator as stewards of the land and waters that have sustained them for thousands of years.

Saint-Laurent

The Saint-Laurent Michif remember and respect the values and teachings of their ancestors by expressing their proud heritage in their everyday lives.

Yakama

Yakama people respect and value their cultural traditions and take responsibility for their Nation's future.

Appendix C

Mission Statement and Goals of the National Museum of the American Indian

Mission Statement

The National Museum of the American Indian shall recognize and affirm to Native communities and the non-Native public the historical and contemporary culture and cultural achievements of the Natives of the Western Hemisphere by advancing—in consultation, collaboration and cooperation with Natives—knowledge and understanding of Native cultures, including art, history and language, and by recognizing the museum's special responsibility, through innovative public programming, research and collections, to protect, support and enhance the development, maintenance and perpetuation of Native culture and community.

Statement of Goals

- Acknowledge the diversity of cultures among the indigenous peoples of the Western Hemisphere.
- Acknowledge the continuity of cultural knowledge among the Native peoples of the Western Hemisphere.
- Acknowledge and incorporate indigenous methodologies for conservation, documentation, and collections care.
- Acknowledge the importance of interpretation of culture within the context of indigenous worldviews.
- Acknowledge and respect that some indigenous communities have restricted cultural knowledge.
- Acknowledge and incorporate Native-based knowledge—such as oral histories and cosmologies—into exhibition- and program-related research.

Exhibition Guiding Principles

Community: *Our tribes are sovereign nations.*
    Stress that Native rights and issues are community-based, and that tribal

communities possess unique rights and inherent powers. The focus is on Native nations that are indigenous to the Western Hemisphere.

Locality: *This is Indian land.*
Show the interrelationship between geographical landscape, spiritual tradition and community identity. The focus is on particular geographical places and their inextricable relationships to indigenous spiritual traditions of the Western Hemisphere.

Vitality: *We are here now.*
Present Native cultures as living cultures that continue through time and across space. The focus is on the continuities within Native communities today.

Viewpoint: *We know the world differently.*
Develop interpretations from interdisciplinary viewpoints, but with indigenous worldviews always central. The focus is on Native philosophical systems, the distinct worldview of each and the Native languages that transmit this information.

Voice: *These are our stories.*
Include stories from multiple and divergent perspectives, but with Native voices always central. The focus is on Native individuals and their personal stories.

Notes

Preface

1. Suzan Shown Harjo, November 23, 2004.

Chapter 1. Anticipation

1. Transcript of co-curator meeting, June 13, 2003. The speakers are Theo Ikummaq (Iglulingmiut) and Terri Iyerak (Iglulingmiut).

2. My in-depth experience with the exhibit-making process in Igloolik prompted the research described in this book. I did not, however, return there for my fieldwork. Unlike my work as an assistant in the Chicago and Kalinago communities, I was the main museum representative and curatorial worker in Igloolik. I felt that this relationship had the potential to make it uncomfortable for Iglulingmiut co-curators to provide me with critical feedback regarding the exhibit-making process.

3. In the NMAI Act, collaboration is not mentioned. For the complete text of the law, see http://nmai.si.edu/sites/1/files/pdf/about/NMAIAct.pdf (accessed December 17, 2012).

4. According to a study conducted by the travel magazine *Travel+Leisure*, in 2010, the Louvre in Paris recorded 8.5 million visitors and the National Air and Space Museum recorded 8.3 million visitors.

5. Referring to the "last spot on the mall" was common before and after the opening of the NMAI. However, more recently, the National Museum of African American History and Culture has claimed the "last available space on the National Mall" and is scheduled to open in 2015 near the Washington Monument. See http://nmaahc.si.edu (accessed April 19, 2014).

6. Some of the material in this section is from Shannon n.d.

7. "Salvage anthropology" or "salvage ethnography" refers to the practice of collecting Native American objects and knowledge (songs, stories, languages) as quickly as possible. Researchers in the nineteenth and early twentieth centuries assumed that Native American cultural knowledges and lifeways, along with Native American peoples, were disappearing and needed to be recorded and preserved for posterity; they needed to be "salvaged," like cargo from a sinking ship. However, the posterity imagined was not the Native people themselves,

but Euro Americans. The preservation efforts removed objects and knowledge from Native communities and placed them in museums and universities, and cultural preservation within Native communities was thought to be futile and acculturation inevitable.

8. Protests of the exhibits *The Spirit Sings: Artistic Traditions of Canada's First Peoples* and *Into the Heart of Africa* (discussed in Phillips 2000) and the controversy over the *Enola Gay* exhibit (discussed in Dubin 1999) show that exhibitions and their subject matter cannot be divorced from the political and social context in which they are made. For an example of "counter-labels," or interventions in museum displays, see Strong 1997.

9. For an excellent discussion of the epistemological reasons for collaboration with indigenous communities, see Wylie 2008. Although she is referring to archaeology, her argument is applicable to knowledge making in general.

10. Here, "native" does not refer to Native Americans, but to the point of view of each actor, in this case, everyone working on museum exhibitions.

11. According to the American Alliance of Museums (2012), "in 2006, 77% of adult museum-goers ranked museums as 'equal or higher in trustworthiness' than any other source of information," and "according to a noted study by Indiana University, museums are considered a more reliable source of historical information than books, teachers, or even personal accounts by grandparents or other relatives."

12. Briefly, "thick description" in anthropology refers to the practice of detailed observation and description with an attention to meaning making.

13. For Laura Nader's call for anthropologists to "study up," or research people and institutions of power, see Nader 1974[1969].

14. Macdonald (2001:94) defines "analytical reflexivity" as "a process of careful reflection upon the cultural context and processes examined with a view to identifying the particular formations of knowledge and practice operating within that organization." Anna Tsing explains that, drawing from feminist theory, "we call our process 'strong collaboration,' that is, a form of collaboration in which explicit attention to the process is part of the project" (Matsutake Worlds Research Group 2009:399n3, 381).

15. Early instances of collaboration include the famous George Hunt–Franz Boas partnership (Berman 1996; Jacknis 2002b) and Michael Ames's efforts at the University of British Columbia Museum of Anthropology, although there are great differences in how these collaborations were structured and who benefited. Native voices were displayed in the Santa Fe Museum of Indian Arts and Culture (MIAC) exhibition titled *Here, Now, and Always: Voices of the First Peoples of the Southwest* (1997). Bruce Bernstein, who would later spearhead the community-curating initiative at the NMAI, was the chief curator and director of the MIAC during the development of this exhibition (see Bernstein et al. 2001). Ann Hedlund's (1994) incorporation of Native commentary in a textile exhibit is an example of what we now think of as Native voice in text panels, and the archaeological literature abounds with descriptions of collaborative practice. For accounts of collaborative museum projects before the NMAI, see, for example, Archambault 1993, 2011; Peers and Brown 2003.

16. In "The Complicity of Cultural Production," Fred Myers recognizes that symposia are a part of the cultural production associated with exhibitions. He writes that a symposium is an "evanescent moment of translation" and a "significant site of cultural practice" (Myers 2006:528). Dominic Boyer (2004:5) discusses the challenges of the anthropology of experts, noting that "since the anthropologist confronting another professional is at once expert and

parvenu, at once colleague and competitor, professionalism and the politics of expertise must be forefronted in our analysis of our ethnographic research in these areas." I devote an entire chapter to the cultures and politics of expertise, but it is a theme that runs throughout the book.

17. Deloria's manifesto includes "Anthropologists and Other Friends," a notorious and satirical criticism of the extractive relations that anthropologists have had with American Indian tribes. When scholars cite Deloria, it is often to indicate a particular recognition of past misdeeds and a commitment to ethical practice with Native nations and individuals. Elizabeth Grobsmith (1997:45) writes, "Those of us 'raised on Deloria' have had built into our knowledge of our discipline issues of ethics and morality, legality and propriety, jurisdiction and self-determination, seldom considered by pre-1950s ethnographers, their offensive and frequently unethical field techniques having been well documented." She explains how Deloria's critique created a new standard for "anthros" working with tribes and made them desperately avoid being "tiresome meddler[s]"; it also made anthropologists defensive about their usefulness and more accountable for their actions (ibid.:37).

18. For the conceptualization of collaboration as subject and method, I am indebted to the work of Hiro Miyazaki, especially *The Method of Hope* (2004). But whereas Miyazaki intends to provide a space for anthropological engagement with philosophy, I seek this engagement in a more mundane sphere—in everyday organizational practice. I am indebted to Annelise Riles and her work on nongovernmental organizations and bureaucratic practice in *The Network Inside Out* (2000) and, as editor, *Documents: Artifacts of Modern Knowledge* (2006c).

19. Kahn was a curator for *Pacific Voices*, an exhibit about the contemporary lives of seventeen "Pacific Rim cultures" that was created in collaboration with leaders of those communities and displayed at the University of Washington's Burke Museum of Natural History and Culture.

20. Drawing from the Boasian concept of culture, cultures of expertise have a shared (technical or perceptual) language, a shared worldview, and a common history (how they got to where they are today) and psychology (how they think about the world around them, or what we might refer to as a shared epistemology).

21. Elaine Heumann Gurian, personal communication, July 1, 2004. "Personal communication" includes phone calls and conversations; otherwise it is a recorded interview.

22. Cynthia Chavez, personal communication, March 31, 2004.

23. See Holmes and Marcus 2005:248 about relationships with collaborators being a "fiction to be sustained."

24. Jessica Cattelino (2008) was "discouraged" from learning the Mikasuki language when she did fieldwork with the Florida Seminoles, so she chose not to study it during her fieldwork. I experienced something similar in Dominica with the local patois when I first arrived, but at the end of my stay, the Kalinagos encouraged me to learn the language. It may seem unusual to choose not to learn a local language when we think about what fieldwork should include, but what you choose to "study" and what you choose not to "study" are important indicators to the community about your intentions and your receptiveness to their concerns. As Cattelino (2008:70) writes, "at stake in this boundary making is indigenous control over cultural forms and representations" and ultimately issues of sovereignty. See also Isaac 2007:7.

25. Field notes, September 3, 2004.

26. Field notes, August 9, 2004.

27. Field notes, June 5, 2006.

28. Deloria's humor and insight created a caricature that may have been accurate only about some anthropologists, and it may feel unfair to contemporary anthropologists with different methods and goals. Nonetheless, his critique encouraged an empowered sense of wariness and an expectation of reciprocity by Native communities working with outside researchers. Linda Tuhiwai Smith's *Decolonizing Methodologies* (1999) not only insists on reciprocity but also provides different models for how to work appropriately with indigenous peoples.

29. I am indebted to Jean-Klein and Riles's (2005:184) discussion of the "anthropological slot" in NGOs. They also discuss how anthropologists can get enrolled, often problematically, in bureaucratic and activist projects.

30. This is an important Americanist anthropology recognition: individuals being interviewed by anthropologists have some control through what they say or in directing what is appropriate for discussion.

31. Suzukovich, January 8, 2005.

32. Boas remains a polarizing figure among Native Americans. Some see his work with Native consultants, his emphasis on language, and his theories of racial equality as positive, while others view him as a grave robber and an extractive scientist.

33. Field notes, January 23, 2005. Garnette Joseph told me later that this young man was not from the Carib Territory.

34. Field notes, September 7, 2005.

35. For example, I would categorize Fred Myers's work on indigenous media as Americanist, although he does not work with US tribes; his emphasis on representation and his "uneasiness" while representing Aboriginal people in an exhibit symposium are indicators. Myers (2006:506) emphasizes indigenous peoples as culture producers rather than culture bearers and considers a focus on cultural *production* to be tied to respect for indigenous agency. He also recognizes that scholars are culture producers as well.

36. Because the Americanists emphasized the importance of Native texts over theorists' interpretations of them, they have often been deemed atheoretical, or even anti-theory. Darnell explains that, in the past, the imperative and urgency of salvage anthropology often displaced theorizing. Boasians considered their top priority to be collecting and recording—there would be time for interpreting the materials later. For examples that detail what I would call a theoretical and Americanist approach outside the American context, see T. Turner 1991 and Hale 2006.

37. I am indebted to Bunzl 1998 and Darnell 2001. See also Jacknis 1985, 2002a; Stocking 1966; and the primary sources Boas 2004[1887], 1887, 1889, 1919, 1920.

Chapter 2. Our Lives

1. The mission statement changed shortly prior to the opening of the museum. Here, I am referring to the NMAI mission statement from around 2002 (appendix C). It was shortened around 2004 to read: "The National Museum of the American Indian is committed to advancing knowledge and understanding of the Native cultures of the Western Hemisphere—past, present, and future—through partnership with Native people and others. The museum works to support the continuance of culture, traditional values, and transitions in contemporary Native life." www.nmai.si.edu/collaboration/files/CS_Guide_English0708.pdf, accessed July 3, 2010.

2. In the anthropology of institutions, three ethnographies provided models for the "field site" as I am using it here: Kathleen Gregory's 1984 study of Silicon Valley computer professionals (cited in Schwartzman 1993), Stacia Zabusky's 1995 study of the European Space Agency, and Georgina Born's 1995 study of a large computer music research and production institute in Paris. These anthropologists focused on collaborative projects between experts and used the social formations of "the project" (Born 1995; Gregory cited in Schwartzman 1993) and "the mission" (Zabusky 1995) to follow the changing contour lines of their field sites, similar to how I view "the exhibit."

3. For similar enrollments in local projects, see Nadasdy 2003:23 and Riles 2000:xv. Nadasdy took meeting minutes and participated in local committees. Riles provided "technical assistance." Each of us found ways to participate and at the same time produce something for both ourselves and our interlocutors.

4. Kerry Boyd, November 17, 2004.

5. One curator urged me, if I wanted to understand where the power in the institution was, I needed to "follow the money." Unfortunately, I did not have access to financial information about the exhibitions.

6. There was a notable division of ethnic backgrounds among the various departments at the CRC: most administrative and security staff were African American (and lived in the Suitland area, which is predominantly African American), and the rest of the departments were a mix of Native and non-Native people, with the Collections Department and the "move team" mainly Native. Most CRC workers lived in Washington, DC; Alexandria, Virginia; or suburbs in Maryland. Downtown staff were also a mix of Natives and non-Natives; when the museum opened, this balance continued, except that all the cultural interpreters who worked on the museum floor with the public were Native.

7. Until the human remains, or Native ancestors, from the NMAI collection were repatriated, the Museum Support Center of the National Museum of Natural History housed them.

8. For samples of his scholarly writing about Native identity, see McMaster 1998; McMaster et al. 2004.

9. The design diagrams from Design+Communication somewhat parallel the internal documents, but there are significant differences. For instance, in a 1998 report, the conceptual diagram was the same—four circles—but the center circle was titled "Introduction; Witness" and the three circles around it were titled "Identity; Dialogue," "Community; Interaction," and "Heritage; Change," with arrows to denote movement from one to the next, in that order.

10. Ann McMullen, March 25, 2004. Ann also noted that Ruth Phillips was at the "scholars" consultation. The negative critique may have been due to the pan-Indian nature of the design and content, since that group of scholars was instrumental in the eventual shift to community-centered exhibits. However, what was "trashed" was never explicitly mentioned by either person who used this term to describe the review.

11. Bruce Bernstein, personal communication, October 4, 2010.

12. This provocative critique of working with "informants," a loaded term in anthropology, can also be read against the NMAI staff's desire to avoid working with the Native people with whom museums usually consulted, in order to access an "authentic Native voice." The recognized/recognizable "experts," in a museum professional sense, were passed over in favor of community curators, who were referred to as "experts of their own experience."

13. Blue Spruce, personal communication, April 1, 2004.

14. Bernstein, personal communication, October 4, 2010.

15. It was not until around 2004 that the full names of the galleries were chosen, circulated among staff, and appeared in literature: *Our Lives: Contemporary Life and Identities, Our Universes: Traditional Knowledge Shapes Our World,* and *Our Peoples: Giving Voice to Our Histories.* The "our" in each case indicates who is telling the stories in the exhibition, signaling the community-curating practice. For a discussion of the semiotics of museum text and inclusive labeling, see Strong 1997.

16. Email from Tristine Smart, January 17, 2001.

17. McMullen, personal communication, July 8, 2004.

18. The NMAI-curated sections also changed a number of times; two guest curators, Gabi Tayac and Jolene Rickard, were responsible for the final installation. However, in this book, I only attend to the community-curated sections.

19. Although Cynthia at first shied away from calling these groups "committees," that was how communities referred to their own co-curator groups in the early stages of the process.

20. The limitations of this approach for a broader representation of Chicago Native experience are addressed by James LaGrand (2002:5), who says that the AIC is often selected by people wanting to work with the Indian population of Chicago for ease of access for research, though it does not and cannot represent or provide access to the more than thirty thousand Native people in the city alone (not counting suburbs and rural areas). For the purposes of the *OL* project, the Chicago "community" was primarily defined as the AIC community, although some co-curators objected to the exhibit being so AIC centered.

21. Wenona Rymond-Richmond, on a contract with the NMAI, was the field worker assigned to this community. She took meeting notes in Cynthia's absence and conducted interviews. Only three communities had field workers assigned: Chicago, Dominica (Susan Secakuku), and Igloolik (me). Ann McMullen was the main NMAI contact for Pamunkey. The rest relied on regular visits and, mainly, group meetings with Cynthia, rather than individual interviews. Having multiple field workers helped to get the *OL* fieldwork and exhibition completed in time.

22. Some elders spoke only Kweyol. The last person to speak some Carib phrases died in the early twentieth century.

23. Terry Turner (1991) documented the formation of cultural consciousness among the Kayapos in the Brazilian Amazon, presenting another way to think about how notions of culture, community representation, and anthropological practice are intertwined.

24. Carib descendants are also found in populations on other islands, such as nearby St. Vincent.

25. Prosper Paris told me on April 24, 2005, that Honychurch, a non-Native white man with a Ph.D. in anthropology and museum studies from Oxford University, was originally asked by the Kalinagos to be a co-curator. The Kalinagos appreciate his work and invite him to speak at Carib Week celebrations each year, and researchers often ask him, rather than the Kalinagos themselves, for information about the Kalinagos. But, Prosper told me, the Smithsonian said no to his inclusion because it wanted *Native* co-curators *from* the community. This was a positive development. Although people like Garnette Joseph were highly educated and Prosper had read all the same materials as Honychurch, their expertise was often overlooked because Honychurch was "the expert" with "a Ph.D." Honychurch was contracted by the Dominican government to make the introductory wall panel exhibit about the history of the

Kalinagos for the Carib Model Village—without consulting the community. The difference between an "expert" and what the Kalinagos call a "resource person" is detailed in chapter 4.

26. Prosper Paris, July 20, 2005.

27. Ibid.

28. Many people do not know that "the US Constitution stops here" on reservations—that federally recognized tribes have their own constitutions, heads of state, and, in many cases, police forces and court systems.

29. This discussion is based on material in the Sol Tax Collection at the Native American Educational Services College archives in Chicago.

30. For historical and sociological accounts of Chicago's urban Indian community, see Beck 1988; LaGrand 2002; Straus and Arndt 1998. See LaGrand 2002 for a detailed breakdown of the city's Native American demographics during relocation times.

Chapter 3. Bureaucracy

1. Casey MacPherson, personal communication, June 2, 2004.

2. Jane Sledge, personal communication, March 16, 2006. By this time, after an institution-wide departmental reorganization, Sledge was associate director of the new Museum Assets and Operations Group.

3. By 2012, the Visitor Services Department was a casualty of another reorganization. Instead, at the request of director Kevin Gover (Pawnee), all NMAI staff members regardless of department do "service hours" each year on a rotating basis. These duties emphasize staff interaction with the public, for example, greeting visitors at the front desk of the mall museum, giving tours, or conducting visitor surveys. Whether this change was based on financial or museological reasons is unclear (NMAI staff member, personal communication, December 11, 2012).

4. I am indebted to Pamela Smart for this apt analogy.

5. CRC staff member, personal communication, March 29, 2004.

6. Research assistants, personal communication, July 9, 2004.

7. Iris Jean-Klein explains her research about Palestine as an attempt to "see past the political" in a place where it is always studied (personal communication, March 27, 2003). This has inspired my wording here.

8. Max Weber is often a starting point and resource for many scholars who study bureaucracy (see, for example, Weber et al. 1947). In his view, the characteristics of bureaucracy include a highly developed division of labor, specialized tasks assigned to each office or department, expert training for those tasks, a desire to be seen as legitimate, and written documents. All of these can be seen in the everyday practices of the museum.

9. I am indebted to Annelise Riles's (2006c) work, which led me to the concept of documents as artifacts of bureaucracy and of modernity more generally.

10. The anthropology of institutions has focused mainly on the state (Alexander 2002; Ferguson 1990; Herzfeld 1992), "total institutions" (Foucault 1979), service bureaucracies (Lipsky 1980), and scientific and academic institutions (Brenneis 1994; Gusterson 1996; Zabusky 1995).

11. Born (1995:24) considers IRCAM within the broader "sphere of subsidized high culture," which she sees as lacking ethnographic engagement. She also notes another oversight: the

lack of distinction, especially in the field of cultural studies, between culture as "lived" and culture as "professionally produced." At the NMAI, however, it is both: culture that is lived by Native communities is represented by culture that is professionally produced by NMAI staff.

12. Andrew Pekarik, personal communication, May 23, 2006.

13. Ibid.

14. Ibid.

15. Field notes, May 23, 2006.

16. Phillips wrote the introduction to *Museums and Source Communities* (2003), a seminal volume about museum–community collaborations edited by Peers and Brown.

17. The *Our Lives* "extended team" included the contracted design firm, Design+Communication, Inc., from Montreal, and a number of staff members who were involved at different stages of the exhibition process: Maria McWilliams (Registration), Erik Satrum (Registration), Liz Brown (Conservation), Dan Davis (Media), and Collections staff members.

18. CRC staff member, October 12, 2004.

19. From Jennifer Miller's meeting notes (February 25, 2002) via *Ohana*, the NMAI intranet website.

20. Jim Volkert, June 13, 2006. At the time of this phone interview, he was no longer working at the museum but was serving as a consultant for the NMAI and other museum projects.

21. NMAI project manager, personal communication, March 23, 2006.

22. Photo Services Department staff member, personal communication, July 30, 2004.

23. Cécile Ganteaume, October 12, 2004.

24. NMAI staff member, personal communication, April 1, 2004.

25. Gurian, personal communication, June 7, 2006.

26. Volkert, personal communication, June 13, 2006.

27. CRC staff member, November 23, 2004.

28. Theresa Burchett, June 18, 2004.

29. Tanya Thrasher, personal communication, April 1, 2004.

30. McMullen, November 23, 2004.

31. Ganteaume, October 12, 2004.

32. Liz Brown, personal communication, June 22, 2004.

33. *OL* media meeting, CRC conference room, May 14, 2003. I was at this meeting as a consultant for the Igloolik exhibit; we were concerned about, among other things, an elder's statement being cut mid-sentence (which Inuktitut-speakers would recognize) and the representational and symbolic issues of talking over an elder's voice rather than providing translation through subtitles.

34. Snowball, June 5, 2006.

35. Email, June 5, 2006.

36. Email, November 22, 2012.

37. Ann McMullen details the NMAI's distribution of honorariums and other payments for Native community curators in "The Currency of Consultation and Collaboration" (2008).

38. NMAI staff member, personal communication, June 9, 2006.

39. NMAI management support assistant, personal communication, June 7, 2006.

40. Ibid.

41. For an example of an NMAI release form, see Shannon 2007b.

42. NMAI management support assistant, personal communication, June 7, 2006.

43. The management support assistant said that there was "still some tension between the heads of museums and cultural centers and people who actually did the work in getting paid," because now, rather than the NMAI staff providing individual payments, the institutions determined who would get paid from the money provided by the NMAI. He said that, in the future, the museum needed to include in the contract an "administrative overhead fee" and be "specific as to how much money goes to community curators," as opposed to leaving that up to the contracting cultural institution.

44. Harjo, November 23, 2004.

45. "Gang of five" was a term coined by Paul Chaat Smith at the NMAI; he also mentions it in "The Terrible Nearness of Distant Places: Making History at the National Museum of the American Indian" (Smith 2007:390). He provides another perspective on community curating from within the institution, which is a valuable counterpoint to my narrative here.

46. Mall Transition Team member, April 6, 2006.

47. The MAC would later be titled the Museum Associates Council. As Tim Johnson explained in an interview on April 13, 2006, four associate directors, the Executive Planning Office (led by Justin Estoche), and Rick West composed the Museum Associates Council. They kept track of "timelines, schedules, [and] workloads cross-departmentally." This was a much smaller group making decisions, he explained, and avoided the cacophony of the eighteen to twenty people who were in the senior management meetings before.

48. NMAI curator, personal communication, July 8, 2004. During the development of the inaugural exhibitions, departmental allocations were reduced. Part of the later reorganization effort was to allocate money to projects/project managers rather than to departments.

49. Email, September 20, 2004.

50. By 2007, Ann McMullen, Mary Jane Lenz, and Cécile Ganteaume were working in collections research, under Collections Information Services in the Museum Assets and Operations Group. Emil Her Many Horses and Paul Chaat Smith were labeled museum specialists and placed with historians and geographers in the research division of the Museum Programs Group. Ramiro Matos became a special assistant to Jim Pepper Henry in the Community and Constituent Services Group. Ramiro continued to call himself a curator, however, because he felt that his new title did not "mean anything" to people. These former curators continued to do what most would consider to be curatorial work. For example, Cécile curated the object-centered, regionally organized exhibition *Infinity of Nations: Art and History in the Collections of the National Museum of the American Indian*, which opened in October 2010.

51. Johnson, personal communication, April 13, 2006.

52. In 2006, when the Curatorial Department was disbanded, a research group was developed under its own associate director. One of the departments that made the NMAI truly stand apart as a "museum different," the Community Services Department, was lost in the reorganizations. But its function was not lost; the department became Constituent Services, with subgroups for cultural protocols, Native arts/radio, and training. Later reorganizations under Kevin Gover established a Museum Scholarship Group, which includes Latin American studies, contemporary art, collections research and documentation, and repatriation (CRC staff member, personal communication, June 29, 2011).

53. CRC staff member, April 6, 2006.

54. This was very different from the experiences of the enthusiastic cultural interpreters newly hired at the mall museum at this time. One cultural interpreter, in a discussion about her training and some of the difficult questions she is asked working on the exhibition floor, told me that it was a "demanding job." Part of her job was allocated to "research time" so that she could prepare her presentations about *OL* and learn more about what is in the other galleries. She could select what she wanted to focus on as she walked people through the gallery, and, unlike the original research assistant positions, the cultural interpreter positions were permanent rather than temporary appointments. Sharyl Pahe (San Carlos Apache/Navajo), October 19, 2004.

55. Langlais, April 21, 2005.

56. Email to McMullen, April 27, 2005.

57. Email to author, April 27, 2005.

58. Like the NMAI, these communities dealt with organizational problems through "consultants," but in very different ways. The Dominican government hired international consultants to bring the Carib Model Village to completion. In Chicago, the community invited an Ojibwe healer to conduct community talking circles to deal with difficult issues, including individuals who were "dividing the community" and people who were "identity policing" at AIC functions.

59. One field worker/curator resigned from the NMAI in 2002 after major changes were made to an exhibition without notifying the Native communities featured in that gallery. He wrote in his letter of resignation that he feared being transformed into a "19th century treaty negotiator": he might make an agreement with a tribe in good faith, but then the museum (like the federal government) could unilaterally change the agreement and expect the negotiator to convince the tribe to agree to the raw deal.

60. This caveat can also be applied to a number of dichotomies that, perhaps problematically though instructively, can be mapped onto downtown and the CRC: Exhibits–Curatorial; consultants–invitational travelers; visitor advocates–community advocates; presentation–research; design–content; visual–textual; audience focused–constituency focused; center of power–center of mission; public face of the museum–heart of the museum; for the public–for the tribes; connection to politics, donors–connection to objects, communities. These dichotomies have been mentioned by many individuals inside and outside the museum over the years, and they also rose to the surface as I mapped the cultures of expertise, speech networks, locations, and personal relations among NMAI staff as they made sense of the conflict and change going on around them.

Chapter 4. Expertise

1. In "Cultures of Expertise and the Management of Globalization: Toward a Re-functioning of Ethnography," Doug Holmes and George Marcus (2005) turn their attention to the "managers of globalization." Their focus on cultures of expertise was influential in the approach I take here. However, my interlocutors were not only doing para-ethnography; they were often trained specifically in ethnographic and interviewing practices through anthropology or other social sciences.

2. In 1927, Paul Radin, a student of Franz Boas, published *Primitive Man as Philosopher*, which can be considered an early exception. In this work, Radin deliberately focused on the "intellectual class among primitive peoples," the "thinkers" who are a subset and not representative of the whole of an indigenous population.

3. While I agree with Robin Boast that we should continue to scrutinize collaborative museum work despite its positive cast, I do not believe that the concept of the contact zone prescribes any particular forms of collaboration, or "contact zone practices" (Boast 2011:57). Instead, the contact zone sets a stage for productive collaboration—in whatever form—through explicitly acknowledging the problematic development of the institution of the museum and the continuing issues of power, which are not eliminated through collaboration. I agree with Boast's caution against thinking that museum collaborative practices somehow negate issues of authority and his request that we "question why we perpetuate only a partial and rosy portrait of the contact zone" (ibid.). In Srinivasan et al. 2010, Boast and his co-authors effectively scrutinize collaborative endeavors and their tendency to elide the tensions that occur in bringing different kinds of knowledge together. For additional critiques of projects between museums and communities and the desire of dominant cultures to include and collaborate with indigenous peoples, see Jones and Jenkins 2008; Mithlo 2004. These scholars question who the collaboration benefits and why. Collaboration is always a fraught contact zone, despite the positive intentions of those involved.

4. NMAI internal memo, August 11, 1997.

5. Doug Evelyn, November 15, 2004.

6. Mark Hirsch, September 8, 2004.

7. Rick West, November 18, 2004.

8. Both Native co-curators and NMAI curators (except perhaps Jolene Rickard, who is an artist) were prohibited from doing any design work, since that was not part of their recognized expertise.

9. The meeting took place on December 14, 2000. Attendees: NMAI staff Cynthia Chavez, Ann McMullen, Bruce Bernstein, and Jennifer Shannon; and Native scholars Angela Gonzales, Wesley Thomas, Inez Hernandez Avila, Paul Chaat Smith, and Gerald McMaster.

10. Vetting session transcript, December 14, 2000, emphases added.

11. There were notable exceptions: two curators, both self-described Native "intelligentsia," were outspoken in their criticism of the NMAI as "anti-intellectual," and they did not agree with the characterization of or commitment to community curators as "experts." One of them, referencing the *OP* gallery, said that, in many cases, Native people "don't know their own history." At the time of this vetting session, however, these curators were not NMAI staff members.

12. Chavez, June 18, 2004.

13. NMAI curator, personal communication, June 7, 2006.

14. Bernstein, November 22, 2004.

15. NMAI curator, November 24, 2004.

16. All quotations from McMullen in this paragraph and the following are from November 23, 2004.

17. McMullen, November 23, 2004.

18. The hiring of a scriptwriter was a surprise to curators at the NMAI, who had assumed that they would be working with the Native communities to write the exhibition scripts and labels. The slash in his title—writer/editor—highlights the contestation over his role in the process.

19. Hirsch, personal communication, September 8, 2004.

20. Elaine Heumann Gurian, June 7, 2006.

21. One downtown staff member described the Curatorial Department's attitude as a "racist conceit" because the curators did not trust other staff to be "sensitive" enough to work directly with communities.

22. I commented in my transcription notes of the interview, "Exhibits and Curatorial sitting back to back, facing their constituents, public and Native tribes, respectively. Makes it hard to communicate, and their philosophies are quite different."

23. Volkert, July 8, 2004.

24. In this interview (November 9, 2004), Jim finally used the term "anthropologist" as an example of an expert, although that was what I always thought he had meant in past discussions when he would say "astronomer" or "biologist." All quotations from Jim in the following pages, except where noted, are from this same interview.

25. Volkert, August 25, 2004.

26. Volkert, November 19, 2004.

27. Barbara Mogel, personal communication, March 23, 2006.

28. Boyd, November 17, 2004.

29. Volkert, July 21, 2004.

30. NMAI curator, personal communication, March 31, 2004; NMAI curator, personal communication, April 11, 2006.

31. Some Native curators were also museum specialists, such as Jolene Rickard, who gave a presentation about the *Our Peoples* gallery at the 2004 Deerfield Symposium. Jolene criticized the press for focusing exclusively on the museum's collaboration with Native "community" curators: "I'm from Tuscarora and a curator—why am I less of a community curator than someone within a community but with less professional experience?" Jolene said that she, Paul Chaat Smith, and Gabi Tayac, who all worked on the NMAI-curated sections in the inaugural exhibitions, were "erased from press presentations" of the exhibits (Deerfield Symposium conference presentation, November 6, 2004). After the symposium, Jolene told me that the NMAI "hasn't dealt with Native people like [her]—they prefer non-experts." Again, she asked, "Why don't they [the NMAI] see us as Native collaborators?" The "NMAI wants ownership" over the NMAI-curated sections, she explained; it's about "territoriality." But we need to be open, to collaborate, to learn.

32. This term was also negatively glossed within the museum in reference to cultural elites, as when Rick West mentioned that non-Natives understand the exhibitions "inversely proportionate to their expertise."

33. Paris, April 24, 2005.

34. Joseph, April 13, 2005. Note the similarity to the categories of "representational experts" that Rick West selected for the consultations.

35. Joseph, March 17, 2005.

36. Suzukovich, personal communication, March 12, 2007.

37. Attendees: Rita Hodge, Cynthia Chavez, Wenona Rymond-Richmond, Ansel Deon, Mavis Neconish, Jayne Blacker, Susan Power, Angie Decorah, Cindy Soto, Cyndee Fox-Starr, David Spencer, Patricia Xerikos, Eli Suzukovich, and Joe Podlasek.

38. Unpublished document in possession of author.

39. Unpublished document in possession of author.

40. Volkert, personal communication, June 13, 2006.

41. I have argued elsewhere that curators' knowledge of *how* to work with communities constitutes a particular kind of expertise (Shannon 2007a).

42. Unwritten codes of ethics in practice are what Meskell and Pels (2005) refer to as "embedding ethics."

43. NMAI curator, November 24, 2004.

Chapter 5. Authorship

1. Transcript of vetting session, December 14, 2000.

2. Originally conceived as a "five-phase" process, the community-curating model was modified for *OL* due to the shorter time frame, compared with the other two galleries. For a detailed description of the five-phase process, see Howe 2001; for an explanation of why it was not feasible for *OL*, see Chavez Lamar 2008.

3. On the shift from objects to reflexive subjects in museum display, see Shannon 2009. For an analysis of labels and the language of inclusion and exclusion, see Strong 1997.

4. Gwyneira Isaac (2005) productively uses the frame of mediation to analyze the making of the A:shiwi A:wan Museum and Heritage Center and its negotiation of the Zuni value of restricting knowledge versus the practice of western-based museums, which assume that all knowledge should be accessible. Here, I am more interested in the intrapersonal dynamics of mediation and how actors' imaginations and assumptions influence their practice.

5. This was inspired by Dornfeld's (1998:179) discussion of the "authorial ideology" of the producers of the *Childhood* series, which was seen as "collegial and negotiated."

6. With a blood quantum requirement of 50 percent, higher than the Canadian government's requirement, the Kahnawake people assert control over their community membership as part of their sovereign right. The co-curators, however, chose to emphasize language immersion, ironworking, and crossing international borders with their own passports. The Oka crisis *was* included by Gabi Tayac and Jolene Rickard in the NMAI-curated introductory section of *Our Lives*. Gabi told me that, in this section, the NMAI curators were able to present topics—like blood quantum and Oka—that no community wanted to author but most would agree were important issues to educate people about. Tayac, October 6, 2004.

7. McMullen, November 23, 2004.

8. Attendees: Cynthia Chavez, Jennifer Shannon, Wenona Rymond-Richmond, Faith Smith (NAES director), R. J. Smith (Faith's son, youth group leader), and Eli Suzukovich III (NAES archivist, youth group leader).

9. From the transcript. Her comments included that Chicago had the oldest urban Indian center, Chicago was a major relocation site, there were no recognized tribal lands in Illinois, and the conference in 1961 that brought so many Native leaders to Chicago was "really one of the...starting points of talking about self-determination" among Native people. She added that, before the federal relocation program, there was "a long history of Native people living" in Chicago. This comment was particularly appreciated by the group.

10. In meetings and within the community, the term "Carib" was most often used by Carib Territory residents. But, in preparing the exhibition, the co-curators decided that they wanted "Kalinago" to displace this term.

11. Attendees: Susan Secakuku, Jennifer Shannon, Prosper Paris, Gerard Langlais, Garnette Joseph, Jacinta Bruney, Irvince Auguiste, Faustulus Frederick (former chief, artist, and Cozier's father), James Frederick (Sineku Development Committee), Eve Sanford (elder), Regina Joseph (banana farmer), Judith Francis (youth representative), Sylvie Warrington (nurse), Murvina Thomas (basket maker), Reny Auguiste (youth representative), Maulyn Stout

(elder), Jerome Octave (elder), Hillary Frederick (former chief), Andel Challenger (teacher), Kevin Dangleben (teacher), and Raphael Auguiste (tourism/driver).

12. Kalinago co-curator meeting transcript, January 17, 2002.

13. The Carib Model Village opened in 2006, and its name was changed to Kalinago Barana Autê: Carib Village by the Sea.

14. Attendees: Susan Secakuku, Jennifer Shannon, Irvince Auguiste, Prosper Paris, Alexis Valmond, Cozier Frederick, James Frederick, Faustulus Frederick, Reny Auguiste, Sylvie Warrington, Andel Challenger, Paulinas Frederick (Karifuna Cultural Group), Louisette Auguiste (Irvince's wife), Lawrence Daroux (former parliamentary representative), Reina Auguiste (youth representative), and Miranda Langlais (Karina Cultural Group member and Gerard's wife).

15. Prosper said during the meeting that the Kalinagos should not "run away from the reality of things": "We don't want to pretend to be what we're not. If we say we are not hungry, no one will want to send food. If we say we are hungry, someone will send food. It's that we have a good meal now but don't know about the next one. It fluctuates, good sometimes, bad sometimes" (from my meeting notes).

16. The following meeting information is based on transcripts and notes recorded by Wenona Rymond-Richmond and Rita Hodge.

17. Attendees: Christine Red Cloud, Wenona Rymond-Richmond, Jennifer Shannon, Cynthia Chavez, Antonia Wheeler Sheehy, Joseph Podlasek, Mary Anne Armstrong, Eli Suzukovich, Megan Bang, Beverly Moeser, Ed Two Rivers, and Vincent Romero.

18. Attendees: Rita Hodge, Cynthia Chavez, Wenona Rymond-Richmond, Ansel Deon, Mavis Neconish, Jayne Blacker, Susan Power, Angie Decorah, Cynthia Soto, Cyndee Fox-Starr, David Spencer, Patricia Xerikos, Eli Suzukovich, and Joe Podlasek.

19. Attendees: Rita Hodge, Joe Podlasek, Dave Spencer, Jayne Blacker, Cindy Soto, Mavis Neconish, Susan Power, Cyndee Fox-Starr, and Jean St. Cyr.

20. Design+Communication staff explained the icon as the significant image or thing that a visitor would remember after seeing an exhibit. It can be thought of as a mnemonic device to recall that community's exhibit, to make it stand out in a visitor's memory.

21. Joseph, April 13, 2005.

22. Paris, April 24, 2005.

23. Burton, April 8, 2005.

24. Joseph, March 17, 2005.

25. Joseph, April 13, 2005.

26. Curatorial staff insisted that the design schematics shown to community curators included the wall quotes and that these statements were also in the scripts the co-curators reviewed. It is possible that the community curators did not have enough training to read these technical documents and therefore did not know that pieces of text would be separated out and displayed on the walls. Regardless, it is significant that this came as a surprise to them.

27. Rita Hodge, November 29, 2005.

28. Langlais, March 16, 2005.

29. Denison, personal communication, June 21, 2004.

30. I wrote the preliminary script for the Igloolik exhibit, and Ann McMullen wrote the one for the Pamunkey exhibit.

31. Chavez, personal communication, September 18, 2003.

32. Davis and Suter, June 21, 2004 (all quotations from Dan and Kathy in the following paragraphs are from this conversation, unless otherwise noted). Exhibits staff told them that 120 seconds should be the maximum length of each video. Kathy said that she was trying to get the Exhibits Department to stop asking, "How long is that piece?" Dan said that he countered with "How long does it feel?" or "What does four minutes feel like to you?"

33. A "script" for the media team was a transcription of the recorded interview, which Dan reviewed to pick out the video segments he wanted to use. For the Curatorial Department, a "script" was the text being prepared for the exhibit labels. One was raw, the other cooked, so to speak.

34. Denison, personal communication, June 21, 2004.

35. The D+C design team, including André Bilodeau and Jean St. Cyr, used Mac G5 computers. Erica Denison told me that the designers often worked together in front of a computer using Adobe Photoshop software. I described an image of a few people gathered around a computer screen, looking over the seated person's shoulder as he or she dragged layers of images around on the screen and saying, "Move this there," and "How about that?" Erica said that it was about right. Denison, personal communication, June 21, 2004.

36. This is a common phrase in Indian country. For example, I was given a curriculum guide for Chicago public schools created by staff associated with the AIC and titled *Learning and Teaching about Indians 101: Teaching Resources.*

37. Office of Policy and Analysis staff Zahava Doering and Andrew Pekarik both criticized the NMAI for not paying enough attention to visitors; Jim Volkert and Carolyn Rapkievian, Zahava noted, were the most "visitor centered" at the NMAI (Doering, November 23, 2006). Carolyn, Jim, Zahava, Andrew, and Elaine Gurian share a speech network and a set of concerns as visitor-centered professionals. Carolyn learned a lot from Zahava, who said that visitors want to interact with the museum in ways that are not always about messages and learning: about one-third want to learn, one-third want a social experience, and one-third is split between those wanting an aesthetic experience with objects and those seeking an introspective experience to reflect on their own lives (see Doering 1999). Carolyn also said that she learned from Zahava that these different expectations do not have to be met in every exhibit but can be satisfied in different places throughout the museum. Rapkievian, personal communication, May 3, 2006.

38. Chavez, July 29, 2004.

39. An unexpected, additional audience was imagined by the three *OL* communities I worked with: the audience for my dissertation. During my fieldwork, one NMAI staff member suggested I read works by anthropologists Clifford Geertz, Keith Basso, and Fred Myers. Another suggested that, to understand a museum's departmental dynamics, I must read *Stigma* (1963) and *The Presentation of Self in Everyday Life* (1956) by Erving Goffman. A Kalinago person suggested that I read historian Hilary Beckles' work for a proper, more politically relevant Caribbean history, rather than the work of the well-known Dominica-born Lennox Honychurch.

40. I am indebted to Hiro Miyazaki for this phrasing and his view of temporality. See, for example, Miyazaki 2006.

41. Paris, April 24, 2005.

42. Joseph, April 13, 2005.

43. Terry Turner explains that cultural identities have become an avenue through which to

assert social power and to struggle for collective social production: "This is a struggle for social production in the broadest sense, not merely 'cultural' politics at the level of 'discourse' or 'imagination.'" (The previous quote is from p. 16 of an unpublished English version of Turner 1999 [pp. 1–19] that Terry provided.) Perhaps this is a way to view the Kalinago exhibit: they represented their own identity through their economic needs and recognized that their survival was tied to an economic future that depends on the production of cultural difference. Their hopes for tourism and concerns about intermarriage—such as the Chicago community's creation of institutional and organizational mechanisms for sustaining difference in the assimilating environment that is the urban context—are indeed about the social (re)production of their own communities.

44. From an internal NMAI document, "W. Richard West: A Vision for the Visitor Experience," prepared for the senior management retreat on June 6, 2002, in possession of author.

45. It is important to note that not all interpretations of the exhibit making at the NMAI considered it to be ethical practice, although that was the majority view. Craig Howe, a strong proponent of the community-curating method, wrote about working on the *Our Peoples* gallery and explored "the problem of collaboration across divergent interests and antagonistic regimes of value" (Meskell and Pels 2005:17). Howe (2005:234) concluded that the failure of this method in the development of *Our Peoples* resulted in a moral and ethical breach: "Developing tribal history exhibits in collaboration with Indian communities proved to be a complex undertaking that necessarily reduced the control that individuals and departments within the NMAI had conventionally exercised. It is not surprising, therefore, that the staunchest opposition to this new, collaborative, community-based process came from within the museum itself." Volume editors Meskell and Pels (2005:19) described Howe's essay as an account of how "this emergent methodology of stakeholder negotiation failed, recalling, for Native Americans, a violent history of broken promises."

46. The NMAI departments acted upon Native knowledge in very different ways: one sought to legitimize it as expert knowledge (Curatorial advocacy), whereas the other wanted to transform it for the general museum-going audience into more recognizable or palatable forms of knowledge (Exhibits translation). Price (2007:173) cites a letter to the editor in the October 12, 2006, *Le Nouvel Observateur* in which an Inuit person (unidentified except for a single name) expresses frustration with the lack of information about the objects on display: "I am Inuit.... At the Musée du quai Branly, I looked for my people. I saw so many beautiful objects in the beautiful dark cases.... Next to our objects there were several lines with brief description.... I came away with the feeling of having been parked in a big reservation for savages without culture who can't be mixed in with the great civilizations of the world that are presented in other museums. —Jo."

Chapter 6. Exhibition

1. Denison, personal communication, June 21, 2004.

2. The designers used Adobe Photoshop to prepare layouts and plan the gallery space, so it was no surprise that it was perceived as a "flat" exhibit. One curator said that it reminded her of a "movie set," where backdrops are painted to give the illusion of depth.

3. NMAI curator, personal communication, June 4, 2004.

4. NMAI curator, personal communication, July 8, 2004.

5. Email to author, February 24, 2008.

6. Paul Chaat Smith, April 11, 2006.

7. Whereas anthropologists are trying to move "beyond the cultural turn" (see, for example, Bonnell et al. 1999; Gupta and Ferguson 1992), indigenous peoples have been embracing "culture" as a legal, political, and economic resource and thus as a source for empowerment. William Mazzarella (2004:347) marks this development with a "slightly bemused recognition that while the culture concept was undergoing an apparently terminal crisis in anthropology the rest of the world was lustily discovering it." And Marshall Sahlins (1999:401) famously wrote, "All of a sudden everyone 'got' culture…. 'If we didn't have kastom,' the New Guinean said to his anthropologist, 'we would be just like White Men.'" As long as culture is considered to be a thing that people have (Handler 1985) and the "postmodern marketing of heritage" continues to render "the display of identity as culture or art" (Clifford 1997:219), the trope of tradition and the notion of culture loss will persist in presentations of Native identity in the museum and elsewhere.

8. Early in the process, *Our Lives* staff had brainstormed about how to show that the communities are not isolated but are instead interconnected. Ideas such as lines on the exhibition floor tying them together or other indicators of cross-cultural influence were never fully developed. Although this criticism of bounded communities was anticipated, in the final exhibition, no strategies were implemented to address it.

Chapter 7. Reception

1. NMAI curatorial research assistant, August 3, 2004.

2. A "soft opening" is a preview of the exhibitions before the official opening. There was one for the press, although, at that time, the exhibitions were not complete (labels and media were not yet in place); another for staff members; and a "preview reception" on September 20, 2004.

3. Co-curators did not relate this experience only to me. Yakama co-curator Arlen Washines, at the 2005 AAM conference, specifically mentioned during his presentation that the Yakama co-curators had done a prayer in their NMAI exhibit space before the opening: "[We] had our own time before others saw it." He added, "[The exhibit] made me feel at home, made me feel good…knowing that people of the world will know who we were, who we are, and see what we have. Maybe not…all of it, but at least some of it."

4. Considered an "icon of the Inuit," an *inuksuk* is a pile of rocks used as a marker for way finding or special places. Inuksuk may have been used to corral animals or as markers for good hunting and fishing places. The way they are constructed, they often look like human beings in the distance. For more information, see Graburn 2004.

5. Paris, February 23, 2005.

6. All the speakers used this phrase, which was new to me, as a reference to the museum.

7. Susan Power, personal communication, October 5, 2005. The Jingle Dress Dance is considered a gift from the Creator to the Ojibwes. The dress itself is slim fitting and covered in rows of metal cones that jingle as the woman dances.

8. A number of journal articles discuss them. See, for example, Lonetree 2006; Lonetree and Cobb 2008; Phillips 2006; Reinhardt 2005.

9. This is from a recording I made of Elaine's speech, which I transcribed and then made available to the NMAI staff by email, with Elaine's permission.

10. Elaine and Rick included the public programs, community outreach programs, theater, and cafe as some of the museum functions making up the 70 percent.

11. Rapkievian, personal communication, May 5, 2006.

12. Tayac, personal communication, October 6, 2004.

13. MacPherson, October 12, 2004.

14. NMAI staff member, personal communication, October 28, 2004.

15. West, interview, November 18, 2004. All quotations from Rick that follow come from this interview.

16. From an NMAI internal survey of the *OL* exhibit, "*Our Lives*: Evaluation of Community Curated Sections" (June 2005), in possession of author.

17. Rapkievian, personal communication, May 3, 2006.

18. One NMAI staff member commented on Rick's statement: "I always wanted to feel like [the] NMAI wasn't just a museum. And to me, a museum is just exhibitions, primarily. So you know, I don't really find that problematic. But I guess I find it problematic—or [do] not find it problematic, but it leaves me wondering—especially since we spent so many years and time working with twenty-four Native communities, that…sort of everything was leading up to the opening of this museum and these new exhibits.… Then just to say, well, they're just 30 percent. Well then, what's the other 70 percent? That's what I want to know. [*laughs*] So I guess that's the only thing that would kind of bother me.… Because I think it was some important work that we did and that we're never ever going to do again. So, you know, we shouldn't just toss it aside so easily." CRC staff member, November 24, 2004.

19. NMAI research assistant, October 15, 2004.

20. Gurian, personal communication, November 17, 2004.

21. However, Cynthia Chavez had a Ph.D. in American studies and was well received by Native communities. Bruce Bernstein and Ann McMullen had Ph.D.s in anthropology, but curators Cécile Ganteaume and Emil Her Many Horses did not. In other words, the lead curators of the exhibitions whom Elaine was generalizing about had very different backgrounds. Everyone, including the curators, mentioned, recognized, praised, and appreciated Elaine's intelligence and insight into museum practice. The problem was that, in this case, as one person explained, she was still operating under assumptions she had developed during consultations in the early 1990s (when these were indeed the sentiments of advisors) and she had not updated her notions based on the actual practices of curators at the NMAI since. A number of people felt that this influential consultant greatly misunderstood the NMAI curatorial philosophy.

22. Suzukovich, January 8, 2005.

23. Fox-Starr, January 16, 2005.

24. As Craig Howe (2001:32–33) notes, intratribal dynamics can be set into play when participating with a museum. The process can also affirm and acknowledge the collective knowledge of the community. Accordingly, communities often want copies of the information developed for exhibition.

25. Whereas I was able to facilitate getting the NMAI bookstore to sell the Chicago community's video, the Kalinagos, unfortunately, did not have the same opportunity. Prosper Paris's wife, Marian, and I spent two weeks creating a "craft catalog" for Smithsonian Business Ventures (SBV), the organization that oversees purchases for Smithsonian bookstores. At SBV's request our reference document included measurements and prices of each craft and photos

of each craftmaker from every hamlet. Unfortunately, during this time, the SBV experienced downsizing and our main contact left the organization. After I returned to the Carib Territory in 2007, I sent additional materials to the NMAI, but the SBV expressed interest not in the crafts but rather in a new booklet that included a number of articles written by Kalinago co-curators. The booklet, published by the Cultural Division of the Dominica government and titled *Heritage of the Kalinago People*, was never in the NMAI bookstore, however. We made repeated attempts to follow up with Cultural Division staff, but they never provided copies of the book to the SBV (see Cultural Division 2007).

26. CRC staff member, personal communication, October 6, 2004.

27. This oversight was corrected by the time *Listening to Our Ancestors* was created; having a separate community event at which the co-curators are honored was suggested in postmortem documents as essential to the process (see epilogue).

28. Chavez, November 24, 2004.

29. Compare this with Michel Foucault's concept of "subjugated knowledge," or knowledge that is "disqualified from the hierarchy of knowledges and sciences" (Foucault and Gordon 1980:82).

Chapter 8. Reflection

1. Radio interview, WESU, August 27, 2009, about Paul Smith's then new book, *Everything You Know about Indians Is Wrong* (2009), available at www.indigenouspolitics.mypodcast .com (accessed December 11, 2009).

2. For more information, see Breidenbach and McAndrew 2006.

3. From January to March 2005, a list of questions reflecting these and other stereotypes was collected by the NMAI Resource Center from the Native cultural interpreters, who heard them in the museum. The questions included "Are you a real Indian?" "Is this the American Indian zoo?" (from a second-grader), "Are there any tribes that practice where a virgin girl goes into womanhood by getting with her father for the first time?" "You as an interpreter, do you get into trouble by the NMAI if you change your look and don't look the part [Indian]?" "Are all of the people in these pictures [*Our Lives* Face Wall] full-blooded Indian?" "Aren't you angry for what has happened to you?" "What is [the] politically correct term for calling you?" "Did you guys start the term 'blood brothers' or exchange blood by cutting your wrists?" "What are advantages and disadvantages of being recognized?" "How did the statue of an Indian man in a bonnet end up in the front of cigar stores?" "What do thirteen-year-old Navajo boys like as gifts?" "Where is the info on the 'black Indians'?" "Are Indians still here today?" and "Does this museum provide a catharsis for you? What does this museum do for you?" (from two anthropologists). One cultural interpreter got the following string of questions: "You don't sound like an Indian. Where are your feathers? Where are your bows and arrows? Are you an Indian?" Another interpreter commented in the log, "Visitor on a VIP tour said that Native people on the Trail of Tears opened casinos at every stop on their trip.... I chose to ignore his comment and proceeded with the tour. I ended up talking about the Trail of Tears in *Our Peoples* and casinos in *Our Lives*."

4. See Kuhn 1996 for a discusson of how paradigms shift.

5. CRC staff member, personal communication, July 8, 2004.

6. Some of this material is based on Shannon 2009.

7. In the final version of the UN document, the removal of the brackets obviated days of

contentious discussions over the meaning of "gender," allowing the text to flow seamlessly and seemingly uncontested (Riles 2006b).

8. I discuss "representational experts" and the "professionalizaton of indigeneity" in Shannon 2011.

9. For an excellent resource about the history and practice of collaboration in cultural anthropology, see Lassiter 2005.

10. See McMullen 2009:86 for a discussion of how collector George Gustav Heye has become an "inconvenient truth and…a victim of [the NMAI's] self-told story"; there has been a "systematic erasure of Heye's purpose and intent in assembling a collection and founding the MAI." McMullen seeks to restore this particular invisible genealogy in the history of the institution and to provide a more nuanced image of Heye than "just a crazy white man."

11. For a discussion of the rise of professions and issues of professional jurisdiction, see Abbott 1988.

12. But whose feedback counts? The NMAI is moving more and more toward being a mainstream mall museum. The Resource Center is now a family-focused activity room, and the library is no longer there for self-directed scholarly research. The cafeteria, lauded by director Kevin Gover as the main icon for the museum, has been expanded into the first-floor gift shop's original location. NMAI employee, personal communication, August 1, 2011.

13. For example, curator John Terrell wrote a notorious and biting commentary on his experience transitioning to the team approach at the Field Museum. Terrell (1991:152) claimed, "[The] era of the curator-driven exhibition is dead. From this day forth, we will give our 'museum visitors' what they want, when they want it, and how they want it…. From now on, museum educators are to be…the lucky ones to decide what visitors may and may not see in museums." Sounding very much like NMAI staff members, he described the Field Museum's "reorganization" to increase "efficiency" and the existence of "two cultures" at the museum: the curators versus everyone else. In a sarcastic tone mocking some common critiques of curators, he said that they do not care about museum visitors and this is why they are being "driven back into their ivory towers."

14. Conversation with a participant in early Smithsonian meetings, July 29, 2011.

15. At the December 2005 AAA meetings in Washington, DC, Rick spoke in the plenary session: "I fully appreciate—and honor—the reality that, in *anthropology's deconstruction and reconstruction of itself in the past two decades, this system of knowledge has repositioned in critical ways that align with much of what I have described.* With respect, specifically, to the involvement of Native peoples in its work, the discipline of *anthropology now has proceeded well beyond the notion of Native "informants" to strike genuinely collaborative and partnering relationships with Native peoples.* It also acknowledges and attempts to incorporate, through this partnering, the subjective tethers and nuances of culture that tell us so much more about the first citizens of the Americas than the excessive devotion to a sometimes empty 'descriptiveness' did a generation ago" (emphases added).

16. See http://www.prm.ox.ac.uk/haida.html (accessed December 19, 2012). In the video, Pitt Rivers Museum curator Laura Peers explains that many Native American objects are in European museums. She says that this is "kind of like removing all the history books" and that these new kinds of collaboration are aimed at "recovering knowledge [that] is important to identity."

17. See Phillips 2004 about Iroquois False Face masks, for example. At the UBC Museum

of Anthropology, a mask was wrapped (and thus concealed) in the display case and flanked by two labels. One label was a statement by the Grand Council of Haudenosaunee forbidding any display of these masks. The other was by a mask maker, who felt that it was fine to display masks not produced for ceremonial purposes. Beyond collaboration and honoring a tribe's request, this display also showed that there is diversity in the community and that the museum chooses to err on the side of caution. Meanwhile, the visitor learns far more about postcolonial dynamics by viewing a concealed object than viewing no object at all.

Epilogue

1. McMullen, personal communication, January 31, 2005.

2. I rely on an unpublished draft Rachel provided in March 2006 during my fieldwork (Griffin 2005; a published version is Griffin 2007).

3. The Bering Strait theory posits that Native Americans' ancestors—the first people in the Americas—migrated from Asia thousands of years ago over the Bering Strait land bridge, which has surfaced occasionally through time in the Bering Sea between Alaska and Russia. Native American communities have origin accounts that often conflict with this theory.

References

Abbott, Andrew Delano
1988   The System of Professions: An Essay on the Division of Expert Labor. Chicago: University of Chicago Press.

Achenbach, Joel
2004   Within These Walls, Science Yields to Stories. Washington Post, September 19: R1, R7.

Alexander, Catherine
2002   Personal States: Making Connections between People and Bureaucracy in Turkey. New York: Oxford University Press.

American Alliance of Museums
2012   Museum Facts. http://www.speakupformuseums.org/museum_facts.htm, accessed October 25, 2012.

American Association of Museums
2002   Mastering Civic Engagement: A Challenge to Museums. Washington, DC: American Association of Museums.

American Indian College Fund
2001   Getting the Word Out: Have You Ever Seen a Real Indian? http://www.collegefund.org/news/news01 /campaign2001.shtml, accessed January 4, 2004.

Ames, Michael
1987   Free Indians from Their Ethnological Fate: The Emergence of the Indian Point of View in Exhibitions of Indians. Muse 5(2):14–25.
1992   Cannibal Tours and Glass Boxes: The Anthropology of Museums. Vancouver: University of British Columbia Press.
1999   How to Decorate a House: The Re-negotiation of Cultural Representations at the University of British Columbia Museum of Anthropology. Museum Anthropology 22(3):41–51.
2000   Are Changing Representations of First Peoples in Canadian Museums and Galleries Challenging the Curatorial Prerogative? In The Changing Presentation of the American Indian: Museums and Native Cultures. R. West and NMAI, eds. Pp. 73–88. Washington, DC: National Museum of the American Indian.

Amit, Vered
2002   Reconceptualizing Community. In Realizing Community: Concepts, Social Relationships and Sentiments. V. Amit, ed. Pp. 1–20. New York: Routledge.

Anderson, Gail
2012   Reinventing the Museum: The Evolving Conversation on the Paradigm Shift. Lanham, MD: AltaMira.

Ang, Ien
1996   Living Room Wars: Rethinking Media Audiences for a Postmodern World. London: Routledge.

Appadurai, Arjun, ed.
1986   The Social Life of Things: Commodities in Cultural Perspective. Cambridge: Cambridge University Press.

Archambault, JoAllyn

1993   American Indians and American Museums. Zeitschrift für Ethnologie 118:7–22.

2011   Native Communities, Museums and Collaboration. Practicing Anthropology 33(2):16–20.

Arndt, Grant

1998   Relocation's Imagined Landscape and the Rise of Chicago's Native American Community. *In* Native Chicago. T. Straus and G. Arndt, eds. Pp. 114–127. Chicago: McNaughton and Gunn.

Atalay, Sonya

2006   Indigenous Archaeology as Decolonizing Practice. American Indian Quarterly 30(3–4):280–310.

Baggioli, Mario

2006   Documents of Documents: Scientists' Claims and Scientific Claims. *In* Documents: Artifacts of Modern Knowledge. A. Riles, ed. Pp. 127–157. Ann Arbor: University of Michigan Press.

Baker, Patrick

1994   Centring the Periphery: Chaos, Order, and the Ethnohistory of Dominica. Kingston, Jamaica: University of the West Indies Press.

Basso, Keith

1996   Wisdom Sits in Places: Landscape and Language among the Western Apache. Albuquerque: University of New Mexico Press.

Batty, Phillip

2005   Private Politics, Public Strategies: White Advisers and Their Aboriginal Subjects. Oceania 75(3):209–221.

Beck, David

1988   The Chicago American Indian Community, 1893–1988: Annotated Bibliography and Guide to Sources in Chicago. Chicago: NAES College Press.

1998   The Chicago American Indian Community. *In* Native Chicago. T. Straus and G. Arndt, eds. Pp. 167–181. Chicago: McNaughton and Gunn.

2002   Developing a Voice: The Evolution of Self-Determination in an Urban Indian Community. Wicazo Sa Review 17(2):117–141.

Beckles, Hilary M.

1992   Kalinago (Carib) Resistance to European Colonisation of the Caribbean. Caribbean Quarterly 38(2&3):1–14.

Berlo, Janet Catherine, and Aldona Jonaitis

2005   "Indian Country" on Washington's Mall—The National Museum of the American Indian: A Review Essay. Museum Anthropology 28(2):17–30.

Berman, Judith

1996   "The Culture as It Appears to the Indian Himself." *In* Volksgeist as Method and Ethic: Essays on Boasian Ethnography and the German Anthropological Tradition, vol. 8. G. W. J. Stocking, ed. Pp. 215–256. Madison: University of Wisconsin Press.

Bernstein, Bruce, Joan Kathryn O'Donnell, and Rina Swentzell, eds.

2001   Here, Now, and Always: Voices of the First Peoples of the Southwest. Albuquerque: University of New Mexico Press.

Blue Spruce, Duane, and the National Museum of the American Indian

2004   Spirit of a Native Place: Building the National Museum of the American Indian. Washington, DC: National Museum of the American Indian, Smithsonian Institution, in association with National Geographic.

Boas, Franz

1887   The Study of Geography. Science 9(210):137–141.

1889   On Alternating Sounds. American Anthropologist 2(1):47–54.

1907   Some Principles of Museum Administration. Science 25(650):921–933.

1911   Handbook of American Indian Languages. Washington, DC: Government Printing Office.

1919   Report on the Academic Teaching of Anthropology. American Anthropologist 21(1):41–48.

1920   The Methods of Ethnology. American Anthropologist 22(4):311–321.

2004[1887] Museums of Ethnology and Their Classification. *In* Museum Studies: An Anthology of Contexts. B. M. Carbonell, ed. Pp. 139–142. Malden, MA: Blackwell.

Boast, Robin

2011   Neocolonial Collaboration: Museum as Contact Zone Revisited. Museum Anthropology 34(1):56–70.

Bodinger de Uriarte, John

2007   Casino and Museum: Representing Mashantucket Pequot Identity. Tucson: University of Arizona Press.

Bonnell, Victoria E., Lynn Avery Hunt, and Richard Biernacki

1999   Beyond the Cultural Turn: New Directions in the Study of Society and Culture. Berkeley: University of California Press.

Born, Georgina

1995   Rationalizing Culture: IRCAM, Boulez, and the Institutionalization of the Musical Avant-Garde. Berkeley: University of California Press.

Bouquet, Mary

2000   Thinking and Doing Otherwise: Anthropological Theory in Exhibitionary Practice. Ethnos 65(2):217–236.

2001   The Art of Exhibition Making as a Problem of Translation. *In* Academic Anthropology and the Museum: Back to the Future. M. Bouquet, ed. Pp. 177–199. New York: Berghahn.

Bowechop, Janine, and Patricia Pierce Erikson

2005   Forging Indigenous Methodologies on Cape Flattery: The Makah Museum as a Center of Collaborative Research. American Indian Quarterly 29(1 & 2):263–273.

Boyer, Dominic

2003   Censorship as a Vocation: The Institutions, Practices, and Cultural Logic of Media Control in the German Democratic Republic. Comparative Studies in Society and History 45(03):511–545.

2004   The Dilemma of the Anthropology of Experts. Paper presented at the American Anthropological Association conference, Chicago, November 17–21.

2008   Thinking through the Anthropology of Experts. Anthropology in Action 15(2):38–46.

Breidenbach, Michelle, and Mike McAndrew

2006   Sign on Indian Land Now Targets Spitzer: I-81 Billboard Repainted to Criticize the Attorney General rather than Gov. Pataki. Syracuse Post-Standard, June 3. http://www.onondaganation.org /news/2006/2006_0603.html, accessed June 22, 2008.

Brenneis, Donald

1994   Discourse and Discipline at the National Research Council: A Bureaucratic Bildungsroman. Cultural Anthropology 9(1):23–36.

Brettell, Caroline

1993   When They Read What We Write: The Politics of Ethnography. Westport, CT: Bergin and Garvey.

Brown, Dee Alexander

1971   Bury My Heart at Wounded Knee: An Indian History of the American West. New York: Holt.

Buntinx, Gustavo, and Ivan Karp

2006   Tactical Museologies. *In* Museum Frictions: Public Cultures/Global Transformations. I. Karp, C. A. Kratz, L. Szwaja, and T. Ybarra-Frausto, eds. Pp. 207–218. Durham, NC: Duke University Press.

Bunzl, Matti

1998   Franz Boas and the Humboldtian Tradition: From Volksgeist and Nationalcharakter to an Anthropological Concept of Culture. *In* Volksgeist as Method and Ethic: Essays on Boasian Ethnography and the German Anthropological Tradition. G. Stocking, ed. Pp. 17–78. Madison: University of Wisconsin Press.

2004   Boas, Foucault, and the "Native Anthropologist": Notes toward a Neo-Boasian Anthropology. American Anthropologist 106(3):435–442.

2005   Anthropology beyond the Crisis: Toward an Intellectual History of the Extended Present. Anthropology and Humanism 30(2):187–195.

Carpenter, Edmund Snow
2005   Two Essays: Chief and Greed. North Andover, MA: Persimmon.

Cattelino, Jessica
2008   High Stakes: Florida Seminole Gaming and Sovereignty. Durham, NC: Duke University Press.

Chavez, Cynthia
2001   Negotiated Representations: Pueblo Artists and Culture (New Mexico). Ph.D. dissertation, University of New Mexico.

Chavez Lamar, Cynthia
2008   Collaborative Exhibit Development at the Smithsonian's National Museum of the American Indian. *In* The National Museum of the American Indian: Critical Conversations. A. Lonetree and A. J. Cobb, eds. Pp. 144–164. Lincoln: University of Nebraska Press.

Chavez Lamar, Cynthia, Sherry Farrell Racette, and Lara Evans
2010   Art in Our Lives: Native Women Artists in Dialogue. Santa Fe, NM: SAR Press.

Christen, Kimberly
2011   Opening Archives: Respectful Repatriation. American Archivist 74(1):185–210.

Clavir, Miriam
2002   Preserving What Is Valued: Museums, Conservation, and First Nations. Vancouver: University of British Columbia Press.

Clifford, James
1988   The Predicament of Culture: Twentieth-Century Ethnography, Literature, and Art. Cambridge, MA: Harvard University Press.

1997   Routes: Travel and Translation in the Late Twentieth Century. Cambridge, MA: Harvard University Press.

Clifford, James, and George Marcus
1986   Writing Culture. Berkeley: University of California Press.

Cobb, Amanda J.
2005   The National Museum of the American Indian as Cultural Sovereignty. American Quarterly 57(2):485–506.

Colwell-Chanthaphonh, Chip
2007   Massacre at Camp Grant: Forgetting and Remembering Apache History. Tucson: University of Arizona Press.

2009   Collaborative Ethics and Epistemology: Collaborative Communities and Multivocality in Archaeology. Paper presented at the American Anthropological Association conference, Philadelphia, December 2–6.

Colwell-Chanthaphonh, C., and T. J. Ferguson
2004   Virtue Ethics and the Practice of History. Journal of Social Archaeology 4(1):5.

2006   Trust and Archaeological Practice: Towards a Framework of Virtue Ethics. *In* The Ethics of Archaeology: Philosophical Perspectives on Archaeological Practice. C. Scarre and G. Scarre, eds. Pp. 115–130. Cambridge: Cambridge University Press.

Colwell-Chanthaphonh, Chip, Stephen E. Nash, and Steven R. Holen
2010   Crossroads of Culture: Anthropology Collections at the Denver Museum of Nature and Science. Boulder: University Press of Colorado.

Cruikshank, Julie
1992   Oral Tradition and Material Culture: Multiplying the Meanings of "Words" and "Things." Anthropology Today 8(3):5–9.

Cultural Division, Ministry of Community Development, Gender Affairs and Information, Commonwealth of Dominica

2007   Heritage of the Kalinago People. Lethbridge, Canada: Paramount Printers.

Darnell, Regna

2001   Invisible Genealogies: A History of Americanist Anthropology. Lincoln: University of Nebraska Press.

Deloria, Vine, Jr.

1988[1969] Custer Died for Your Sins: An Indian Manifesto. Norman: University of Oklahoma Press.

Denny, J. Peter

1999   Current Extensions of Sapir and Whorf in Cross-Cultural Cognitive Science: Cognitive Styles and Ontological Categories. *In* Theorizing the Americanist Tradition. R. Darnell and L. P. Valentine, eds. Pp. 365–379. Toronto: University of Toronto Press.

Doering, Zahava

1999   Strangers, Guests or Clients? Visitor Experiences in Museums. Curator 42(2):74–87.

Dornfeld, Barry

1998   Producing Public Television, Producing Public Culture. Princeton, NJ: Princeton University Press.

Dubin, Margaret

1999   Native American Imagemaking and the Spurious Canon of the "Of-and-By." Visual Anthropology Review 15(1):70–74.

Echo-Hawk, Roger

2002   Keepers of Culture: Repatriating Cultural Items under the Native American Graves Protection and Repatriation Act. Denver: Denver Art Museum. http://www.denverartmuseum.org/sites/all/themes /dam/files/nagpra.pdf, accessed December 11, 2012.

Erikson, Patricia Pierce

2004   "Defining Ourselves through Baskets": Museum Autoethnography and the Makah Cultural and Research Center. *In* Coming to Shore: Northwest Coast Ethnology, Traditions, and Visions. M. Mauzé, M. E. Harkin, and S. Kan, eds. Pp. 339–362. Lincoln: University of Nebraska Press.

Erikson, Patricia Pierce, Helma Ward, and Kirk Wachendorf

2002   Voices of a Thousand People: The Makah Cultural and Research Center. Lincoln: University of Nebraska Press.

Errington, Shelly

1994   What Became Authentic Primitive Art? Cultural Anthropology 9(2):201–226.

1998   The Death of Authentic Primitive Art and Other Tales of Progress. Berkeley: University of California Press.

Evelyn, Douglas, and Mark Hirsch

2006   At the Threshold: A Response to Comments on the National Museum of the American Indian's Inaugural Exhibitions. Public Historian 28(2):85–90.

Ferguson, James

1990   The Anti-politics Machine: "Development," Depoliticization, and Bureaucratic Power in Lesotho. New York: Cambridge University Press.

Fine-Dare, Kathleen

2002   Grave Injustice: The American Indian Repatriation Movement and NAGPRA. Lincoln: University of Nebraska Press.

Fisher, Marc

2004   Indian Museum's Appeal, Sadly, Only Skin-Deep. Washington Post, September 21: B1.

Fitzhugh, William

1997   Ambassadors in Sealskins: Exhibiting Eskimos at the Smithsonian. *In* Exhibiting Dilemmas: Issues of Representation at the Smithsonian. A. Henderson and A. L. Kaeppler, eds. Pp. 206–245. Washington, DC: Smithsonian Institution Press.

Force, Roland

1999   Politics and the Museum of the American Indian: The Heye and the Mighty. Honolulu, Hawaii: Mechas.

Foucault, Michel

1979   Discipline and Punish: The Birth of the Prison. New York: Vintage.

Foucault, Michel, and Colin Gordon

1980   Power/Knowledge: Selected Interviews and Other Writings, 1972–1977. Brighton, England: Harvester.

Fricker, Miranda

2007   Epistemic Injustice: Power and the Ethics of Knowing. New York: Oxford University Press.

Friedman, Jonathon

2001   Museums, the State and Global Transformation: From Temple of the Muses to Temple of Amusements. Folk 43:251–268.

Gable, Eric

2010[2009] Ethnographie: Das Museum als Feld *In* Museumsanalyse: Methoden und Konturen eines neuen Forschungsfeldes. J. Baur, ed. Pp. 95–120. Bielefeld, Germany: Transcript.

Gerard Hilferty and Associates

1995   National Museum of the American Indian Smithsonian Institution Mall Facility Exhibition Master Plan, Phase I Interim Report: Orientation and Research. Unpublished document in possession of author.

1997   National Museum of the American Indian Smithsonian Institution National Mall Museum Exhibition Plan, Revised Review Draft. Unpublished document in possession of author.

Ginsburg, Faye

1996   Mediating Culture: Aboriginal Media and the Social Transformation of Identity. Paper presented at the Conference on Communication and Empowerment: Uses of Media and Information Technologies in Developing Countries, Los Angeles, April 11–13.

2002[1995] Mediating Culture: Indigenous Media, Ethnographic Film, and the Production of Identity. *In* The Anthropology of Media: A Reader. K. Askew and R. E. Wilk, eds. Pp. 210–235. Malden, MA: Blackwell.

Graburn, Nelson

2004   Inuksuk: Icon of the Inuit of Nunavut. Études/Inuit/Studies 28(1):69–82.

Graburn, Nelson, and Kathryn Mathers

2000   Museums Inside and Out. Current Anthropology 41(4):691–692.

Great Lakes Research Alliance for the Study of Aboriginal Arts and Cultures

2008   About GRASAC. https://grasac.org/gks/gks_about.php, accessed July 16, 2012.

Gregoire, Crispin, and Natalia Kanem

1989   The Caribs of Dominica: Land Rights and Ethnic Consciousness. Cultural Survival Quarterly 13(3):52–55.

Griffin, Rachel

2005   Aesthetics and Authenticity at the National Museum of the American Indian. Unpublished document in possession of author.

2007   The Art of Native Life: Exhibiting Culture and Identity at the National Museum of the American Indian. American Indian Culture and Research Journal 31(3):167–180.

Griffin, Rachel, and Lindsey Martin

2005   The Art of Native Life along the North Pacific Coast: Eleven Communities, One Exhibit. Paper presented at the Native American Arts Studies Association conference, Phoenix, October 25–30.

Griffins, José-Marie, and Donald King

2008   Interconnections: The IMLS National Study on the Use of Libraries, Museums, and the

Internet—Conclusions: Study by the Institute of Museum and Library Services. http://www.sla.org
/content/SLA/alignment/portal/documents/explore/industry-reports/IMLS%20Study.pdf, accessed
October 25, 2012.

Grobsmith, Elizabeth
1997   Growing Up on Deloria: The Impact of His Work on a New Generation of Anthropologists. *In*
        Indians and Anthropologists: Vine Deloria Jr. and the Critique of Anthropology. T. Biolsi and
        L. J. Zimmerman, eds. Pp. 35–49. Tucson: University of Arizona Press.

Gupta, Akhil, and James Ferguson
1992   Beyond "Culture": Space, Identity, and the Politics of Difference. Cultural Anthropology 7(1):6–23.
1997   Anthropological Locations: Boundaries and Grounds of a Field Science. Berkeley: University of
        California Press.

Gurian, Elaine Heumann, and Ken Gorbey
2003a   Gurian-Gorbey Report 3-03. Washington, DC: National Museum of the American Indian.
        Unpublished document in possession of author.
2003b   National Museum of the American Indian Mall Museum Transition Office Summary Action Steps.
        Unpublished document in possession of author.

Gusterson, Hugh
1996   Nuclear Rites: A Weapons Laboratory at the End of the Cold War. Berkeley: University of California
        Press.

Hale, Charles
2006   Activist Research v. Cultural Critique: Indigenous Land Rights and the Contradictions of Politically
        Engaged Anthropology. Cultural Anthropology 21(1):96–120.

Handler, Richard
1985   On Having Culture: Nationalism and the Preservation of Quebec's *Patrimoine*. *In* Essays on Museums
        and Material Culture. G. Stocking, ed. Pp. 192–217. Madison: University of Wisconsin Press.

Handler, Richard, and Eric Gable
1997   The New History in an Old Museum: Creating the Past at Colonial Williamsburg. Durham, NC:
        Duke University Press.

Haraway, Donna
1991   Situated Knowledges: The Science Question in Feminism and the Privilege of Partial Perspective. *In*
        Simians, Cyborgs, and Women: The Reinvention of Nature. Pp. 183–201. New York: Routledge.

Hedlund, Ann Lane
1994   Speaking for or about Others? Evolving Ethnological Perspectives. Museum Anthropology 18(3):32–43.

Hennessy, Kate
2009   Digital Matters: Anthropology, Disciplinarity, and Repatriation in a Northern Athapaskan
        Community. Paper presented at the American Anthropological Association conference, Philadelphia,
        December 4.

Herle, Anita
2000   Torres Strait Islanders: Stories from an Exhibition. Ethnos 65(2):253–274.

Herzfeld, Michael
1992   The Social Production of Indifference: Exploring the Symbolic Roots of Western Bureaucracy.
        Chicago: University of Chicago Press.

Holmes, Doug
2000   Integral Europe: Fast-Capitalism, Multiculturalism, Neofascism. Princeton, NJ: Princeton University
        Press.

Holmes, Doug, and George Marcus
2005   Cultures of Expertise and the Management of Globalization: Toward a Re-functioning of
        Ethnography. *In* Global Assemblages: Technology, Politics, and Ethics as Anthropological Problems.
        A. Ong and S. J. Collier, eds. Pp. 235–252. Malden, MA: Blackwell.

Honychurch, Lennox

1984   The Dominica Story: A History of the Island. Roseau, Dominica, West Indies: Dominica Institute.

1997   Carib to Creole: Contact and Culture Exchange in Dominica. Ph.D. dissertation, University of Oxford, St. Hugh's College.

Hooper-Greenhill, Eilean

2006   Studying Visitors. *In* A Companion to Museum Studies. S. Macdonald, ed. Pp. 362–380. Oxford: Blackwell.

Howe, Craig

2001   Exhibiting Indians: Communities, Collaboration and Control. Exhibitionist 20(1):28–33.

2002   Keep Your Thoughts above the Trees: Ideas on Developing and Presenting Tribal Histories. *In* Clearing a Path: Theorizing the Past in Native American Studies. N. Shoemaker, ed. Pp. 161–179. New York: Routledge.

2005   The Morality of Exhibiting Indians. *In* Embedding Ethics. L. Meskell and P. Pels, eds. Pp. 219–238. Oxford: Berg.

Hymes, Dell, ed.

1972   Reinventing Anthropology. New York: Vintage.

Intellectual Property Issues in Cultural Heritage

2012   About Us. http://www.sfu.ca/ipinch/about, accessed July 16, 2012.

Isaac, Gwyneira

2005   Mediating Knowledges: Zuni Negotiations for a Culturally Relevant Museum. Museum Anthropology 28(1):3–18.

2007   Mediating Knowledges: Origins of a Zuni Tribal Museum. Tucson: University of Arizona Press.

Jacknis, Ira

1985   Franz Boas and Exhibits: On the Limitations of the Museum Method of Anthropology. *In* Objects and Others: Essays on Museums and Material Culture. G. Stocking, ed. Pp. 75–111. Madison: University of Wisconsin Press.

2002a   The First Boasian: Alfred Kroeber and Franz Boas, 1896–1905. American Anthropologist 104(2):520–532.

2002b   The Storage Box of Tradition: Kwakiutl Art, Anthropologists, and Museums, 1881–1981. Washington, DC: Smithsonian Institution Press.

Jean-Klein, Iris, and Annelise Riles

2005   Introducing Discipline: Anthropology and Human Rights Administrations. Political and Legal Anthropology Review 28(2):173–202.

Jones, Alison, and Kuni Jenkins

2008   Rethinking Collaboration: Working the Indigene-Colonizer Hyphen. *In* The Handbook of Critical and Indigenous Methodologies. N. K. Denzin, Y. S. Lincoln, and L. T. Smith, eds. Pp. 471–486. Los Angeles: Sage.

Jones, Anna Laura

1993   Exploding Cannons: The Anthropology of Museums. Annual Review of Anthropology 22:210–220.

Joseph, Garnette

1997   Five Hundred Years of Resistance. *In* The Indigenous People of the Caribbean. S. M. Wilson, ed. Pp. 214–222. Miami: University Press of Florida.

Joseph, Garnette, and Jennifer Shannon

2009   The Carib Liberation Movement: The Legacy of American Indian Activism in Dominica. *In* Visions and Voices: American Indian Activism and the Civil Rights Movement. T. Straus and K. Peters, eds. Pp. 408–425. Chicago: Albatross.

Kahn, Miriam

2000   Not Really Pacific Voices: Politics of Representation in Collaborative Museum Exhibits. Museum Anthropology 24(1):57–74.

Kilian, Michael

2004   DC Museum Honors Indian Spirit, Identity. Chicago Tribune, September 16: 1.

Kirshenblatt-Gimblett, Barbara

1998   Destination Culture: Tourism, Museums, and Heritage. Berkeley: University of California Press.

Kopytoff, Igor

1986   The Cultural Biography of Things: Commoditization as Process. *In* The Social Life of Things. A. Appadurai, ed. Pp. 64–91. New York: Cambridge University Press.

Kratz, Corinne, and Ivan Karp

2006   Museum Frictions: Public Cultures/Global Transformations. *In* Museum Frictions: Public Cultures/ Global Transformations. I. Karp, C. A. Kratz, L. Szwaja, and T. Ybarra-Frausto, eds. Pp. 1–33. Durham, NC: Duke University Press.

Kreps, Christina

1988   Decolonizing Anthropology Museums: The Tropenmuseum, Amsterdam. Museum Studies Journal 3(2):56–63.

2003a   Curatorship as Social Practice. Curator 46(3):311–324. Art Full Text (H. W. Wilson), EBSCOhost, accessed June 3, 2013.

2003b   Liberating Culture: Cross-Cultural Perspectives on Museums, Curation, and Heritage Preservation. New York: Routledge.

Kuhn, Thomas

1996   The Structure of Scientific Revolutions. Chicago: University of Chicago Press.

Kurin, Richard

1997   Reflections of a Cultural Broker: A View from the Smithsonian. Washington, DC: Smithsonian Institution Press.

LaGrand, James

2002   Indian Metropolis: Native Americans in Chicago, 1945–75. Urbana: University of Illinois Press.

Lassiter, Luke

2005   The Chicago Guide to Collaborative Ethnography. Chicago: University of Chicago Press.

Latour, Bruno

1990   Drawing Things Together. *In* Representation in Scientific Practice. M. Lynch and S. Woolgar, eds. Pp. 19–68. Cambridge: Massachusetts Institute of Technology Press.

1993   We Have Never Been Modern. Cambridge, MA: Harvard University Press.

Latour, Bruno, and Steve Woolgar

1986   Laboratory Life. Princeton, NJ: Princeton University Press.

Lederman, Rena

2006   Papering Ethics, Documenting Consent: The New Bureaucracies of Virtue. PoLAR Symposium, Cornell University, October 26–28.

Linenthal, Edward

2001   Preserving Memory: The Struggle to Create America's Holocaust Museum. New York: Columbia University Press.

Lipsky, Michael

1980   Street-Level Bureaucracy: Dilemmas of the Individual in Public Services. New York: Russell Sage Foundation.

Lobo, Susan

2001   Is Urban a Person or Place? Characteristics of Urban Indian Country. *In* American Indians and the Urban Experience. S. Lobo and K. Peters, eds. Pp. 73–84. Walnut Creek, CA: AltaMira.

Lonetree, Amy

2006   Missed Opportunities: Reflections on the NMAI. American Indian Quarterly 30(3–4):632–645.

2012   Decolonizing Museums: Representing Native America in National and Tribal Museums. Chapel Hill: University of North Carolina Press.

Lonetree, Amy, and Amanda J. Cobb

2008 The National Museum of the American Indian: Critical Conversations. Lincoln: University of Nebraska Press.

Macdonald, Sharon

2001 Ethnography in the Science Museum, London. *In* Inside Organizations: Anthropologists at Work. D. N. Gellner and E. Hirsch, eds. Pp. 77–96. New York: Berg.

2002 Behind the Scenes at the Science Museum. New York: Berg.

Macdonald, Sharon, and Roger Silverstone

1990 Rewriting the Museums' Fictions: Taxonomies, Stories and Readers. Cultural Studies 4(2):176–191.

1992 Science on Display: The Representation of Scientific Controversy in Museum Exhibitions. Public Understanding of Science 1(1):69–87.

MacMillan, Kyle

2004 DC Indian Museum Keeps Dialogue Alive. Denver Post, November 14.

Mankekar, Purnima

1999 Screening Culture, Viewing Politics: An Ethnography of Television, Womanhood, and Nation in Postcolonial India. Durham, NC: Duke University Press.

2002 National Texts and Gendered Lives: An Ethnography of Television Viewers in a North Indian City. *In* The Anthropology of Media. A Reader, K. Askew, and R. Wilk, eds. Pp. 299–322. Malden, MA: Blackwell.

Marcus, George

1998 Ethnography through Thick and Thin. Princeton, NJ: Princeton University Press.

Marcus, George, and Michael Fischer

1999[1986] Anthropology as Cultural Critique: An Experimental Moment in the Human Sciences. Chicago: University of Chicago Press.

Marstine, Janet

2006 Introduction. *In* New Museum Theory and Practice: An Introduction. J. Marstine, ed. Pp. 1–36. Oxford: Blackwell.

Matsutake Worlds Research Group

2009 A New Form of Collaboration in Cultural Anthropology: Matsutake Worlds. American Ethnologist 36(2):380–403.

Mazzarella, William

2004 Culture, Globalization, Mediation. Annual Review of Anthropology 33(1):345–367.

McMaster, Gerald, ed.

1998 Reservation X. Ottawa: Canadian Museum of Civilization.

McMaster, Gerald, Clifford E. Trafzer, and National Museum of the American Indian

2004 Native Universe: Voices of Indian America. Washington, DC: National Geographic.

McMullen, Ann

1996 Culture by Design: Native Identity, Historiography, and the Reclamation of Tradition in Twentieth-Century Southeastern New England. Ph.D. dissertation, Brown University.

2008 The Currency of Consultation and Collaboration. Museum Anthropology Review 2(2):54–87.

2009 Reinventing George Heye: Nationalizing the Museum of the American Indian and Its Collections. *In* Contesting Knowledge: Museums and Indigenous Perspectives. S. Sleeper-Smith, ed. Pp. 65–105. Lincoln: University of Nebraska Press.

McMullen, Ann, and Bruce Bernstein

2004 Mall Museum Reviews: An Overview and Analysis. Unpublished document in possession of author.

Merrill, William, Edmund Ladd, and T. J. Ferguson

1993 The Return of the Ahayu:da: Lessons for Repatriation from Zuni Pueblo and the Smithsonian Institution. Current Anthropology 34(5):523–567.

Meskell, Lynn, and Peter Pels, eds.

2005   Embedding Ethics. Oxford: Berg.

Mihesuah, Devon

2000   Repatriation Reader: Who Owns American Indian Remains? Lincoln: University of Nebraska Press.

Mithlo, Nancy Marie

2004   "Red Man's Burden": The Politics of Inclusion in Museum Settings. American Indian Quarterly 28(3/4):743–763.

Miyazaki, Hirokazu

2004   The Method of Hope: Anthropology, Philosophy, and Fijian Knowledge. Stanford, CA: Stanford University Press.

2006   Documenting the Present. In Documents: Artifacts of Modern Knowledge. A. Riles, ed. Pp. 206–225. Durham, NC: Duke University Press.

Mogel, Barbara

2006   Summary of Listening to Our Ancestors Debriefings. Unpublished document in possession of author.

Myers, Fred

2006   The Complicity of Cultural Production: The Contingencies of Performance in Globalizing Museum Practices. In Museum Frictions: Public Cultures/Global Transformations. I. Karp, C. A. Kratz, L. Szwaja, and T. Ybarra-Frausto, eds. Pp. 504–535. Durham, NC: Duke University Press.

Nadasdy, Paul

2003   Hunters and Bureaucrats: Power, Knowledge and Aboriginal-State Relations in the Southwest Yukon. Vancouver: University of British Columbia Press.

Nader, Laura

1974[1969] Up the Anthropologist. In Reinventing Anthropology. D. Hymes, ed. Pp. 284–311. New York: Vintage.

Nash, Stephen, and Chip Colwell-Chanthaphonh

2010   NAGPRA after Two Decades. Museum Anthropology (special issue) 33(2):99–104.

National Museum of the American Indian

2004   Welcome Center on the National Mall: Information Panels. http://www.nmai.si.edu/subpage.cfm ?subpage=visitor&second=dc&third=welcome, accessed January 4, 2004.

Nicks, Trudy

2003   Museums and Contact Work: Introduction. In Museums and Source Communities: A Routledge Reader. L. L. Peers and A. K. Brown, eds. Pp. 19–27. London: Routledge.

Noah, Timothy

2004   The National Museum of Ben Nighthorse Campbell: The Smithsonian's New Travesty. Slate, September 29. http://www.slate.com/id/2107140, accessed December 20, 2012.

O'Hanlon, Michael

1993   Paradise: Portraying the New Guinea Highlands. London: British Museum Press.

Ortner, Sherry

2006   Anthropology and Social Theory: Culture, Power, and the Acting Subject. Durham, NC: Duke University Press.

Paine, Chris, dir.

2006   Who Killed the Electric Car? Sony Pictures Classics.

Peers, Laura, and Alison Brown, eds.

2003   Museums and Source Communities: A Routledge Reader. London: Routledge.

Phillips, Ruth

2000   APEC at the Museum of Anthropology: The Politics of Site and the Poetics of Sight Bite. Ethnos 65(2):172–194.

2003   Community Collaboration in Exhibitions: Introduction. *In* Museums and Source Communities: A Routledge Reader. L. L. Peers and A. K. Brown, eds. Pp. 155–170. London: Routledge.

2004   Disappearing Acts: Traditions of Exposure, Traditions of Enclosure and Iroquois Masks. *In* Questions of Tradition. M. S. Phillips and G. J. Schochet, eds. Pp. 56–87. Toronto: University of Toronto Press.

2006   Disrupting Past Paradigms: The National Museum of the American Indian and the First Peoples Hall at the Canadian Museum of Civilization. Public Historian 28(2):75–80.

Phillips, Ruth, and Christopher Steiner

1999   Art, Authenticity and the Baggage of Cultural Encounter. *In* Unpacking Culture: Art and Commodity in Colonial and Postcolonial Worlds. R. B. Phillips and C. B. Steiner, eds. Pp. 3–19. Berkeley: University of California Press.

Powell, Timothy

2007   A Drum Speaks: A Partnership to Create a Digital Archive Based on Traditional Ojibwe Systems of Knowledge. RBM: A Journal of Rare Books, Manuscripts, and Cultural Heritage 8(2):167–179.

Price, Sally

1989   Primitive Art in Civilized Places. Chicago: University of Chicago Press.

2007   Paris Primitive: Jacques Chirac's Museum on the Quai Branly. Chicago: University of Chicago Press.

Public Broadcasting Service

2006   Indian Country Diaries. http://www.pbs.org/indiancountry/history/relocate.html, accessed December 14, 2009.

Radin, Paul

1927   Primitive Man as Philosopher. New York: Appleton.

Reinhardt, Akim

2005   Defining the Native: Local Print Media Coverage of the NMAI. American Indian Quarterly 29(3–4):450–465.

Richard, Paul

2004   Shards of Many Untold Stories: In Place of Unity, a Melange of Unconnected Objects. Washington Post, September 21: C1, C2.

Riles, Annelise

2000   The Network Inside Out. Ann Arbor: University of Michigan Press.

2006a   Anthropology, Human Rights, and Legal Knowledge: Culture in the Iron Cage. American Anthropologist 108(1):52–65.

2006b   [Deadlines]: Removing the Brackets on Politics in Bureaucratic and Anthropological Analysis. *In* Documents: Artifacts of Modern Knowledge. A. Riles, ed. Pp. 71–94. Ann Arbor: University of Michigan Press.

Riles, Annelise, ed.

2006c   Documents: Artifacts of Modern Knowledge. Ann Arbor: University of Michigan Press.

Roberts, Lisa

1997   From Knowledge to Narrative: Educators and the Changing Museum. Washington, DC: Smithsonian Institution Press.

Rosoff, Nancy

1998   Integrating Native Views into Museum Procedures: Hope and Practice at the National Museum of the American Indian. Museum Anthropology 22(1):33–42.

Rothstein, Edward

2004a   Museum with an American Indian Voice. New York Times, September 21.

2004b   Who Should Tell History: The Tribes or the Museums? New York Times, December 21.

Rowley, Susan, Dave Schaepe, Leona Sparrow, Andrea Sanborn, Ulrike Radermacher, Ryan Wallace, Nicholas Jakobsen, Hannah Turner, Sivia Sadofsky, and Tristan Goffman

2010   Building an On-Line Research Community: The Reciprocal Research Network. Paper presented at the Museums and the Web 2010 conference, Denver, CO, April 13–17.

Sahlins, Marshall

1985   Islands of History. Chicago: University of Chicago Press.

1999   Two or Three Things That I Know about Culture. Journal of the Royal Anthropological Institute 5:399–421.

Sandell, Richard, and Eithne Nightingale

2012   Museums, Equality, and Social Justice. New York: Routledge.

Schwartzman, Helen

1993   Ethnography in Organizations. Newbury Park, CA: Sage.

Scott Brown Venturi and Associates

1991   The Way of the People: National Museum of the American Indian. Master Facilities Programming, Phase 1 Draft Report. Washington, DC: Smithsonian Institution Office of Design and Construction.

Shannon, Jennifer

2007a   Artifacts of Collaboration: The *Our Lives* Exhibition at the National Museum of the American Indian. Paper presented at the American Anthropological Association conference, Washington, DC, November 29–December 2.

2007b   Informed Consent: Documenting the Intersection of Bureaucratic Regulation and Ethnographic Practice. PoLAR: Political and Legal Anthropology Review 30(2):229–248.

2009   The Construction of Native Voice at the National Museum of the American Indian. *In* Contesting Knowledge: Museums and Indigenous Perspectives. S. Sleeper-Smith, ed. Pp. 218–247. Lincoln: University of Nebraska Press.

2011   The Professionalization of Indigeneity in the Carib Territory of Dominica. Paper presented at the American Anthropological Association conference, Montreal, Canada, November 17.

N.d.   Projectishare.com: Sharing Our Past, Collecting for the Future. *In* Museum as Process: Translating Local and Global Knowledges. R. Silverman, ed. New York: Routledge.

Shelton, Anthony

1995   Introduction: Object Realities. Cultural Dynamics 7(1):5–14.

2001a   Museums in an Age of Cultural Hybridity. Folk 43:221–250.

2001b   Unsettling the Meaning: Critical Museology, Art, and Anthropological Discourse. *In* Academic Anthropology and the Museum: Back to the Future. M. Bouquet, ed. Pp. 142–161. New York: Berghahn.

Simon, Nina

2010   The Participatory Museum. Santa Cruz, CA: Museum 2.0.

Simpson, Moira

1996   Making Representations: Museums in the Post-colonial Era. New York: Routledge.

Smart, Pamela

2007   Aesthetic Experimentation and Catholic Modernism. Paper presented at the American Anthropological Association conference, Washington, DC, November 29–December 2.

2010   Aesthetics as a Vocation. *In* Art and Activism: The Projects of John and Dominique de Menil. L. Schipsi and J. Helfenstein, eds. Pp. 21–39. Houston, TX: Menil Collection.

2011   Sacred Modern: Faith, Activism, and Aesthetics in the Menil Collection. Austin: University of Texas Press.

Smith, Claire

2005   Decolonising the Museum: The National Museum of the American Indian in Washington, DC. Antiquity 79(304):424–439.

Smith, Claire, and Gary Jackson

2006   Decolonizing Indigenous Archaeology. American Indian Quarterly 30(3–4):311–349.

Smith, Linda Tuhiwai

1999   Decolonizing Methodologies: Research and Indigenous Peoples. New York: St. Martin's.

Smith, Paul Chaat

2007   The Terrible Nearness of Distant Places: Making History at the National Museum of the American Indian. *In* Indigenous Experience Today. M. de la Cadena and O. Starn, eds. Pp. 379–396. New York: Berg.

2009   Everything You Know about Indians Is Wrong. Minneapolis: University of Minnesota Press.

Smithsonian Institution, Office of Public Affairs

2004   Office of Public Affairs press release: National Museum of the American Indian Announces Grand Opening on Sept. 21. http://www.nmai.si.edu/press/releases/opening_release.pdf, accessed January 15, 2004.

Special Projects Assistance Team

2000   Carib Identity in the New Millennium. Koudmen: Issues in Development (special issue) 9(2).

Srinivasan, Ramesh

2006   Indigenous, Ethnic and Cultural Articulations of New Media. International Journal of Cultural Studies 9(4):497–518.

Srinivasan, Ramesh, R. Boast, J. Furner, and K. Bevar

2008   Digital Museums and Diverse Cultural Knowledges: Moving Past the Traditional Catalog. Information Society 25(4):265–278.

Srinivasan, Ramesh, R. Boast, K. Bevar, and J. Enote

2010   Diverse Knowledges and Contact Zones within the Digital Museum. Science, Technology, and Human Values 35(5):735–768.

Stanley, Nick

1998   Being Ourselves for You: The Global Display of Cultures. London: Middlesex University Press.

Stocking, George, Jr.

1966   Franz Boas and the Culture Concept in Historical Perspective. American Anthropologist 68(4):867–882.

Straus, Terry, and Grant Arndt, eds.

1998   Native Chicago. Chicago: McNaughton and Gunn.

Straus, Terry, and Debra Valentino

2001   Retribalization in Urban Indian Communities. *In* American Indians and the Urban Experience. S. Lobo and K. Peters, eds. Pp. 85–94. Walnut Creek, CA: AltaMira.

2003   Gender and Community Organization Leadership in the Chicago Indian Community. American Indian Quarterly 27(3–4):523–532.

Strong, Pauline Turner

1997   Exclusive Labels: Indexing the National "We" in Commemorative and Oppositional Exhibitions. Museum Anthropology 21(1):42–56.

Stuever, Hank

2004   In Tonto, the Museum Comes Face to Face with Its Biggest Faux. Washington Post, September 18: C1, C2.

Tayac, Gabrielle

2009   IndiVisible: African–Native American Lives in the Americas. Washington, DC: Smithsonian Institution's National Museum of the American Indian in association with the National Museum of African American History and Culture and the Smithsonian Institution Traveling Exhibition Service.

Terrell, John

1991   Disneyland and the Future of Museum Anthropology. American Anthropologist 93(1):149–153.

Thomas, David Hurst

2000   Skull Wars: Kennewick Man, Archaeology, and the Battle for Native American Identity. New York: Basic.

Thomas, Nicholas
2010   Commentary: Museum as Method. Museum Anthropology 33(1):6–10.

Traweek, Sharon
1988   Beamtimes and Lifetimes: The World of High Energy Physicists. Cambridge, MA: Harvard
            University Press.

Trouillot, Michel-Rolph
1991   Anthropology and the Savage Slot: The Poetics and Politics of Otherness. *In* Recapturing
            Anthropology: Working in the Present. R. Fox, ed. Pp. 17–44. Santa Fe, NM: SAR Press.

Tsing, Anna Lowenhaupt
2007   Indigenous Voice. *In* Indigenous Experience Today. M. de la Cadena and O. Starn, eds. Pp. 33–68.
            New York: Berg.

Turin, Mark
2011   Salvaging the Records of Salvage Ethnography: The Story of the Digital Himalaya Project. Book 2.0
            1(1):39–46.

Turner, Christopher
2011   Making Native Space: Cultural Politics, Historical Narrative, and Community Curation at the
            National Museum of the American Indian. Practicing Anthropology 33(2):40–44.

Turner, Terence
1991   Representing, Resisting, Rethinking: Historical Transformations of Kayapo Culture and
            Anthropological Analysis. *In* Colonial Situations: Essays on the Contextualization of Ethnographic
            Knowledge. G. W. Stocking, Jr., ed. Pp. 285–313. University of Wisconsin Press: Madison.
1992   Defiant Images: The Kayapo Appropriation of Video. Anthropology Today 8(6):5–16.
1999   Indigenous and Culturalist Movements in the Contemporary Global Conjuncture. *In* Las Identidades
            y las Tensiones Culturales de la Modernidad. F. Fernando de Riego and T. Turner, eds. Pp. 52–72.
            Santiago de Compostela, Spain: VIII Congresso de Antropologia: Transcript.
2001   The Yanomami and the Ethics of Anthropological Practice. Paper presented at the Science–Ethics–
            Power: Controversy over the Production of Knowledge and Indigenous Peoples colloquium, University
            of Michigan. March 23.
2002   Representation, Politics, and Cultural Imagination in Indigenous Video: General Points and Kayapo
            Examples. *In* Media Worlds: Anthropology on New Terrain. F. Ginsburg, L. Abu-Lughod, and
            B. Larkin, eds. Pp. 75–89. Berkeley: University of California Press.

University of British Columbia
2011   The Reciprocol Research Network: Online Access to First Nations Items from the Northwest Coast.
            http://www.rrnpilot.org, accessed June 23, 2011.

Vergo, Peter
1989   The New Museology. London: Reaktion.

Waziyatawin and Michael Yellow Bird
2012   For Indigenous Minds Only: A Decolonization Handbook. Santa Fe, NM: SAR Press.

Weber, Max, A. M. Henderson, and Talcott Parsons
1947   The Theory of Social and Economic Organization. New York: Oxford University Press.

West, Richard
2000   A New Idea of Ourselves: The Changing Presentation of the American Indian. *In* The Changing
            Presentation of the American Indian: Museums and Native Cultures. Richard West and NMAI, eds.
            Pp. 7–13. Washington, DC: National Museum of the American Indian.
2004   The National Museum of the American Indian: A Historical Reckoning. Remarks presented at the
            National Press Club, Washington, DC, September 9.
2005   The National Museum of the American Indian: Journeys in a Post-colonial World. Paper pre-
            sented at the World Archaeological Conference, Canberra, Australia, July 8, and at the American
            Anthropological Association conference, Washington, DC, December 2.

West, Richard, and the National Museum of the American Indian, eds.

2000   The Changing Presentation of the American Indian: Museums and Native Cultures. Washington, DC: National Museum of the American Indian.

Wilson, Angela Cavender, and Michael Yellow Bird

2005   For Indigenous Eyes Only: A Decolonization Handbook. Santa Fe, NM: SAR Press.

Witcomb, Andrea

2003   Re-imagining the Museum beyond the Mausoleum. New York: Routledge.

Wylie, Alison

2008   Legacies of Collaboration: Transformative Criticism in Archaeology. Paper presented at the American Anthropological Association—Archaeology Division: Patty Jo Watson Distinguished Lecture, San Francisco, November 21.

Zabusky, Stacia

1995   Launching Europe: An Ethnography of European Cooperation in Space Science. Princeton, NJ: Princeton University Press.

2002   Ethnography in/of Transnational Processes: Following Gyres in the Worlds of Big Science and European Integration. *In* Ethnography in Unstable Places: Everyday Lives in Contexts of Dramatic Political Change. C. J. Greenhouse, E. Mertz, and K. B. Warren, eds. Pp. 113–145. Durham, NC: Duke University Press.

Zafar, Aylin

2012   The World's Most-Visited Museums. Time, January 5. http://newsfeed.time.com/2012/01/05/the -worlds-most-visited-museums, accessed December 17, 2012.

Index

Mogel, Barbara, 196–197, 203
Mohawk people, 42, 111, 114, 119, 145
Morning Star Institute, 74
multisensory environments, 35–36
Musée du quai Branly, 142, 222n46
museology: and anthropology, 13; audience-centered, 62–63; critical, 5–7, 12; expertise in, 86, 97, 99–100, 170, 187; language of, 87; "new," 5–7, 168; of NMAI, 9; and reception studies, 154; tactical, 139–140
Museum Anthropology (Thomas), 190
Museum Assets and Operations, 72, 77, 215n50
Museum Associates Council, 215n47
Museum Frictions: Public Cultures/Global Transformations (Kratz and Karp), 139
Museum of Indian Arts and Culture (MIAC, Santa Fe), 39, 208n15
Museum of Natural History's Museum Support Center, 33
Museum of New Mexico (Santa Fe), 39
Museum of New Zealand: Te Papa Tongarewa, 69, 72–74
Museum of the American Indian (New York City), 4, 28, 62, 68, 74
Museum Programs Group, 215n50
Museum Scholarship Group, 215n52
museum studies, 14, 65, 83, 90, 111, 113, 163, 178, 184, 191
museums: of anthropology, 7, 10, 14, 16, 190; changing role of, 6–8, 10–12, 88; as educational/participatory space, 6–7; as elite institutions, 86–87; ethnographic approach to, 65; increasing professionalization of, 66; and intratribal dynamics, 224n24; literature about, 111; and Native communities, 8–9, 60, 81–82, 86–87, 141; as object-centered, 7–9; primary role of, 186; private vs. federal, 68. *See also* specific names; specific topics
Museums and Community Collaborations Abroad grant, 198–199
Museums and Source Communities (Peers and Brown), 111, 139
Myers, Fred, 13, 208n16, 210n35, 221n39

Nakota people, 161
Naranjo, Tessie, 39
National Air and Space Museum, 4, 137, 207n4
National Congress of American Indians, 161
National Indian Youth Council, 51
National Mall (Washington, DC), 2, 4–5, 30, 32–34, 37, 151, 153–155, 160–161, 207n5
National Museum of African American History and Culture, 207n5
National Museum of American History, 8, 64
"National Museum of Ben Nighthorse Campbell: The Smithsonian's New Travesty, The" (Noah), 169–170
National Museum of Natural History, 8, 60, 167, 211n7
National Museum of the American Indian (NMAI): as artifact of collaboration, 189; board members of, 74, 167–169; buildings of, 12, 32–36, 177; changing gallery of, *plates 5a–5b*; as civic space, 184; committed to Native peoples/voice, 4–5, 7–13, 27, 32–33, 35, 38–39, 60, 62, 65–66, 80, 86, 90, 92, 106–108, 140, 167, 170, 182, 186, 188–189, 205, 210n1; as community museum, 140; criticism of, 218n31, 221n37; curatorial practices of, 23; description of, 147–149; donors to, 155, 158, 166, 177, 181, 196; funding of, 32, 62–63, 70, 76; history/background of, 2–5; impact of, 129–130, 138, 154, 163, 172–176, 197–198; importance of, 87, 193; legitimizing of,

140–141, 186; literature about, 19, 28; mission of, 27, 31–32, 35, 69–70, 90, 100, 106–108, 154, 170–171, 179, 182, 184–185, 188, 205, 210n1; and paradigm shift, 2, 6, 23, 28, 65, 83, 86; praise of, 161, 164–166, 168–170, 172, 177, 181; principles/purpose of, 2–3, 5, 12, 24–25; public influence on, 163; reorganization of, 75–77, 80, 165, 173, 186, 196, 213n2, 213n3, 215n48, 215n52; shifts focus of, 163, 173; success of, 142, 164–165, 177, 182, 184; tribal visits to, 34–35
National Taiwan Museum, 198
Native American Art Studies Association, 65, 81–82, 106
Native American Educational Services (NAES) College, 122, 124, 174, 219n8
Native American Graves Protection and Repatriation Act (NAGPRA, 1990), 4, 8, 193
Native co-curators. *See* community curators
Native Modernism: The Art of George Morrison and Allan Houser (exhibition), *plates 5a–5b*, 147
Native Nations Procession, *plate 18*, 153–154, 160–161, 163–164, 166, 174, 176
Native peoples: ancestors of, 4, 8, 34, 193, 211n7, 227n3; and anthropology field, 20–24; and broken promises, 81, 222n45; campaigns against, 57, 184; collaboration with, 14, 24, 27, 35, 88, 111, 226n15; contemporary lives of, 2–3, 37, 41, 110, 118–119, 149, 151, 171, 182, 184, 189, 206, 210n1; control own images, 189–190; cultural institutions of, 196; and education policies, 40; and exhibit content, 91–94, 96–100; exhibits about, 12, 17, 139, 193, 224n18; histories of, 2; increasing participation of, 28; lifeways of, 5, 9, 36, 57, 149, 183, 207n7; literature about, 19, 57; as noble savages, 46; as "objects of knowledge," 86; origin accounts of, 227n3; primary institution for, 25; reception of, 153–154; respect for, 24; and selection of co-curators, 86; traditional view of, 114
Native place, 3, 25, 169, 171, 184
Native representation: accuracy of, 187, 197; control of, 46, 139, 141, 190, 209n24; and decolonizing practices, 191, 193; emphasis on, 210n35; in ethnographic texts, 22–23; of identity, 222n43; of indigenous peoples, 9, 141, 176; in museums, 3–4, 7–9, 12, 17, 24–25, 51, 82, 90, 101, 137, 141, 180, 182–184, 186–187, 199; and Native voice, 179; online, 198; politics of, 4, 9, 47, 100, 138; and power, 8, 87; solutions to, 14; unfiltered, 185
Native rights, 9–10, 31, 47, 49–51, 148, 184, 188, 205–206
Native scholars, 36, 89, 91, 110–111, 148, 170, 217n9
Native voice, 2–3, 5, 8–9, 12; and authenticity, 141, 176, 211n12; as authority, 107, 167–168, 179–180, 183–184, 189; commitment to, 90, 167, 179, 189–191; communicating through, 28, 161, 165, 170, 179, 189; and community curating, 25, 39, 91–92, 176, 186; construction of, 110–113; definition of, 74–75, 141–142; emphasis on, 140, 170, 206; and exhibit content, 37–39, 69, 94–95, 98, 124, 142, 150, 167, 168, 172, 176, 182–183; and exhibit process, 81–82; as expert knowledge, 177–179, 191; filtering of, 98–99, 141–142, 170; and media production, 105, 135; mediating of, 131–136, 142, 196; in museum context, 60, 90, 208n15; and NMAI's mission, 170–171; value of, 188
Navajo/Diné people, 8, 53, 122–123, 198–199
Navajo Nation Museum, 198–199